Carp and the Carp Angler

Carp and the Carp Angler

George Sharman

with contributions from Rod Hutchinson,
Fred Wilton and Chris Yates

Stanley Paul
London Melbourne Sydney Auckland Johannesburg

Stanley Paul & Co. Ltd

An imprint of Century Hutchinson Ltd
Brookmount House, 62–65 Chandos Place, London WC2N 4NW

Century Hutchinson Publishing Group (Australia) Pty Ltd
16–22 Church Street, Hawthorn, Melbourne, Victoria 3122

Century Hutchinson Group (NZ) Ltd
32–34 View Road, PO Box 40–086, Glenfield, Auckland 10

Century Hutchinson Group (SA) Pty Ltd
PO Box 337, Bergvlei 2012, South Africa

First published 1980
Reprinted 1984, 1985

Set in VIP Times
Printed and bound in Great Britain by
Anchor Brendon Ltd, Tiptree, Essex

British Library Cataloguing in Publication Data
Sharman, George
    Carp and the carp angler.
    1.   Carp fishing
    I.   Title
    799.1'7'52   SH691.C3

ISBN 0 09 141440 7 (cased)
        0 09 141441 5 (paper)

Dedicated with love to my wife, Anne Marie, and
my children, Richard, Andrew, Catherine and David

Contents

Acknowledgements

One thing that stood out during the preparation of this book was the co-operation of my contributors and personal friends. Each supplied what was asked of them without prompting or prodding and gave such encouragement in the process, lightening my own personal fears of not being able to complete the task.

First, then, let me thank Rod Hutchinson for his contribution on particle baits; a topic of major interest to most carp anglers. And Fred Wilton, a modest man who preferred photographs of an angling companion to accompany his contribution on high-nutritional-value baits, rather than some of himself. To both these principle contributors I offer my sincere gratitude.

To Chris Yates for his enchanting story of the pot of gold he caught, only to find later that a much smaller fish left him with an unforgettable memory. To Kevin Roberts for his informative and amusing letter in the winter-fishing chapter; and to Bob Chambers writing in the same chapter in a similar vein must go my thanks for supplying such quality to the book. And I must not forget to thank Paul Snepp, Kevin Roberts and Andrew Hughes for supplying some of the data in the list of 'known' carp.

From the technical side thanks are due to my friend of long standing, Ron Barker, A.Met., M.I.M, both for his contributions on the striking power and stiffness in nylon lines, and for reading and correcting the chapter as a whole. Also to my life-long friend, Ron Dewsnap, A.Met., M.I.M, for assistance with the angles and forces involved in hook penetration; for advice on heat treatment and its effect on small section steel samples; and for correcting the relevant parts of the text.

I would also like to thank my fellow Hallamshire Group members. Ernest Colley, a professional photographer, for advice and assistance with some of the photographic content; Pete Evans who has given me advice on general photography for several years; and Kevin Clifford for supplying a negative of his 20 plus linear mirror and that of my good friend Dave Booth with his beautiful fully scaled mirror. My thanks to Robin Monday for the wide selection of negatives he sent to help illustrate Fred Wilton's contribution and likewise to Rod Hutchinson, Chris Yates and my good friend Bob Ford for their supply of negatives. Many thanks too for the last minute photographic material provided by Kevin Clifford, Trevor Moss and Jim Tyree; and also to Rodney Paull for providing the line drawings. Grateful thanks are also given to Dr F. R. M. Elgood (Rex), the quiet man of carp-angling, who has helped many people without thought of any personal gain; and also Dr D. Cragg-Hine for assistance and tuition with scale reading.

Finally I must record my gratitude for the advice, assistance and encouragement that Brian Harris has given me over the years. A busy man who has successfully run one of the best monthly magazines, *Angling*, for many years but a man who also finds time to look after the interests of the angler in general, whether it be frank assessment in a tackle revue; outspoken comment on pollution; misguided river authority 'improvements'; the rape of the inshore fisheries; or just acting as a wet nurse to occasional contributors like me.

PARKER GEORGE SHARMAN

Foreword
by Richard Walker

The words 'it gives me great pleasure' have become hackneyed by constant use, but I can think of none better to express my feelings at being asked to introduce George Sharman's book.

When my book *Still-Water Angling* was published in 1953, I liked to think that it made a useful contribution to angling knowledge generally and to knowledge of carp-fishing particularly. No book, however, can be right about everything with which it deals, and much has been learned about carp fishing in more than a quarter of a century. Consequently, the time is ripe for the publication of this book, which will carry forward our knowledge of carp and how to catch them by another long stride.

George Sharman has added much to our knowledge by his own experience and logic, but he has not hesitated to draw upon that of others, thus making his book all the more valuable. While it is devoted to carp, there is much to be learned from it that is of value to anglers interested in other kinds of fish. It will take another quarter-century, perhaps much longer, for it to be superseded.

RICHARD WALKER

Introduction

As I had never written a book before, I looked at many introductions in the books on my shelves to try to get some idea of what an author is supposed to say when faced with writing one. I met with such variety that left me confused rather than informed. So, reverting to basics, I will use this short chapter to introduce my attitude to carp-fishing and give some brief description of the content.

While due thanks have already been given to my contributors and the friends who have helped in many ways to produce this book, there are others who, indirectly, have given enlightenment for years and who I must not forget to include. First I must pay tribute to Richard Walker, who unknowingly was my private god during the late fifties and much of the sixties. It is no coincidence that my first-born – a son – is called Richard. Occasionally my own observations are at variance with some of Dick's past pronouncements but he must take the blame for it. His writings gave me a solid base to work from, such that allows the Master's word to be questioned occasionally.

Jim Gibbinson must also accept my gratitude for the tuition he has given with his prolific writing over the years. As a silent worshipper of this Adonis of the carp-anglers' world, I came face to face with him at the first British Angling Conference at Chelsea College in 1968 and found the meeting too much, making a complete fool of myself.

To Fred J. Taylor, Maurice Ingham, Jack Hilton, 'B.B.' and many other carp anglers who have written so well of their own experiences I owe a debt of gratitude. I have read their books and articles so many times that if, accidentally, I have used one of their phrases in the text it is because they have had such profound effect. To my many personal friends up and down the country who have passed on so much information during our correspondence; to the members of the Hallamshire Group, from whom I have learnt so much of fishing over the years, must go my sincere thanks. All have contributed to the memory store of this electronic computer called a brain, erasing the more random thoughts and rationalizing the more acceptable ones.

This book has been in the making for several years. I started it in 1972 when a number of the more technical chapters were completed. I then stopped writing for various reasons, the main one being that I doubted my own ability to finish a whole book. I hope that the text has not suffered because of this and that the knowledge I gained in that time has led to a more factual and accurate book.

The carp-angling scene has its conventions – the customs and traditional explanations of events like any other sport or pastime. Fortunately, perhaps because carp-fishing is still a comparatively young sapling that is still growing vigorously from the seed planted from the angling tree, little deadwood has accumulated. But any 'tree of convention' is subject to weak growth and deadwood in some areas, which blocks light and reduces growth. What I have tried to do here is gently prune away some of the weaker areas without damaging the sapling, for I respect and admire all the people who have tended and promoted its growth to a level such as it blossoms with increasing abundance each year – even into winter. There have been some areas of neglect that have caused poor fruition due to a lack of understanding. These are the places that have received the most attention in the hope that such light as may enter will promote healthy growth in place of stagnation.

I have tried to keep each chapter reasonably complete and because of this there is some repetition. There has been no conscious effort to pad the book in any way; my problem has been to compress, rather than expand, material. I have tried hard to deal with the more technical aspects in a readable manner, illustrating them, where possible, with fishing or observed examples. In other chapters, such as the Woldale one, I have dropped the enquiring attitude – as well as I am able – and written from the heart rather than the head. Woldale made such an impression on me. It typified all that a carp angler should need for complete satisfaction. At the same time it cast such a spell over me that it stopped me from making an all-out effort on its carp. To me it has a magical appeal; just to walk the banks and fish the swims that Walker, Ingham and

Taylor trod and fished is enough. To 'hammer' the carp it contains might just spoil my private vision of this paradise.

'No man is an island' and this book is far from complete as a guide to carp angling. Where possible I have avoided direct teaching (or preaching!). The book is intended for the more experienced carp angler who has already served some years of apprenticeship and, like many of my friends and correspondents, has reached a stage where the habits of the fish and the methods of catching it are equally interesting. Carp anglers who have said so often in their letters, 'I'm fed up with the "how to catch 'em" books, I want something with a bit more "meat" in it.' With modesty, this is what I have tried to supply. Carp-fishing is so many things to so many people. To me it is principally an exercise in observation that results in first catching carp and secondly, absorbing all the facts of nature which, unfailingly, present themselves at each visit to the waterside. There is so much of interest to absorb once you have progressed beyond the stage where mere size or numbers of carp have influence on your approach. I love to catch carp. This is the primary drive that takes me to a pond or lake. Yet there is so much more going on, asking to be observed. Things that often point the way to a behaviour pattern; happenings that can be missed or overlooked or misinterpreted because the mind is occupied with catching a bigger or better fish than the last, or improving upon last year's total. In common with most specimen hunters I have gone through this stage of carp-angling and, while I would not deny anyone the same experience, there is so much more to carp-fishing. I can now look upon the size or number of carp I catch in relative terms. A 10 pounder is big where the average is 6 or 7 pounds and a 16 pounder is only average in waters that contain a fair head of 20s. That one man is destined to fish the first water while another is privileged to fish the second has no bearing upon the angling abilities of either. Only when the two anglers fish the same water for a season could any sensible comparison be made ... if it had to be.

My own fishing has improved since I have relaxed the rigid specimen-hunter approach that once motivated me. Now I can warmly congratulate a friend who has banked a good fish and really mean it. When I go fishing I try to catch the better fish from a given water instead of chasing from water to water looking for monsters. That I hold two separate water records shows that there is no jealousy in my remarks and indicates, too, that a relaxed attitude can also produce the 'goods'. The size of these fish of which I am so proud? Well, by modern standards, only average. The best one would have just broken Albert Buckley's old National Record.

This book is about carp, carp-fishing and carp anglers. In writing it I have tried to bring into the text as many of my friends as possible, for the sessions spent with them have often been as rewarding as the actual fishing. The main theme is that of close observation and personal interpretation of what has been seen. It is the story of an average carp angler who tries to find satisfactory answers to the mysterious goings-on that occur in any carp pool every year; personal views presented not as hard fact, since fact in fishing is often hard to prove, but rather as an accumulation of ideas based on sound reasoning.

As a nature lover I can do no better than close this introduction with two sentences penned long ago by a man very much in tune with nature:

'Nature will bear the closest inspection. She invites us to lay our eyes level with her smallest leaf, and take an insect's view of its plane.' *H. D. Thoreau*

Part One

1 Weedbed fishing

There are many ways to present baits to a carp when weedbed fishing. However, the term 'weed bed' can be used to describe anything from a small straggly patch to a weed bed so dense and solid that a 1 ounce lead will make no impression other than a 'thunk!' as it hits the surface. The weedbed fishing I describe here concerns the dense, impenetrable sort.

I can still remember, vividly, the first week I spent on the banks of this particular pond. For years I had read about carp-fishing and my copies of *Still-water Angling* by Walker; the *Drop Me a Line* book by Walker and Ingham; and, of course, Fred J. Taylor's *Favourite Swims* had become quite tatty by the constant re-reading of the accounts given by these exciting writers. For years I wanted to try my hand at carp-fishing, but in the 1960 period there seemed little chance of this in the Sheffield area. We all talked of carp, yet no one seemed to know any waters that contained them. Apart from a few exclusive places that, it seemed to us, a chosen few were allowed to fish, little else from the carp-fishing angle was available. We used to discuss with envy the odd double that these few local anglers caught from their exclusive waters, and they were elevated to near gods if they landed a carp weighing 14 or 15 pounds.

My chance to catch carp came in 1965. It came quite by accident too as I had set off for a week's holiday intending to fish for barbel in the Yorkshire Ouse. When I arrived at the caravan site near the river, I unloaded the car as quickly as possible, and made my way down to the river with the suppressed feeling of excitement any angler understands. The sight that met my eyes was far from encouraging. The river, it appeared, had been over the banks the previous week and was still far from being in the best fishing condition. Watching the peat-coloured water smoothly flowing by just below the bank level, I cursed my luck at picking *this* particular week for a holiday. And talking to two anglers who had already spent the previous week there didn't help; one had caught nothing and the other only two roach! Putting up a rod, I began stret-pegging as close to the bank as I could manage – a method which produced four roach to half a pound after a couple of hours' diligent angling. It was no good though, I could catch roach three times this size nearer home, so I could see no future here at present – my heart wasn't in it anyway. Packing up, I went back to the caravan site to get things organized and cook a meal. This proved to be a most fortuitous move for, while bemoaning the state of the river to the chap in the next caravan, he told me of the pond just up the road where 'big fish' were caught. My informant was no angler, not even knowing what species of fish the pond held, yet to a specimen-hunter this is not too important, the mere mention of 'big fish' being enough. Gulping down a hastily prepared meal I was off, without tackle, for a recce.

It was a beautiful part of the country for anyone who had time to stop and admire it. The trees that grew on either side of the narrow, twisting lane formed an arch of branches overhead, while the thick well-trimmed hawthorn hedges and tall walls gave me a slightly claustrophobic feeling and deadened my quickly hurrying footsteps. Soon I came to an even smaller lane that forked left off the metalled surface. It was little more than a cart-track. I walked along this for a hundred yards or so with still no sight of a pond through the mass of vegetation until, suddenly, there before me lay the most enchanting pond it has been my pleasure to fish. Little did I know that this small pond would occupy my thoughts for seasons to come. Even as I write, ten years on, many of the things I witnessed there are as fresh in my mind as if they happened yesterday.

Completely enraptured, I began a tour of inspection, hardly able to believe the good fortune that had brought this angling paradise to my notice. The 4-foot-high banks were completely deserted and appeared little used by anglers, only a few worn bank areas showing signs of angling activity. Starting out from the north-eastern corner I walked along the east bank. The first impression was one of weed – masses and masses of it. Dense beds of spiked-water milfoil covered a greater part of the water surface, the little pointed fingers of its coloured flowers pushing up about four or five inches above water level. There was just one lily patch, a small circle of pads near the margin, that seemed to be fighting a losing battle with the encroaching milfoil.

As I continued along the bank the massive weed bed gave way, within a couple of strides, to the largest area of open water the pond contained, an area of perhaps 20 by 30 yards. The water in this first open area was about 4 feet deep and gin clear; there were no signs of any fish at all. Standing at this point, approximately half-way along the eastern bank, a broad vista of the pond could be obtained. There were dots of islands only a few square feet in diameter, while others were long thin strips, broken here and there by narrow channels passing through to more massive weed beds beyond. The islands were all but covered with willow trees, whose supple branches trailed down into the water below. A little further along the bank the shallows, an area of dense weed interspaced with small open pieces and strips of water, began. From the south bank ran a few small prominences, which formed shallow bays. But, again, the general aspect was one of weed, broken only by the odd small hole or island.

The west bank was, in the main, completely unfishable. The bank was sheer for most of its length and growing right on its very edge was a line of close-spaced hawthorn trees. Their gnarled, twisted, roots were bare and stuck out from the bank. Under the thick cover of these overhanging branches ran a long strip of open water where insufficient light penetration had kept the rank weed growth in check. In common with most other inaccessible places seen in many ponds and lakes, it had that indefinable touch of mystery that made one sure it was the haunt of big fish. Only at the northern end of this bank was it possible to get at the water. But even here the willow trees that grew from the water's edge left only small gaps. Most of these gaps were of little use for fishing because more dense weed completely blocked the swims.

At the junction of the west and north banks was a small bay. The water of this bay looked as though it might be the deepest in the pond, for no weed grew there and it was too deep to see the bottom; the slight colour in the water stopping light penetration. Later checks proved it was 7 to 8 feet overall, much deeper than average. The rounded bay led on to the northern bank, the least attractive part of the pond. An acre or so of land ran back from this bank and formed the 'dry-dock' of a thriving boat-yard. There were all sorts of river craft in various stages of repair. They looked unsafe, balanced on their keels and propped, seemingly in a casual way, with odd bits of timber along each side. Fortunately much of the main activity in this boat-yard was a considerable distance from the water's edge. Each week-end saw an army of enthusiasts, armed with saws and hammers, copper plates, red lead and paint of all hues, clambering about their particular pride-and-joy. The noise was never excessive though, seeming to be absorbed by the natural profusion of trees that enclosed the whole area. In any case it had a pleasant sound when heard in unity, and the smell of melting tar that drifted occasionally over the pond was far from objectionable. The boat people seemed a happy crowd, and they never bothered the angler, always being too busy to walk round the banks asking questions.

Now the tour of inspection was complete I was sure that the 'big fish' must be carp, even though I had seen no signs of any. In spite of never having fished for, or seen, carp in the wild the oft-read descriptive passages of my angling 'bibles' told me that here was the ideal carp water. My only problem was how to obtain permission to fish the pond, for I had seen a 'private' notice on my way round the banks. With sinking spirits I made my way towards the low buildings to one side of the boat-yard to find someone who might enlighten me. What a blow it would be if the answer to my plaintive question was an emphatic *no!*

One of the small buildings turned out to be a café, selling meals and refreshments to the boat enthusiasts. Occupying most of the right wall of the café was the counter with the usual range of wrapped goodies on display. Behind the counter stood a buxom, homely-looking lady, who I felt might be sympathetic to my questions. As I took the few strides towards the counter it flashed through my mind that I ought to order a cup of coffee or something, while I weighed up the situation. 'Is there any chance of fishing the pond?' I blurted out, in the direct way Yorkshire people have, cursing myself inwardly for lack of finesse.

It transpired that the lady behind the counter was the wife of the man who owned the lot; café, boat-yard and pond. The pond was private, the fishing rights belonging to a club who hired the water. 'Oh,' said I, even more crestfallen. 'But,' said the lady, 'we do keep a few permits to issue to our customers.' I pleaded that I had come a long way for a week's fishing holiday only to find the river almost unfishable and that I had been told the pond was a wonderful fishery. The look of abject misery on my face was enough and I was issued with a fishing permit for the week.

There are on record several cases of people who claim to be able

A pair of long, lean Northern Torpedoes. The strength and speed of these small fish was breathtaking

to levitate. One case that seems indisputable concerned a nun who subconsciously levitated when very happy, sometimes ending up touching the ceiling. There may be some truth in this rather unbelievable ability to defy the laws of gravity, for haven't we all felt as if we were 'walking on air' in some moment of supreme happiness at some time or another? All I can say is that as I walked back down the narrow twisting lane, clutching my paper permit, I would swear the ring of my footsteps on the metalled surface was much quieter than it was when I walked up it two hours earlier.

The following week passed all too quickly. But before it ended I had caught five carp and had seen half a slice of bread sucked *through* the matted surface of a dense weed bed. It went with a terrific gurgling slurp just as the light faded, and left me wondering as to the size of the carp that had taken it. The dense weeds were to cause the loss of many carp in the years to come.

The pattern of the season's carp-fishing at this water varied considerably. During the first few weeks the carp could be tempted with crust, flake or worms fished in the open patches of water. Floating crust was often quite deadly in the early mornings, particularly if a slight breeze rippled the water. In these conditions standard text-book fishing, of crust cast to the edge of a weed bed with the line flicked back over the weed, produced quite a high percentage of the fish caught. It had a certain charm about it that seems to be lacking in these days of high-pressure carp-fishing. And it was exciting too! Crouched behind a small bank-side willow and watching through the sparse branches as a carp swallowed the free offerings lined, by the wind in almost regimental precision, along the edge of the weed bed until at last it was the turn of the one that contained your hook! So many times have I crouched there shaking, waiting, thinking the fish had eaten enough and wasn't going to take my crust, then 'cloop', and down it went. The fish were only small, having a rather poor growth rate in spite of the richly weeded water that one would normally expect to be a good environment for aquatic fauna. However, in spite of the average fish being only 5 or 6 pounds in weight, I have yet to fish a water which produces carp that can accelerate as fast off the mark or fight as hard, pound for pound, as these fish did during the period my friends and I fished there. After being broken time after time on 8 pound lines, line strength was gradually increased to 11 pounds. Even then breakages happened far too often. Had it just been I who suffered the breakages it would have been easy to say my angling was at fault, but we all had our share of exasperation.

The problem was, of course, the small amount of room available in the open water areas to play the fish. The dense, unyielding nature of the surrounding weed beds was tough opposition if a carp once managed to enter them. Sometimes we fished 15 foot diameter holes in big weed beds and had our crust baits taken at the right-hand side of the holes. When the carp took the crust, it was relatively easy to strike and heave the fish away from the right-hand side all in one movement. That was when the trouble started, though! These fish accelerated so fast on feeling the hook, that they often covered the few yards across the open water and were 3 yards into the weed on the opposite side before you had time to get the rod over from left-hand to right-hand side-strain. There was no finesse about playing these carp. None of the text-book niceties of a finger applying delicate control to the spool-lip as the carp went off in the first mad rush. It was 'clutches screwed down tight boys' and line given grudgingly from the reel handle. The average carp rod, which when bent into a full test-curve, gives two yards of line to the fish without any line being given from the spool, did not help either. In a hole only 5 yards across the loss of 2 yards in bending the rod is often the difference between landing or losing the fish. We tried slackening off when a carp became weeded but it did not work. The carp just took the opportunity offered and ploughed further in the weed. The only way to extract them was to use a boat to get above them and net them, weed and all. Not very exciting really, but it made sure the carp was not swimming around with yards of line trailing behind it.

Sometimes we were lucky though, for the carp would pass through a small patch of weed, picking some up on nose and eyes. Then, like magic, the fish stopped as if possessing inboard disc-brakes, usually coming to the net easily, with that peculiar rocking, rolling motion as they were pumped along the surface. One has to be careful with fish landed in this way as they have a habit of going berserk when netted or on being lifted on the bank. They have used little energy in fighting and are liable to damage themselves badly while thrashing about. We found that reels fitted with roller bail-arms were best for this heavy 'heave-ho' sort of fishing, allowing more 'feel' through the reel handle.

As the season progressed the carp became shy of floating crust. Apart from the odd brief, but concentrated, feeding spell common to all carp waters, they ignored the bait. The procedure then was to soak half a bucket of stale bread in water the night before a planned session. The bread was mashed to a soupy liquid with the hands and groundbait was added to make it into a throwable consistency. At the start of a session this lot was dumped into the swim and off-bottom crust fished on the hook, about 3 inches above the lake bed. Flake would also work too, the only trouble being that it was often pinched by the roach before the carp moved in. For some reason the roach seemed less inclined to bother with crust. By using crust, worms or maggots, we could still catch a few carp in the open swims until about the middle of July. After that it became progressively harder to catch them in the open water and they appeared to spend more and more time under the dense weed beds.

It was so frustrating to stand looking at a weed bed, its thick matted surface revealing little, yet know that carp were under it, stuffing themselves to the gills with food while you were powerless to present a bait. At the edge, where the weed gave way to open water, we could see clouds of sediment billowing out like smoke, a sure sign that quite a few carp were active. And often, in the few small holes in the weed, we would see bursts of bubbles coming to the surface too; a further pointer that carp were feeding underneath. It seemed futile to drop a baited hook into one of the small holes and expect to get a carp up through its 2 foot diameter space. Yet that was what we decided to try.

It was *easy* enough to hook a carp under the weed bed. The takes were solid, no-nonsense, ones that suggested the carp were quite secure and unafraid in their underwater jungle. The problem was trying to get them to the surface. No matter how we crammed on the pressure, it proved impossible to force one of these tough little fish up through the opening before the tackle became snagged and forced us to pull for a break. The S/U carp rod just didn't have enough poke for the job, which seems ridiculous when you consider it could, in more favourable circumstances, deal easily with any carp that ever lived. After losing a number of fish I gave it up, for there was no pleasure in hooking carp, becoming snagged, and then pulling until the line broke. You have to be some kind of a nut to enjoy that. While the attempt ended in failure, it did prove that the carp were there, were feeding, and were quite easy to hook. There had to be some way to get them out....

As it happened an outbreak of foot and mouth disease during the 1967–8 season curtailed visits to the pond, and, like many anglers, we suffered an enforced 'close season'. We all moaned like mad of course. But our loss was small compared to the heartbreak seen on the farmers' faces when they saw a lifetime's hard work shot, burned, and dug into the very ground they had trod during those long years. The sight of grown men being interviewed on television, close to tears, after seeing a prize dairy herd slaughtered that had taken years of graft to acquire, was enough to keep any right-thinking man away from the rural areas. After all, who would like to think that by fishing a river or lake they had introduced the disease to a previously unaffected area? Apart from the grief such an unthinking action could cause, it would not do anything to endear the anglers to farmers in general. Without permission from the many farmers whose land encloses thousands of miles of rivers and countless lakes up and down the country, anglers would be in serious trouble.

During the months of the long close season I thought about the weedbed problems at the pond and wondered if a heftier rod would solve them. It was obvious that some of the carp we were losing were bigger than the average of 5 or 6 pounds. If a way could be found to get a higher proportion of hooked fish on the bank we might break the official pond record of 9 pounds 1 ounce. So, after thinking about the sort of rod required, I went ahead with the construction.

The weapon that evolved was bordering on the obscene. My reasoning that a short, stiff, rod was required to provide terrific initial power resulted in a rod of 8 foot in length, with a staggering test curve of 7 pounds! This was used with 20 pound breaking-strain line and No. 2 low-water salmon hooks, which were the strongest hooks I knew of in 1967. The power of this combination was frightening and the jarring, arm-wrenching thump of a simulated strike had to be felt to be believed. I spent many hours of mental and physical practice trying to re-condition the normal strike into a slower, more powerful heave, the idea being that all the available power must be used in one smooth movement before the carp could accelerate away and wrap the line around the weed roots. The rod was a poor caster, as might be expected, but this was no real problem as the holes in the weed beds were mainly close to the bank and plenty of weight had to be used to get the bait down anyway. Tests proved that casts of 10 to 15 yards could be made with reasonable accuracy once the strange stiffness of the rod was allowed for and one got the 'feel' of rod and thick line. I waited for 1 June – the start of the Yorkshire season – with increasing impatience, thinking it would never arrive.

The last day in May saw me and my friend Ted Cornish on our way northward, full of enthusiasm for the start of the new season. We settled down in our chosen swims, rigging up two rods each. Ted chose an open area, while I chose a smaller open patch of water, close to a big weed bed that had several likely-looking holes to choose from; intending to fish the heavy rod in the weed and the normal tackle in the more open water. Although the conditions that promoted the construction of the rod didn't normally occur until later in the year, I just *had* to try this powerful gear to see if it worked as planned.

I always find the start of a new season tremendously thrilling: the quiet buzz of conversation between friends as the night's prospects are reviewed; the re-living of last year's opening night and some of the more exciting or laughable incidents that we had shared; the final half-hour of waiting, sat close to the rods, previously assembled with care before dusk, waiting for the midnight start that is announced by the chiming of the local clock at so many waters up and down the country; the swish of rods and the plop of lead, as anglers around the pond or lake make the first cast of the season into a baited swim – it is all pure magic to me. To cheat by starting before time is unthinkable, yet cheat I did. As dusk approached it was obvious that to cast accurately into a 2 foot diameter hole would be impossible in the dark. So, just before it became too dark to see properly, I selected a hole in the weed bed and made the cast. The practice paid off; the bait landed smack in the hole and the three swan-shot had enough weight to pull the braided line along the surface of the weed, showing that the bait had gone down to the lake bed. This is the only time I have broken the midnight start rule and I hoped that a run would not develop until the early hours of the morning. When, eventually, twelve o'clock came, my other rod was cast into the baited swim and I felt free to shoot maggots into the general area of the weed bed, where my brandling-baited hook lay at the bottom of the hole.

The night passed all too quickly. It seemed only a short while from midnight to the time when the swallows, which roosted at dusk in the willows that grew on the islands, began their first sleepy twittering as a greeting to the coming dawn. There is much argument among naturalists as to which bird starts the dawn chorus, to my mind the swallow has it by a piece, though one can hardly call their untuneful twitter a song. It is as though all the effort of creation went towards providing the beautifully streamlined body, leaving just enough over for a splash of colour and a squeak of a song. Perhaps there is more to the swallow than meets the eye though, for I have many times seen them on the wing apparently feeding along with the bats before it has been properly light. Just how they locate the flies they feed upon is a puzzle, unless like the bat they use a form of echo-location.

During the night the indicator on the open-swim rod buzzed twice, providing an unwanted tench on each occasion. But the weedbed indicator remained silent. Ted and I were fishing from the east bank of the pond. Behind us lay a thickly wooded area composed of tall, tightly-packed trees, each trying to outgrow its neighbour in a natural competition for the available light. Because of this dense mass of foliage dawn had a peculiar effect. As the sun began to brighten the eastern horizon the thick backcloth stopped the light

Newstead Abbey's lower lake, a more 'carpy' water would be hard to imagine

rays reaching the water in a direct way. From about 3 a.m. onwards, one became aware of strange suffusion of light that slowly increased in intensity. First one object then another emerged from the darkness, while minute by minute as the light strengthened, more and more detail in the objects could be seen. By 4 a.m. it was quite light and the thick lines, hanging limp, could be clearly seen. It was at this point that the transistor indicator of the weedbed rod peeped out its 1000-cycle warning note – action at last!

Pouncing on the rod, in a frenzy of anticipation, I put in the smooth, practised, heave of a strike. The effect was amazing – shattering – for a carp rose, with the grace of a Polaris missile, through the hole in the weed bed, to clear the surface by some 3 feet before landing in the margins with a huge splash! From the indicator sounding to the fish being on the bank took about ten seconds. I was left trembling; not by the size of the 4 pound 10 ounce carp but by the vicious power of the rod. Here, surely, was the right weapon to tackle this problem of dense weed. All I wanted now was for one of the bigger fish, for which the rod was intended, to take the bait and test the tackle to the full.

The rod did all that was asked of it, providing several above-average fish that, hooked on normal tackle, would certainly have been lost. Yet there was a niggling uneasiness in my mind all the time I used it. The short, stubby rod seemed ludicrous when one looked at the average size of the carp it landed. It offended my sporting instincts, making me feel the carp deserved a better chance. But we were still losing fish on our standard carp rods. There must be another way though, something that had a little more finesse than this billiard-cue of a rod. The experiment had been interesting and, to a degree, successful. But it was time now to try a different approach; something still unusual in carp-fishing circles, yet something I had become convinced would provide an answer to the 'solid' weedbed problem that had cost us so many fishless hours and so many lost carp.

In the hours I had spent watching the activity in and around the vast weed beds, I had begun to visualize what the pattern of life under the dense mass must be like. To a casual glance the whole bed of weed seemed solid, impenetrable. Yet it was quite obvious that this solid appearance was just an illusion. The light that all plants require for healthy growth could penetrate only a few inches below the surface in these overgrown areas. And then there was the oxygen and carbon dioxide cycle of plants: oxygen given out under bright light conditions and carbon dioxide taken in. If much weed did exist *under* the thick surface layer, then surely it would be in perpetual night-time conditions and not removing the carbon dioxide? The water would only be oxygenated in day time by the upper few inches of weed. It did not seem right that nature would arrange things in this way; nor did the visual evidence support the thought that the water was seriously de-oxygenated under the weed beds – the carp spent far too much time under them. So it slowly dawned upon me that there must be plenty of room under the thick covering. I began to view weed beds in a completely different light. Before this revelation they had appeared, on casual examination, to be completely choked areas of water and I visualized carp literally forcing their way through them in a search for food; now I suddenly understood it wasn't like that at all. The underwater aspect was much like a wood composed of beech trees, whose wide-spread leafy branches stop most of the light and warmth reaching the ground so that little grows there. In such a wood there is plenty of space between the trees and the branches and leaves are so dense that the sky is completely obscured. If we were to fly over a wood in an aircraft we would assume, if we had not walked through woods before, that it was a solid mass. Such was the case with the weed beds. They were composed of numbers of rooted stems that carried the majority of their foliage to the surface leaving, between the tough, anchoring stems, adequate room for big fish, like carp, to swim. Only when the carp were 'tenting' in the upper layer was it possible to say that a carp was definitely in the weed. Other clues were more subtle, billowing clouds of sediment and small patches of bubbles filtering through the weed.

Several questions began to form in my mind: would it be possible to smash a way through the surface weed and obtain access to the interconnected feeding areas that lay beneath? If one did tear away the cover, would it drive the carp away and scare them so much that they would not return? If they did return, would they be suspicious of the altered aspect of the weed bed? How long would it take them to return after dragging out a swim? The questions began to form in my mind at an alarming rate, but as usually happens a funny side presents itself! I began to picture the underwater scene as a thriving metropolis: there were roads and lanes with intersections, each having varying status. On duty at each main junction was a

'Sergeant Perch' with the bold, black stripes of authority on each flank and resplendent red fins, all extended to make him look bigger than he really was. I could see in my fantasy a shoal of roach fingerlings who, having entered a main thoroughfare from one of the minor feeding lanes, were swimming along with a lost look in their eyes. As they reached the junction the Gladstone bag of a mouth of Sergeant Perch opens: ' 'allo 'allo, what 'ave we 'ere? You roachlings know full well you are not 'h'-allowed on a carpway. Be-orf with you to your roachlane before I gobbles you up!' At which the roachlings flee in panic, turning left down a narrow lane marked 'No Entry' where they are swallowed in their entirety by a mugging pike. Such is the fantasia born from days continuous fishing with only little sleep!

I decided to make a decent rake so that we could try dragging out a swim in one of the big weed beds. Dave Mottram and I were due to spend a few days' holiday later in the year at the pond; it would be a good time to try the experiment. The rake was quickly constructed using the strong, light alloy tubing and fittings of a television aerial. The major problem of attaching the head to the shaft to form the T-section for the rake was already solved with the TV aerial fitting, as it had a stout die-cast part to join the two pieces together with high-tensile $\frac{1}{4}$ inch bolts. The 'design' then consisted merely of deciding the width of the head, the length of the shaft and the spacing of the tines along the rake head. The fitting of the tines to the head was simple indeed. 4 inch nails were used as tines to be fitted into fractionally undersized holes. The nails were then knocked through the tube from alternate sides to form a double-sided head, making a light rake that, with the right technique, could be thrown considerable distances. This was the reason that alloy tube was used as I had foreseen that the rake would have to be thrown up to 60 or 70 feet if my assault on the weed beds was to work. To keep the weight down I left off the additional cross-bracing often featured on rake heads. I thought these braces would add weight and reduce the efficiency of the rake, though I must confess I had misgivings as to whether the omission would drastically reduce the strength. A fine thing if the first throw into a dense weed bed resulted in just the shaft being retrieved!

On my next visit to the pond I took the newly constructed rake, with its 25-yard-length of thin plastic-coated washing line, along with me to test it after the fishing session was over. I quickly found that one could not throw the rake very far when using the arm alone. Perhaps a well-developed 14-stone individual might have managed the full throw with ease – as a 10-stone weakling I found it very difficult. With continued trial I found the best way of throwing long distances was to lean back, with the rake touching the ground, and using the whole of the body, swing the rake in a long, increasingly accelerated arc over my head; similar, in fact, to the throw used for a hand-grenade – something I had been trained to do many years before. Moving to a weeded area on the shallows of the pond, well away from the places earmarked for the real experiment, I made one throw, and succeeded in getting all the 75 feet of line out first go. As I pulled the rake back towards the bank I could see it was leaving behind a broad, clear path through the densely packed weed. I continued pulling, thinking that as the weed clogged the tines and head, it would stop collecting it. Nothing of the sort! The rake collected more and more weed until it arrived in the margins containing so much that I was unable to lift it up the bank, having to pull it off in the water at my feet.

My journey home passed quickly, the 55 miles of travel seemingly reduced in length by my optimistic attitude. After testing the rake so effectively I was convinced that taking the action to the carp, rather than waiting for them to come to me, was going to work. The removal of half a ton of weed to make a swim was not going to be such a massive task after all.

My plan of assault was quite simple: select a big weed bed known from observation to be a productive feeding area. Then tear out a large rectangular hole, 10 yards into the weed and 6 yards wide. From three sides of the rectangle I would cut long 'fingers' into the surrounding weed bed. The 'fingers' would be as long as the length of rope on the rake permitted. I hoped these 'fingers' would intersect as many of the feeding lanes as possible. I would then feed into the 'fingers' bait samples leading to the large rectangle, where most of the bait was concentrated. It was so simple it *must* work. My only doubt was that the terrific commotion caused by throwing a large rake time and time again into the pond might scare the carp away for good. Ah well! Nothing ventured, nothing gained. . . .

The five day holiday Dave Mottram and I had planned earlier in the year arrived at last. We headed for the pond as soon as we had sorted and loaded the gear into the car. . . . Five days of complete 'immersion' in the problems of capturing that superb adversary, the carp! We had both looked forward so much to this visit and as we motored northwards we were in high spirits.

As the miles slid by, we talked of our plans. What would we do if the water was really dead, or if things did not go to plan? Well, there was always the river and the barbel if the pond proved completely useless; while neither of us minded having a crack at barbel, we both hoped that it would not be necessary. We turned off the narrow lane and down the cart-track to see again the little pond that had given both of us so many hours of absorbing fishing. There were six anglers already fishing when we arrived; something of a record that, for I never remembered seeing so many before – even on opening day. Our plans for dragging out two swims immediately on arrival had to be abandoned for fear of upsetting carp anglers already settled in their chosen swims. We fished through the night in the more open areas, catching one carp between the eight of us. It was significant that the angler who caught the carp was fishing a swim that contained a fair amount of weed growth – the carp were following their usual pattern of ignoring the open water.

The following day we expected the other anglers to pack up and leave us some privacy so that we could begin to drag swims. We found to our immense disappointment that five of these anglers were stopping for the week. I felt the disappointment most. Dave was more adaptable than I and much more ready to make the best of things. But then, had I not spent hour after hour assessing which weed beds contained feeding carp? Had I not gone to the trouble of making a special rod and then a big rake to try to solve this problem? It was natural, perhaps, that I was more upset by this, the least expected setback to our planned experiment.

There was nothing for it but to explain to the five anglers what we were trying to do. This way we could excuse, to some extent, the turmoil of dragging out the four areas I had earmarked for trial during our five days' holiday. As it turned out the other anglers did not appear to mind when we outlined the details of this somewhat unusual approach to carp-fishing. Dave and I went back to the caravan at lunch-time to have a meal and snatch a couple of hours' sleep. After preparing some sandwiches and flasks of coffee, we were back at the pond by late afternoon, equipped with the rake to begin dragging swims. We timed things just right, for the other anglers were sleeping still and, if we got a move on, we could drag our swims before they started fishing. It always annoys me when some idiot upsets *my* fishing and I am always the first to moan about it; perhaps this was why I was so worried. Dave and I got stuck in and, to my intense relief, cleared two swims before our companions started fishing. We soon established a working routine between us and an hour's hard work saw both swims dragged and baited.

At some time during that second night it occurred to me that things were not so bad after all. If our experiment of taking the offensive to the carp was going to provide any useful information, we must have a 'control', in the form of standard carp-fishing, to compare our results with. What better control than five anglers all fishing similar techniques to those we had used for two seasons. It was too good to be true, and I suddenly felt a surge of happiness at this thought.

During the next four days and nights, fishing in the four widely spaced swims we had dragged out (one on the west bank, one on the south bank and two on the east bank), Dave and I hooked fourteen carp between us, nine of which were landed. In the same period the other five anglers hooked four carp and landed three. However, two of the three carp they caught came from the swims we had vacated on the west and south bank when we abandoned them to make new swims on the east bank.

We still lost some carp, beaten by speed alone. But when you consider that I logged only eighteen hours' proper sleep and Dave had about twenty-three in five days of fishing, it is not really surprising that we were, at times, somewhat sluggish in playing a fish correctly. I have two outstanding memories of the holiday that no doubt I will continue to bore friends with until my particular bell tolls. By the fourth night I was suffering badly from the lack of sleep. We had no bed-chairs or anything 'fancy' to sit upon, my particular seating arrangement being an air-cushion to sit on, with my rucksack as a back-rest. About 2 a.m. my back really began to hurt. I tried various sitting positions to ease the pain, but it was no good, it hurt no matter what. The only thing was to lay down to get some relief. So, arranging the air-cushion in the middle of my back, and using a loaf – one of those long, uncut ones – for a pillow to keep my head off the damp grass, I obtained some measure of comfort. So much so that I fell asleep....

The human body is a wonderful thing and said to possess five senses; there is a *sixth* I am sure. As I lay deep in sleep I began to feel all was not well. There was no sudden transition from contentment to fear, more a gradual change to a deepening oppression. In the short time I had slept I must have turned on to my right-hand side, for when the alarm within awoke me from my slumber, I opened my eyes to see a very large rat only inches from my nose. I was quite unable to suppress the jerk of fear from this noted disease-carrying rodent, at which it slipped down the bank and plopped into the water. It was the loaf that interested it, of course, for during the twenty minutes or so that I had slept, it had started eating at one corner, managing to eat its way about 3 inches into my 'pillow'. After that it seemed that I passed through the 'sleep barrier', for whenever I started to doze off I had dreams that entailed a large rat chewing its way through my right ear.

The other memory concerns the final night of this short holiday. Dave and I had dragged a new swim each on the east bank. We had them dragged out and baited before dusk, ready for the last 'onslaught' before returning home. At dusk it started to rain and there was a light, facing breeze. Rain is no problem to anglers equipped with large umbrellas, as we were, except when the wind is in your face. Then the umbrella must be set as low as possible to stop the rain blowing too far under it. I had managed to angle my brolly correctly and was nicely settled when Dave came down the bank to say he had to catch up on some sleep. So he retired to the car, intending to have a couple of hours sleep until the time when the swim became active ... he crawled out two hours *after* dawn!

The rain was not too heavy and I was quite snug and happy, being worried only by the low positioning of my brolly. If I had a run on either rod it would mean that I would have to duck under the front of the umbrella to strike, although the rods were in reach of my sitting position. I would have preferred a better arrangement, but as there was a deep ditch behind me, not allowing movement away from the pond, and rain blowing in my face, I had to make the best of what the conditions offered. I was fishing the $2\frac{1}{2}$ pound test-curve rod right in the middle of the rectangular patch cleared earlier, while the heavy rod was cast at the edge of the right-hand side of the weed that bordered the swim. Some concessions had been made to the heavy rig earlier in the day. The 20 pound braided terylene line was pale green when first bought; fearing that it was too light in colour, I had dyed it a dark greeny-brown by mixing two different Dylon dyes. The colour had been reasonably fast during the shorter sessions, but the previous four days of almost continual immersion had removed most of the dye, leaving the line too light again. To rectify things a little I had tied, using a full blood-knot, a short cast of about 2 foot 6 inches on the end of the main line, using 15 pound breaking strain Damyl-camouflaged line.

The choice of this particular weed bed was no accident. Many times I had seen or heard a big carp roll or jump before it entered this weed bed to feed. It entered from an open patch of water to the right of this very big dense bed. The open area it rolled in was inaccessible, as a large cabin cruiser blocked a cast from the bank. However, I had seen this carp 'tenting' in the very area that I had chosen to drag out my new swim and, although I had never actually seen the fish, I could tell from the surface movement of the weed that it was 'big' by the general standards of this water. It would have been about a quarter to twelve when a big splash to my right told me a carp had rolled in the open patch ... it was coming.

Dave would be warm and dry in the car, no doubt snoring his head off ... wonder if he was having his usual dream of that big carp ... the one he had hooked so often in his dreams and has always woken up before landing? Be interesting to see how big it is if one of these days he manages to finish the ... peep ... pe-e-e-e-ep.' The heavy rig! It's here! At this split second I made the mistake that cost me a big carp. Pouncing on the rod, I struck while still under the umbrella. The rod hit the low-set brolly and I desperately tried to duck under it to get clear and pressure the fish away from the right-hand side of the swim. In that fraction of time the fish was into the weed and fast. Not even the tremendous power of the rod could move it. I did all the usual things, of course: hand-lining, slackening the line, giving quick jerks to try to make the fish move, but things remained solid. Quite suddenly I felt wretched. My trousers were wet and water was running down my neck from my hair, but above all I felt very, very tired. Placing the rod back in the rest so that the fish could take line if it wanted, I sank back in a mood of black despair.

As near as I could say the carp had sucked in my bunch of brandlings about 1 a.m. It was now a quarter to two, and after trying everything I knew in an effort to free the fish, the only positive thing to happen was me getting very wet – 'if only Dave was here, we could get a boat out'. About two o'clock a couple of yards of line whipped out very fast. Once more the routine trial of hand-lining but still the fish remained stuck solid ... 'wish dawn would come sooner ... might stand some chance of sorting out the problem once I had some light on the subject ... perhaps the carp has come unstuck by now anyway'. The time passed slowly, until there was some splashing on the surface of the weed bed about 2 yards in and only 5 yards from the bank; so near but yet so far. The fish was still on, so I stood up once more and took hold of the rod. Hardly had I done so before all hell broke loose. The fish, seemingly tired of being tethered, decided to do something about it.

What I remember more than anything else was seeing the surface erupt in a fantastic upheaval as water and bits of weed were sent flying in all directions. It was great to see such power unleashed in a bid for freedom. It succeeded too, for all was quiet after that, though I was still unable to retrieve my line from the weed. When dawn finally arrived I clambered into an old rowing boat on the north bank and rowed round to my swim. Following the line down to where it was anchored I found the end wrapped round a bunch of weed stems, in all a total of seven turns. The stems had been drawn together in a tight bunch. The roots had been torn loose as the fish drove upwards to escape and the 15 pound line had snapped cleanly about a foot from the hook. I had to replace the hook-link, for the line had become kinked where it had been wrapped around the stems.

At 8 a.m. I had another run on the same rod cast to the same position. This time there was no mistake with the strike and the fish, a 6 pounder, was soon in the net. The last session had not been a complete failure after all, though it had cost me a fish that, even at a conservative estimate, would surely have bettered the pond record.

The holiday had, however, proved the success of our experimental weed-clearing.

One of the main worries I had before the experiment was the fear of scaring carp away from the area completely. I need not have worried on that score at all. The first fish into the cleared swims were perch. They were something of a problem in a way, as we invariably had brandlings or lobs on one rod and there isn't a fish that swims that has a larger appetite than a small perch! It really is amazing how a 4 inch perch can get a No. 2 hook baited with three lobworms right down the gullet. We had some better ones of course; the best went 2 pounds, 2 ounces, a very good fish under normal circumstances, but here classed only as 'bonus' fish.

From the information obtained during the five-day holiday, plus that from later sessions, it seemed that the carp took approximately four hours to move into the swim. At least, this was the sort of time that passed before a run developed. And the carp did not seem to notice any change in the weedbed formation either. During the daylight hours it was often possible to follow the progress of a carp down one of the 'fingers' by watching patches of bubbles coming to the surface, marking the fish's progress towards the main swim.

We found that the first night and morning appeared to produce the best results in a cleared swim. After that there was less activity until by the third day the swim seemed completely dead. We tried re-raking, but caught only unwanted tench. Sometimes a new 'finger', dragged on arrival, would produce a run if the bait was cast into the new channel. The only way to ensure success was to drag out a new swim. Why, or how, the carp became wise to what was going on, I have no idea. But they did and quickly learned to avoid the new 'open' area.

During this period we removed a lot of weed from the water, several tons in all. A close examination of the weed revealed little in the way of aquatic fauna for the fish to feed upon. On several occasions I had seen carp sucking down the emergent flower stalks of the weed (spiked water-milfoil) and thought at first they were eating the flowers from the stem. Continued observation showed that this was not correct, for after several minutes of submersion the stalk usually emerged complete with flowers. I did find the answer later. Some of the flower stems were infested with a sap-sucking larvae similar to green-fly. If the carp were forced into this means of obtaining food, it suggests that little other, apart from the blood-worm group, was available in any real quantity in the weed bed. Perhaps the blood-worm that lived in the lake bed did not like all the light let in when we dragged the covering weed away and promptly migrated along the bottom to find new homes in the protecting darkness of the remaining weed. This might be a reasonable answer as to why the carp quickly stopped using the swim – who knows?

In these days of conservation some anglers might be worried at the removal of so much weed. To put your minds at rest, let me say that within a month the weed re-established itself in the places we dragged. Apart from a slightly greener look, it was impossible to tell that the weed bed had been disturbed at all. We did make one mistake that was rectified subsequently. We actually lifted all the weed out of the water and piled it on the bank before we found, that for several reasons, it was better to leave it in the margins. First of all if there are any eggs or minute forms of insect larvae not readily seen on the weed, they are given a chance to escape back into the main body of the water. Secondly, there were a number of times when my attention was attracted to the pile of weed by flapping noises – often in the dead of night! Inspection would reveal a small roach or perch trying with every ounce of energy its small body contained to find a way back to the water. Now, along with many other carp anglers, I *hate* small roach and perch. But where club rules dictate that the water should be a mixed fishery, these fish must be returned to give pleasure to other, less selective, anglers. This way all get some satisfaction from the decreasing number of ponds and lakes available. Even if these small fish do die enmeshed in the weed, it is better that both their bodies and the weed that contains them is returned to the nutrient cycle of the lake. It is wasteful to throw weed and good protein up the bank, for the material used in the construction of both is then lost from the water for good.

Dave and I fished that small Yorkshire pond for a total of three seasons. Since then we have moved on to waters that give us the chance of catching larger carp. But, personally, I will always have a soft spot for this little pond. We failed to improve the official pond record of 9 pounds 1 ounce but Dave came very close with a 9 pound mirror and I had an 8 pound 12 ounce mirror. Small game compared to 20 pounders but enjoyable none the less. Much time is wasted by some anglers in the quest for that elusive 30 pounder . . . and much of the real joy of angling can be overlooked.

Yes, I will always be grateful for having the opportunity to fish for the tough, fast, carp this water produced. I spent so many hours of complete 'immersion', happily involved in the problems they presented, while the rest of the world went by a thousand light years away. There was always so much to see, so much to ponder upon, so many things witnessed for the first time until I came to think those carp were something special, a cut above the rest. I coined the name 'Northern Torpedoes' to describe the long, slim, fast fish we caught; they earned every syllable of it.

The most outstanding thing I will remember is my introduction to that enigmatic carp – the 'bubbler'. In the following chapter I will try to convey to you the thoughts and satisfaction that went into, and was gained from, observing, presenting a bait to, and catching such fish.

2 Bubbling carp

Those gassy bubbles rising light,
Often in the dark of night,
Gives the watchful eye no glance,
Till the angler sees the chance –
With the coming of the dawn.

G.S.

Of all the various feeding patterns that emerge in a season's carp-fishing, I find that observing 'bubblers' is the most interesting. Apart from the thrill of catching them, I find them so interesting and absorbing because of the clues they give in the form of bubbles reaching the surface. If only we had the same information for all other feeding areas I am sure we would catch a lot more carp. When I think of all the hours I have wasted fishing in what had been productive swims earlier in the season, only to find the carp had moved elsewhere, then I think how lucky we are to have those convenient bubbles rising to the surface.

My first encounter with a bubbler was in August 1967. The pond I was fishing at this time had produced a fair number of carp from the recognized swims, but as the season progressed it became very 'difficult' during late July and most of August. The local anglers said that this was the usual pattern in most seasons and assured me the fishing would pick up in September. Meanwhile, we had to be stoical in outlook and look forward to the time when things would improve. Well this particular day I was feeling browned off, and a great deal of my stoicism had been evaporating during the last few sessions. And what had this present session produced so far to excite the imagination? Nothing! Not even a twitch-bite to ponder upon – and this was my fifth visit without a carp. So about 10 a.m. I decided to go 'walkies' to see if there were any signs of activity in other parts of the pond. I had crept only about 50 yards or so along the bank when I saw some bubbles rising, quite close to the margins, under a clump of overhanging bankside trees. I sat down behind the trees and smoked a cigarette while observing the rising bubbles through the gaps of the tree trunks. The bubbles appeared at the surface in small, intermittent streams. Slowly I felt the excitement mounting inside me as I realized this activity was caused by a 'bubbling carp'. I had read about such activity but until now never really bothered to look for bubblers, as they were considered more or less uncatchable. Perhaps it was sheer desperation that forced my hand now, as I carefully collected a rod and bait from my previous pitch.

The fish was still sending up an intermittent stream of bubbles when I returned to the scene. Pausing only to impale seven or eight brandlings on the hook, I cast the free-line tackle just beyond the last lot of bubbles and sat, like a tightly wound spring, wondering, but not knowing what to expect.

It was a rather tight swim under the trees. The overhanging branches cast heavy shadows upon the surface of the water. The surrounding area was covered with dense, unyielding, weed beds and only under the central, most shaded, part of the trees had weed failed to grow from lack of light. It was in this 'hole', roughly 5 feet in diameter, that the carp was working. I knew the water wasn't very deep at this point, perhaps 3 feet at the outside, yet the dark surface and coloured water revealed nothing, other than the odd stream of bubbles, to indicate a fish was feeding. As I sat there the usual frenzy of mental activity was taking place, trying desperately to interpret the little visual information being received to form a mental picture of what might be happening under the water: 'surely,' I thought, 'the carp must be very hungry to ferret about all this time for a few fiddly little bloodworms? Yet it won't look at my nice juicy brandlings. All very queer,' I mused. Then I realized that there might be a few stunted strands of weed under the surface and my carefully placed cast had ended in being hung up well off the bottom. So gently reeling in, I fixed a swan-shot about 3 inches from the hook, waited for the next bubbles as a casting point, and cast just beyond them. Again I waited, but not long this time, for the line began twitching where it entered the water, causing me to shake with excitement as my hand hovered over the rod-butt. 'Steady lad,' I said to myself, 'it's probably only his tail hitting the line – wait for something more positive.' Then, quite suddenly, there came a quick snatch as the line lifted about 3 inches as the fish located and sucked in the bait. This was followed by an equally fast strike from me and the $2\frac{1}{2}$ pound test curve rod whammed over with this close-range hooking. I held the fish at short rein in the tight swim. It was a tough little mirror carp a fraction under 4 pounds. Not very big I know, but a start. My first bubbler, fished for and caught.

This little fish set me off on the bubbler trail and since then I have tried to catch any carp I have seen bubbling, providing the fish was in reasonable casting range. Sometimes it has been very successful and other times it has failed. But overall results have shown enough bubblers on the bank to suggest that the key to catching them is correct bait presentation. Sorting out the problems involved have provided me with many hours of interesting and absorbing fishing – and that is what it is all about, isn't it?

Once you start fishing for bubblers you will soon begin wondering about the composition of the lake bed and how the bubbles are caused. As your experience increases you will begin to form some sort of mental picture of what might be happening on the bottom of the lake. This is a very important part in the approach to good bubbler-fishing. A fair understanding of the conditions the fish is feeding in, i.e. the nature of the lake bed and surrounding environment, can be of tremendous help in correct bait presentation.

My own observations lead me to believe that the lake bottom is comprised of three layers: the top layer is mainly the decaying remains of recent vegetable and animal life. The middle layer is the one in which the large eruptions of gas are probably formed. The bottom layer is mainly inert material which we normally call mud. This is the residue of all the previous years of decay. Of these three layers the uppermost is the most important, both in the ecology of the lake, and in the presentation of baits to a bubbler. In the deeper parts of a lake, like holes, or areas between shelves or underwater ridges, and in the true deep water, the upper layer has the consistency of soup. It is vital to remember that it is comprised of animal, vegetable and mineral remains that have become *slightly denser than water* and so sunk to the bottom. The fact that many of these remains are very 'light' in the water means that they are easy to displace. Within this layer live many of the animal forms of life a carp seeks when bubbling. It is in this layer you must present your bait to stand a good chance of hooking a bubbler.

The second layer of sediment, which is at its thickest each

November, is the remains of the previous season's deposits. Throughout the winter little decay takes place because the temperature is too low. As soon as the temperature begins to rise in March or April the decaying process begins again. Very often this results in what anglers call 'the bottom coming up', when pieces of dark green mossy-looking vegetation can be seen floating on the surface. This process plays an important part in mixing the vital minerals on the lake bed, for as they rise much of the mineral elements from the bottom are left in fine suspension in the water, and are distributed around the lake to fertilize all areas. As the new season progresses into the animal and vegetable explosion of summer, this still-active layer becomes buried under the new influx of detritus.

The third, and deepest layer is of little interest to the angler, or of use to the ecology of the lake. It is comprised of very fine particles of detritus and, while it contains many of the vital elements that are of use in promoting good growth of lower food-chain organisms, many of these remain locked within it due to chemical changes. It is inert and plays little or no part in producing gas, the main function being to supply secure rooting for pond weeds. Now we have a rough idea of the composition of a lake bottom we can go on to the life that dwells in it.

In a good lake the two upper layers will be rich in the various vegetable materials and minerals needed to promote good growth in the amazingly abundant range of larvae that inhabit this region. As anglers we are not particularly interested in knowing the complete range, or the life cycles of these often-microscopic forms of life; it will be sufficient to realize that the two main groups that bubbling carp seek live in the confines of the lake bed. These are the bloodworm, annelids and the various nymphs that consume the vegetable element present. There are many predators, living in the soupy bottom, that live by stalking and eating the nymphs and bloodworm. But as many of these are free-swimming forms we cannot think of them as 'bottom-dwellers' in the true sense of the word. However, when a carp sticks his head into the bottom and begins to feel, with the four sensitive barbules, for living, pulsating, bodies all is grist to the mill. Any form of life present, along with considerable amounts of the detritus supporting it, is sucked in and chewed up by the pharyngeal teeth.

I have been fortunate enough to observe the actions of some monster bloodworm in the shallow parts of a lake I fished. This particular group of 'worms' were about three-quarters of an inch long, a sixteenth of an inch in diameter, and a bright reddish-brown in colour. When all was quiet they appeared to be anchored by the tail section in the upper layer, while the top part of the body protruded from the mud, swaying back and forth in unsynchronized undulations. Bankside vibration would cause them to withdraw sharply into the upper layers of the detritus. Even in life at this lowly level there are signs of intelligence. Continued stamping on the bank produced less reaction as the bloodworm realized no danger was forthcoming, till eventually my stampings were completely ignored. I had no way of knowing just how far their holes went into the sediment, but thought it might be a considerable distance in relation to the size of the bloodworm. The impression I gathered from watching this activity was that if a fish came into the immediate locality the bloodworm would do a fast disappearing trick on feeling the pressure waves created by the fish's body. After the fish had passed by, they would cautiously emerge to begin feeding in their peculiar swaying manner as they sifted minute organisms from the water. Such action ensured them good protection from roach, rudd and dace, etc., which have no means of locating movement in the sediment. Those in the surface film of the sediment would be fair game to tench and gudgeon, while bream, which suck in and digest the whole of the top layer complete with animal and vegetable contents, would do quite well in finding sufficient sustenance. But only the carp, which has greater power and longer barbules than the tench or gudgeon, would be able to probe deep enough into the two upper layers to reach any living food organisms present.

I have never actually seen carp feeding on bloodworm. Usually the water has been too coloured, or I have been too engrossed in trying to catch the fish and not show myself. I have seen carp in what might be described as a 'bubbler attitude'. These were a group of fish that I observed once in clear water under some trees that grew from the sheer, unfishable bank of a small pond. The fish were engaged in what might be termed a 'group-browsing' as each one was in an almost vertical position, apparently browsing the surface of the top layer of sediment. It seemed unlikely that the carp were digging into the lake bed, particularly since five or six carp were present in an area of only a few square feet. If they had been digging the water would have been too coloured to see the fish. I have no idea what the fish were feeding on, nor was I able to present a bait to them. Others have claimed, however, to have seen, and described, the feeding activity of a bubbler. It would appear that when feeding on bloodworm, the carp pushes a great deal of its head into the sediment in an effort to locate, with its barbules, the organisms it contains. In doing so it causes a release of the gas trapped in the upper layers of the sediment. This gas enters the fish's mouth and leaves via the gill openings. It is said that the gill-rakers break up the large gas bubbles into smaller ones, and, because the gill-raker spacing varies with different species, one is able to tell the species of the fish by the size of the bubbles reaching the surface.

From my own observations I am prepared to accept that the feeding attitude and activity described are correct. Yet I am in some doubt about the second part of the description, concerning the way the bubbles are produced. For a carp has *two* gill openings and it would seem unlikely that the bubbles would come from only *one* of them. If we accept that the bubbles do leave via the gill openings, then surely we would expect to see two *lots* of bubbles reaching the surface. Also, it would not be unreasonable to assume they would be spaced a fair distance apart – say 5 or 6 inches – when a decent-sized carp was causing the emission. I cannot recall such an event while watching bubblers. I have only ever witnessed a single stream of half a dozen or so bubbles reaching the surface at intermittent intervals, when I have both observed, and caught, a *true* bubbler.

Another thing I have found puzzling while observing bubblers working along the bottom, is the complete lack of accidental triggering of gas emissions near the fish. Gas, in any areas where it is trapped in rotting material, is normally quite unstable and a bank stick pushed into the lake bed often triggers off a remote gas emission, sometimes several feet away. One would expect a carp that is ploughing a groove in the lake bed to cause more disturbance than a thin bank stick and so cause remote triggering of marsh gas. It is this lack of gas emission and the fact that the true bubbler sends up only a small stream of intermittent bubbles that suggests things do not happen as we are led to believe. Here is my interpretation of what causes the 'bubbler' to 'bubble'.

I believe that there are only small quantities of gas in those areas of the lake bed which support the highest numbers of larval, pupal and nymphal stages of the various insects. Life under water is tenuous enough without the insect having to combat noxious gas and the continual unstable upheavals that go with it. When a carp

Figure 1 A potherer. Head deep in silt this bubbler probes for annelid and bloodworm, disturbing large amounts of sediment. Note relative position of the two bubble streams mentioned in text

begins to feed in these areas a small amount of gas enters along with the food items and a mixture of the detritus from the lake bottom. This collection of food, gas and detritus passes into the alimentary canal of the fish and is mixed with digestive acids as it travels through the system. The acids work on this mixture producing additional gas while breaking down the various combinations. By the time the waste matter reaches the intestines, it is interspaced with a considerable amount of gas. In due course the waste matter leaves the vent, along with the gas; the waste falling to the bottom and the gas rising to the surface. The result of this would be frequent streams of bubbles, generally small in size, reaching the surface as the carp vacated the intestines while still feeding. This theory fits the situations I have observed while bubbler-fishing. I am not saying that the bubbles *never* issue from the gill-covers, but it does seem odd that I have never noticed two separate streams from a single fish.

You are no doubt thinking: 'What the hell! Is it really important exactly where the bloody bubbles come from as long as they give me a clue where to cast?' To which I would answer with equal emphasis: 'Yes, it *bloody well is* if you want to be in with the best chance of hooking a bubbler!' For consider: in one explanation the bubbles leave the gill openings, in the other, the vent. Each position being relatively close to opposite ends of the body. Although the fish is in a near-vertical position, the distance would still be considerable in a double-figure carp. Perhaps the reason bubblers were once classed as 'impossible preoccupied fish' was because the placing of the bait was not accurate enough, and little or no weight was used to get the bait into the medium in which the bubbler was feeding. The trick with bubbler-fishing, as I see it, is to place the bait as exactly as possible into the very *confined feeding area*. After you have observed which way the carp is moving, by following the bubble pattern on the surface, your cast must end up only 2 or 3 inches in front of the fish's nose. To achieve this sort of accuracy it is important to know exactly where the bubbles leave the fish's body, or else the lead may hit the fish and scare it. It is far better to allow a cast to fall farther in front of the fish. For if my assumption is wrong and the bubbles *are* emitted from the gill openings, the bait is still only a foot or so further in front of the fish than is desirable for the best chance of a take.

You will now have realized that the extreme accuracy required to

float attached with valve rubber

Figure 2 Brandlings on float tackle. The lighter terminal weight presents the bait in the upper layer and is suitable for browsing bubblers. Over-shotting of float will ensure correct presentation; set too deep the float lays flat, too shallow and it will sink beneath the surface

put a bait 'on the nose' means that long-distance casting is out. Beyond a range of 10 or 12 yards it is very hard to judge accurately if a cast is in the correct position. Most of the bubblers I have caught, or seen caught, have come from within this distance of the bank. To obtain good, accurate positioning, even at close range, I advise the use of the following tackle arrangements – both are modifications of the 'lift-method'. The first is little different from the lift-method except that heavier shotting is used to get the bait down into the sediment the carp is feeding in. It is suitable for fairly open areas and consists of a good sized float that will barely support two or three swanshot. These are set a few inches from the hook. The float is set as near to the depth of the swim as possible. The ideal cast should land about 2 feet in front of the last sighting of bubbles. Fortunately the surface film of the water often retains the bubbles for some time. Ease the tackle back until the float is about 4 to 6 inches in front of the surface bubbles. The float is not just a means of indicating a bite – its real purpose is two-fold: it tells you, by cocking, that the bait has reached the bottom correctly and is not hung up on a strand of weed and it also gives you a means to position the bait as accurately as possible in front of the carp below. I know of no other way to obtain the precise positioning needed for regular success at bubbler-fishing.

The second method differs only in that a cork is used in place of the float. This arrangement was devised for use near a weed bed, or in a hole within the weed bed. I am never happy using a float near a weed bed no matter what form of attachment is used, as there is too much chance of snagging for my liking. So in place of the float a small cork is used, set to the required depth as before. The cork is slit down the length with a penknife. The slit should be as deep as the centre of the cork. The cork will remain firmly in place when the line is wedged in the slit. When a fish is hooked and the line 'chungs' tight on the strike the cork obligingly leaves the line. It often flies many yards into the air, so freeing the line of any encumbrance that might snag in the weeds. The cork need only be three-quarters of an inch long and half an inch in diameter; it is positioned over the fish in the same way as the float. Always use a cork, never polystyrene.

When to strike can be a problem. The common type of bite, when using the cork, is usually a rocking motion. But sometimes the cork will bob under the surface, rather like a pike float when the livebait is spooked by an approaching pike. A float usually bobs up and down but on occasions will lift a little, or shoot just under the surface. The lift or undersurface movement are readily identifiable as bites, yet many good takes will be missed if only such are struck. The reason why the bite indication is rather vague will be readily understood if we think of what the carp is doing. As the carp probes the sediment and, hopefully, feels the carefully placed bait, a clear-cut bite will not develop: he did not have to move far before while sifting out bloodworm, so he will not when he picks up our bait. I can only advise that you strike at some reasonably definite or prolonged movement of the float or cork. There are times when the carp is very close to the bait without actually locating it. This produces a trembling motion on the surface indicator, as the 'wash' created by fin movement, or contact with the line, moves it. If you strike at such movements a carp is sometimes hooked, often outside the mouth and usually under it. This suggests the cast was too long and the carp touched the line somewhere between bait and float.

My own research indicates that bubblers are not easily scared. My nephew, Dave Mottram, is a much better bubbler-fisher than me and often uses a half-ounce bomb to get the bait down when he suspects the lake bottom is weedy. I do not recall him complaining of an undue number of fish being scared. Naturally some fish will occasionally be scared by a bad cast. Anglers are not machines and errors are bound to occur. But if we bear in mind that these fish are not normally available to standard techniques, and that bubblers are really exciting 'bonus' fish, then we ought not to be worried by the odd scared fish. I believe the bubbling carp is less aware of what is going on around him than a carp who is just nosing around the swim. Many of the fish's primary sense organs are likely to be buried in the sedimentary deposits and out of action. In fact, if the fish's head is pushed into the sediment as far as some suggest, then smell, sight and part of the hearing system might well be of little use as warning devices. This only leaves the sensitive lateral line in action. As this organ is thought to be concerned with the reception of low-frequency sound, like footsteps and bank vibrations, pressure waves caused by current and the proximity of underwater bodies, it seems unlikely that the 'plop' of a lead would be noticed. Provided you are not silly enough to drop a 1-ounce bomb in the middle of the carp's back, or wind it over him, I shouldn't worry too much about the scaring effect. Concentrate more on getting the bait down to the fish's feeding level using one, two, three swan-shot, or even a bomb,

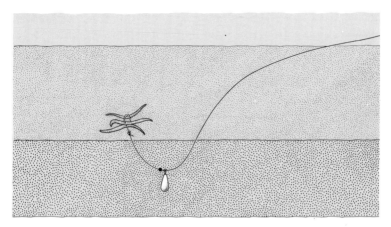

Figure 3 Brandlings on ledger tackle. Ledger presentation normally gives deeper penetration of the sedimentary layers and is suitable for bubblers seeking annelid or bloodworm

to take the bait *into the sediment*. You will not catch many bubblers with the bait hung up a foot off the bottom!

Over the years I have made a special study of bubbling carp and the various forms of bubble activity the carp angler is likely to see. But before I deal with these, let us have another look at bubbler-fishing in action.

Much of my information on bubbler-fishing was obtained from a study of a Yorkshire pond. The methods and thoughts that evolved at this water have been put into practice elsewhere with good results. I was fishing a lake in Cheshire, for instance, that had a completely different character to the Yorkshire pond. It was a larger, more open, water with little weed apart from a tiny bed of amphibious bistort, and a thin fringe of horse-tail and bulrush in the extreme shallows. The bottom was hard, with a thin layer of sand covered by a rich, shallow sediment. The Yorkshire water was more compact, having many little islets, covered with willow trees, scattered about it. The silt was deeper, particularly where it had gathered in the holes and depressions of the lake-bed. From the fertile bottom of these areas grew abundant quantities of spiked water-milfoil, forming dense weed beds that covered a greater part of the water surface. There was often considerable bubbler activity around and under the weed beds. In the hard-bottomed Cheshire lake it was a rare event to see any bubblers working the bottom.

During this particular session at the Cheshire water, I had caught a double in the early hours of the morning – a not-too-frequent event at this water – and I was feeling relaxed and reasonably satisfied. Away to the east the sun rose over the high peaks of the Pennine range and began to burn away the early morning mist. There was little sign of activity, the lake and the inhabitants seemingly lulled into sleep as the morning progressed into a hot, late-July day. I was now resigned to going home with just the one carp for the session. Then, as if by magic, a little line of bubbles arrived at the surface 5 yards out. As the morning light had strengthened I had reduced my hook and bait size, casting both baits farther out from the shallow, bare, marginal regions. Keeping an eye on the continued bubbling, I carefully reeled in the line of one rig. The necessary changes for this close-range bubbler were quickly made, and brandlings replaced the luncheon meat on the hook. A pause for the next set of bubbles to arrive at the surface, then the short cast. I settled the rod in the rest and closed the reel bail-arm, watching the slackened line where it entered the water. Only a few minutes passed before the line began to twitch and, with quickened heartbeat, my right hand took a firm grip around the slim rod-butt. The line lifted a couple of inches and I struck, the rod taking on the lovely Avon rod action curve. It would be nice to end by relating that it was a very big fish, but it was not. Just a little over the average for the water that is all, yet welcome just the same. Shortly after it was time to begin the hot, dreary, twisting drive back over the Pennines into Yorkshire.

If I may be permitted one further example – that of Dave in action with a long-range bubbler – it may help to show that the normally undesirable long-range bubbler can sometimes be caught.

This particular incident occurred on another Cheshire lake and lobworm was the bait. This was a large water of four or five acres, with the low density stocking that is so common in many Northern waters. With only a few carp per acre the angler has to be very careful to select the right swim, or a season might pass with little to show for it. This lake had a fair sized island just off the western bank, with a small channel between the two. A collapsed footbridge of light planks sagged just far enough into the murky water to stop all but the brave making an attempted crossing. In any case the island was out of bounds to the angler, so the 'brave effort' would have risked expulsion from the club as well as life and limb. Our interest in the island had been heightened by seeing carp patrol the margins along the northern side where heavy, overhanging branches from the tree-crowded island cast a dark, mysterious shade on the lake surface. On occasions the hump of a carp could be seen cleaving the surface under the overhanging branches and it seemed as if the carp had a private feeding area, which they were loath to leave, along these island margins. To reach this side of the island required a cast from the northern bank of between 40 and 50 yards.

About half past ten in the morning a carp began profuse bubbling just outside the sanctuary of the tree branches. Had we not seen the bow-wave of a carp approach, and the vortex of displaced water as the big tail pushed downwards, we would have classed the release of gas as a 'natural' emission, so profuse was the bubbling. I have never witnessed such bubbling before, or since and can only conclude that the fish was triggering off general gas release in the feeding area. Dave made the long cast but it fell short. It was a rather tricky situation. Too much effort and the cast ended in the overhanging trees; too little and it landed short. Unlike Goldilocks, Dave needed only two attempts – the second landed just right. Some time passed before the silver-paper foil began a slow trickle along the ground-sheet placed under the rod. There was a considerable 'tow' between the two banks, due to wind action on the larger body of the lake surface. Bits of weed and debris were swept along in this underwater tow. Dave thought these were causing the trickle of a run and did not bother striking. He pulled more slack off the reel to replace that taken. An instinctive angler, he had nagging doubts and finally ended them by reeling in to inspect the bait. The big lobworm was well and truly chewed, only a few mangled remains were left threaded on the hook shank. Cursing his stupidity, Dave re-baited and cast again. Once more a wait before the slow run developed, and the foil began, as if moved by unknown force, to trickle along the ground sheet. This time there was no mistake. Picking up the rod and cranking the reel handle to pull the bow out of the line, Dave made a tremendous strike and hooked the fish. 'It's a slimy —— bream!' he cursed, pumping in the fish, which made no real effort to resist.

An uninvolved onlooker and seeing the curve of the rod, I advised him that 'No bream in England would put a bend like that in the 2½ pound test-curve rod you are using.' Adding as an afterthought,

'Unless it was a 3 pounder hanging *dead* from the end!' Dave continued pumping the fish in and without any semblance of resistance it swam, almost with relief, into the net I was holding. It was a carp all right. A carp of rarely seen proportions, measuring 19 inches in length and weighing 11¼ pounds. At a later date I caught a fish of identical weight from the same swim. It gave the same sort of 'fight' and differed only in body shape and length – the length being 20 inches, the body being triangular in shape. Unfortunately I cannot say if this fish was a bubbler or not as it was caught at night, yet I include it because of the unusual appearance. These fish are not diseased, they are a particular strain bred to be short, fat and, from the angler's point of view, useless.

Let us return now to the subject of bubble patterns reaching the surface and see what they represent.

Many times I have found myself puzzled by the different forms of bubble activity seen while fishing. It is important to know what these various surface patterns mean if the best bait presentation is to be made. It also helps to know the difference between a bubbler and a natural gas-release. The following description of the different forms I have seen and analysed may be of some help to the bubbler-hunter. The conclusions have been reached after a great deal of thought and an initial study of something like two years; I don't claim they are entirely correct, but they have often made it possible to select the right presentation.

Some ponds and lakes often produce a large amount of natural gas-emission – particularly the ones that are deeper than average. One lake I fished often appeared 'alive' with bubblers in the latter half of October and early November. Many of these natural gas-emissions were so like bubbler activity that I have often been caught out and fished hard for non-existent carp. Most anglers know the usual heavy 'boil' of a natural release of gas, but this particular lake produced a lot of tiny emissions that appeared to move along the surface just like a true bubbler. I find it best to study the bubble patterns for a considerable time before deciding if fish are responsible. A natural release of gas is normally more profuse than that from a carp. What happens is that gas builds up in fair quantities between the upper layers of the sediment on the lake bed. Eventually this reservoir of gas reaches a level where it becomes so buoyant that it lifts the matted sedimentary remains, much like a trap door, and releases most of the gas. The gas rushes to the surface to cause

Dave's bubbler – 19 inches long, weighing 11¼ pounds

the familiar boil, the bubbles all bursting within the ring of ripples made by the previous ones. If the gas is accumulating fairly rapidly the whole sequence will be repeated at regular intervals – but always in the *same place*.

When a carp is causing the bubbles the surface pattern is very different. The bubbles arrive at the surface in batches of half a dozen or so, and are generally quite small in nature, being approximately a quarter of an inch in diameter. As the carp grubs along the bottom, releasing small emissions as it feeds, there is a similar apparent movement of bubbles along the surface, telling the angler how far, and in what direction, the carp is moving. It is this movement *along* the surface that tells us that a fish is feeding below, and gives the information required to place the cast correctly.

Another form of bubble pattern often seen is a patch, a foot or so in diameter, of very small bubbles. These rise to the surface all at once – one moment nothing, the next a big patch. If it is very quiet and the release is near the bank, it is sometimes possible to hear the 'swis-s-s-sh' announcing their arrival – a most exciting sound that sets a tremble of anticipation running through the body! This sort of pattern is usually associated with swims that have been well ground-baited. Both tench and carp will produce identical patterns. In both species the release is more or less involuntary. I think that what happens is this: the swim contains a certain amount of sub-surface weed. This weed collects considerable amounts of gas under the foliage and this, along with oxygen released by the weed, makes the foliage quite buoyant and unstable, lifting the branched fronds in the water. During the groundbaiting various bits of food become trapped in the weed fronds making tempting, easily obtained morsels, for a fish attracted into the swim. The fish, seeing the food, pushes the weed. Or, grubbing in the groundbait, knocks a weed stem and triggers the already unstable conditions resulting in a sudden release of gas trapped under the fronds. Up comes a large patch of tiny bubbles.

These fish are *not* bubblers, so it is no use fishing a bait in the sediment. If the swim has been heavily groundbaited there is a good chance that a run will occur soon after one or more of these patches appear. If, however, only small amounts of hookbait have been thrown in, it might be that the fish is just passing through and picking up only those pieces suspended in the weed. I usually expect some action when I see these patches and if it does not come fairly quickly, it is quite likely that the bait presentation is wrong. If I am using lead on the line for casting to the swim, I would alter the length of the trail to 4 feet or more if no runs came. This would ensure the bait had a better chance of being draped over the weeds, rather than being on the bottom. If you are using lobworm it is a simple matter to fish a 'junky' lob by injecting air into it, or, if range permits, fish it in conjunction with a float. Many carp anglers are loath to use a float, thinking that a carp will be put off by seeing the line rising to the surface. All I can say is that I have caught quite a lot of carp in weed beds using float tackle and up to 20 pound test braided line, without feeling the line has reduced the number of takes. And this has been on hard-fished, low-stocked club waters too. Perhaps the thicker braided lines are less scaring than monofil, looking similar to weed stems when in the water.

Then there is the bubbler activity which occurs when anglers fish meat baits. This activity is not seen all that often, perhaps needing just the right bottom conditions for it to occur, but it can be puzzling. There have also been many occasions when using particle bait in deep soft-sediment waters that the following might apply. What happens is that bubbles come to the surface directly over the place where you have cast and thrown bait samples. The bubbles are rather large when compared to a true bubbler's emission, and come up in 'boils' similar to small natural releases. They differ from the natural gas-releases, being scattered about the surface in small batches, rather than all arriving in one place. The angler is usually aware that carp are in the swim and causing the bubble activity. Sometimes the line will twitch two or three times and a small amount of line is taken. Other times the twitches will cease. When the line is reeled in, the bait has often gone. This happens frequently with meat-based pastes fished in areas that have 'soupy' sediment.

I think the problem is that the bait is sinking into the soft upper layer of sediment and disappearing from sight. The top layer, little denser than water, is easily displaced by the weight of the hook and bait. Although the bait is out of sight, it still gives off an oily smell that is permeating through the sediment into the water above. A carp entering the swim is attracted by the free offerings which, without the weight of the hook, are laying partly submerged in the sediment. After eating those that are easily located, it can still smell others, including the hookbait, so begins poking about in the 'soup' to obtain them.

Although a carp has sensitive barbules for probing in the bottom layers, the barbules are responsive only to live, moving organisms, being of little use in locating a 'dead' bait. Smell is of little use to the carp once it has pushed its mouth and nostrils into the stinking sediment. It has no real means of locating an unnatural but very desirable bait, in a medium where it normally 'feels' for living forms. So it is reduced to stab-in-the-dark activity, attempting to locate the bait in the area of highest smell. If this area should contain any gas trapped between the layers of sediment then you can expect to see bubbles rise as the fish releases them. The bubbles can be profuse at times. The fish, however, cannot be classified as a true bubbler. I think a true bubbler is a fish that is seeking natural food items using its own specialized locating techniques, and not one that has been induced to bubble by unnatural baits.

The problem facing the angler is that of correct presentation. The carp is willing to take the bait – if only it can *find it*. Obviously the odd fish will be hooked, even with the bait sunk in the sediment, but by using a slightly different presentation the takes can be made more positive. One improvement is to use the balanced-crust method that the Carpcatchers Club perfected many years ago. This consists of putting crust on the hook and loading it up with paste until the buoyancy of the crust is just overcome. Thus the bait only *just sinks* and, arriving on the bottom, is left nicely settled on top of the upper layer. This presentation has worked quite well for me on a number of occasions, though I must confess that I find getting the correct balance a fiddling job. I use a different method now.

The same sort of presentation can be obtained by fixing a swan-shot 2 inches from the hook. The hook is then baited, first with the crust, which is slid up the line, followed by the meat paste. By putting the hook through the bread from the crumb side first and then pushing the crust up the line, the meat paste can be moulded around the hook. The bread is then slid back down the line until the crust part of the bread is touching the meat paste. This combination makes a buoyant bait that would float if it were not for the weight of the swan-shot. When the bait reaches the bottom of the swim, the swan-shot sinks into the 'soup' leaving the bread slightly sunk into it and the meat paste attractively displayed. This method really works.

Peter Evans unhooks a nice double

Apart from use with meat pastes, luncheon meats, etc., it might be of advantage when using dense particle baits particularly in swims that contain soupy detritus or silk-weed. The method is very good with plain crust too, especially after heavy pre-baiting with a bucket full of mashed bread soaked in Oxo or Bovril.

The last type of bubble activity I have seen when carp fishing is entirely due to bait action. In 1968 I was using brandlings as hook-bait, putting between six and ten on the hook. These were cast and fished close to a weed bed under which bubbler activity was taking place. The weed beds were very dense indeed, yet careful observation would reveal little batches of bubbles here and there, forcing upwards through the tangled mass of weed fronds. Further confirmation of fish could be seen at the edges of the weed, where suspended silt came billowing out like underwater clouds. To try to entice these weed-bound bubblers out from under the weed beds, I catapulted large quantities of maggots. Most landed at the edge of the weed, where my brandlings wriggled enticingly on the hook; while others were shot into the weeds, hoping they would, as maggots instinctively do, work their way downwards to avoid the light and end up on the lake bed.

It was a patient sort of fishing this. The carp were there and feeding; it was just a matter of putting maggots in at regular intervals and waiting for them to be located. It was during this waiting period that the peculiar form of bubbler activity took place. At least I thought it was bubblers that were responsible at the time. I had chosen the swim after spending an hour observing the activity in and around the weed bed. If any bubbles had been coming to the surface *outside* the weeds I would have seen and noted them. All the activity was *under* the weed but, within an hour of first starting to catapult maggots into the swim, little patches of odd bubbles started popping up on the surface. In size and nature they looked very similar to those we knew were made by bubbling carp. We were at a loss to explain why no runs materialized when the baited area appeared alive with carp. Three or four hours would often pass before a run would occur with a suddenness that even now, many years on, I still find startling. But how to explain why it took so long? The answer came slowly after a number of similar sessions had progressed in an almost predictable sequence. It was the maggots of course that were causing the bubbles to appear. That it took so long to realize this can only be put down to my slow thinking or engrossed state of mind.

A rewarding morning's fishing, three carp better than average for the water

Once realized, it was a simple matter to throw a handful in a selected marginal area and observe the effects.

The maggots would sink slowly to the bottom, being only slightly denser than the surrounding water. On reaching the bottom they would immediately attempt the difficult task of trying to bore into the lake bed. It was not that the sediment was hard, as I had selected a soft area for the experiment; it was just that the maggots suffered from a lack of weight in the water and, like a man in space, found difficulty in carrying out a simple task without the help of gravity. Eventually though, most of them would get the point of their bodies into the sediment and with the wonderful fluid transfer they possess, pump the internal body liquids back and forth, forcing their way downwards, away from the offending light. Inside an hour all but the weaker individuals had disappeared. These slowly drowned on the surface of the sediment. This downward-drilling in an area that contained natural gas trapped beneath the detritus, resulted in some maggots tapping the trapped bubbles and releasing the gas.

Dave and I used mainly lobworms or brandlings when fishing for true bubblers, Dave's preference being for lobs and mine for brandlings. I have no doubt that the vast range of baits, many with strong smells, that have arrived since 1967 might prove successful with bubblers, particularly when the fish pulls its head from the sediment as it moves along the bottom. But, for me, using baits other than live ones would spoil some of the pleasure. The bubbler is undoubtedly a hungry fish, willing perhaps to accept any bait it can successfully locate. But the way in which the sensitive barbules probe the silt, feeling for the pulsating body that desperately tries to escape as it shrinks from the touch of certain death, is the whole charm of bubbler-fishing. It seems right to me to have those probing barbules intercept a bunch of squirming brandlings with my hook fixed in the middle of it.

Whether bubbling carp were totally engrossed while feeding in the sediment was a matter of conjecture when we first tried to catch

A well-known north-eastern carp water at Brandsburton in Yorkshire. It has produced good catches of double figure carp for many carp anglers from all over the country

them. The consensus of opinion was that they were more or less a waste of time, too preoccupied to tempt with baits of a size suitable for the large hooks used. After several years of bubbler-hunting I concluded that the carp were preoccupied all right, not with the small size of the food items they were feeding on, but with the method of feeding. There is a difference. In the first case we must use identical food items as bait; in the second, we can use any sort of bait providing it is presented correctly. Now it may be that a bubbler will take more or less any bait it recognizes as food. But seeing that the fish were seeking live food the obvious choice was worms. I felt these must be a better choice than an inanimate lump of 'something' the fish might not locate, or recognize, when sunk in the silt. By using worms, relying on accurate casting, using sufficient weight to sink the bait into the sediment and hold it there against the 'wash' created by the pectoral fins, we could sit back and await some results. We found the results well worth the effort. The actual fishing was among the most exacting and exciting forms I have ever experienced.

Since writing this chapter I have witnessed bubbles leaving the vent of a fish in exactly the same way that they surface from true bubblers in the wild. This observation was made in an aquarium. The fish was a large goldfish that had an enormous appetite for bread. After it had gulped down large amounts from the surface, it went down to polish off what remained on the bottom of the tank. While in the typical head-down position of a bubbling carp, I twice saw two separate streams of small bubbles leave the fish's vent. I think the bubbles were air that was trapped in the bread when it was swallowed. While this observation does not prove the same thing happens under natural conditions, it is evidence that bubbles can leave the vent in the manner outlined earlier in the chapter.

3 Of bites and feeding patterns

Before we can properly understand how a carp feeds we must first look at the way it breathes. This may seem an unusual way of approaching a chapter on feeding yet the two separate functions of breathing and feeding are very closely related. The time spent in understanding the breathing mechanism will provide valuable information to help interpret some of the weird feeding patterns that emerge during the season.

At first sight the breathing would appear simple: the fish sucks in water through its mouth, shuts the mouth and pumps the water out through the gill openings. It is not, however, so simple. The carp (or any bony fish) takes in water through the mouth all right, but careful observation will show that the mouth is already opening again before the gills are fully closed. It is impossible to pump water with a system like that. There are things happening within the mouth that cannot be appreciated by external observation. Inside the mouth cavity are working muscles, unseen even when the fish is on the bank. If you stick your finger into its mouth for a while you may feel the muscles tighten around your finger. Do not put it *too far* in though, for if you get your finger into the pharyngeal teeth it may come out looking like a sucked maggot.

The water entering the mouth is pushed back, by the internal muscles, towards the gills as the muscles undulate in a rippling movement. The first intake of water is flushed through the gill filaments at the back of the mouth cavity, while the muscles pushing it through seal off the front of the mouth, allowing more water to be taken in. The pumping system is very efficient and it is possible for the fish, under normal breathing conditions, to keep a constant flow of water passing the gills. The gill covers never shut completely, as they appear to do when watching normal breathing, but are rather like a door that looks closed on casual examination, until a push clicks the latch. Because of the unique pumping action and the incredibly complex gill structure, the fish's breathing system is very much more efficient than man's. The fish is able to extract something like 80 per cent of the oxygen from the water while man only manages to take around 25 per cent of the oxygen out of each lungful of air.

If we turn now to the feeding aspect we can see the similarity between the two functions. As anglers we say a fish gives us a 'bite' when it takes our bait. This is rather a misnomer since the carp has no teeth in its mouth to bite with. Even pike do not bite. They, like the carp, *suck*, the teeth being holding rather than biting teeth. Mind you it wouldn't sound the same saying, ''as thar 'ad any sucks, mate?', would it? However, the carp does suck in the bait and this is the way it happens: to us a suck is a simple expansion of the lungs to draw air through the mouth. The fish has no lungs to suck with and must 'suck' in a different way. It does this by first closing the mouth completely, then pushing all the water in the mouth out through the gills before shutting the gill-covers tight. The muscles in the mouth contract, leaving a large internal cavity and creating a vacuum. When the fish opens its mouth the water rushes in to fill the vacuum and carries with it the bait, hook and line in the terrific 'suction' available. You will note that suction is in inverted commas, since the fish is not really sucking as we do, but has instead created a vacuum. The degree of vacuum can be adjusted to suit different sizes of food or feeding spells. When the fish is really hungry it will take the bait right into the back of the mouth, push the water through its gills, and then pass the food to the pharyngeal teeth in the throat for chewing. If it is not so hungry it might take the bait quite slowly then eject it, causing several twitches on the line. A wide range of takes is possible simply by the fish adjusting the muscles in its mouth to a greater or lesser degree of 'cavity'. So simple, but so beautifully designed and executed.

When carp are 'twitching' it pays, if possible, to watch the line where it enters the water particularly with long-range twitchers. Most carp anglers have suffered the exasperation of having a quick 'beep' on the indicator and seeing the tell-tale silver paper leap up 6 inches or more. Even when the angler hovers over the rod many of these takes are completely unhittable, being so fast the angler is unable to respond. I have noticed many times that if you ignore the indicator and concentrate on the line where it enters the water, there is often a crafty tightening of the line before the fast twitch. The line might lift only an inch or so, but striking then sometimes results in a carp being well hooked. I think what is happening is that the carp is taking in the bait in a quite slow and positive manner. But after taking it finds something not to its liking and violently ejects the bait, causing the fast twitch as the bait is *blown out*. Some might doubt that this is possible. Stop and consider that the system which allows a carp to take in a bait fast can be reversed, allowing it to eject the bait with almost the same force. Big carp ejecting upwards of a pint of water from the mouth can easily 'blow' the bait and hook several feet through the water at high speed. If small carp and goldfish are able to eject little, unwanted food particles several inches, think of the power of a fish weighing a hundred times more.

A nice brace taken by touch-ledgering. Note the loose scale on upper fish — many scales are lost in this way on linear-type mirrors

And do not forget that a bait has mass but is very buoyant in water. The ejection current in a dense medium like water would 'carry' the bait quite well, the resulting amount of twitch movement of the indicator being decided mainly by the range.

Twitchers in the dark are a different proposition. When you are unable to see the line at the rod end the gentle tightening that signals a take is denied you. There is one method you can try that might bring you success. I have only caught a handful of carp using the method, but this has been due to lack of opportunity rather than inefficiency of method. Some years ago I was bothered one night with carp taking about 3 inches of line, setting the indicator going, but nothing more. I was fishing at about 20 yards' range and each time a twitch came I waited, hand on rod, for further movement that never came. When, after waiting for a while, the line was wound in I found the bait had gone. I had several twitches and each time slackened the line in front of the bite alarm to stop the alarm while waiting to see if a run would develop. It was while slackening off after a twitch that I felt the peculiar grating vibration, reminiscent of a barbel bite when touch-ledgering, coming up the line. The thought flashed through my mind that a carp was chewing the bait. On went the bail-arm and I struck, feeling the solid thump as the hook found hold. The fish that caused the tremble on the line was a 13 pound linear mirror. Some while later came a similar bite. This time I just grasped the line between finger and thumb, feeling the same peculiar sawing vibration. The strike connected and the fish was a $13\frac{1}{2}$ pound scattered mirror. Since then I have had several carp that might not have been caught were it not for feeling the fish chewing the bait. The carp giving this sort of bite is usually hooked well inside the mouth, proving it is a 'confident twitcher'.

The nervous twitcher offers a more serious problem. Here the fish is suspicious of the bait, perhaps having been caught with it a number of times. The fish knows the bait is good to eat, much better than its natural food. Yet, having been subject to several uncomfortable experiences while eating the bait, it sucks it in and blows it out, trying to decide if it is safe. Under these circumstances I have used float tackle with some success. But it becomes difficult to control the tackle properly beyond a range of about 30 yards. A change of bait can often work wonders in a situation like this. I remember fishing a water in Cheshire where the carp had become very suspicious of luncheon meat. The first month three friends and

I fished this water we hammered out sixty carp between us in five or six visits. After that we fished another water for a while but still called at the first lake for an odd session now and again. The lake was not all that big and by the end of the season we reckoned we had caught almost every carp in the water – some of them a number of times! The luncheon meat went well all season so, naturally, we fished it at the start of the following season too. Again we caught a fair number of carp, though we never hit the same peak reached during the first season. We had the water to ourselves from the carp-fishing point of view. Few other anglers seemed to bother with the carp and those that did used floating crust. So we continued using luncheon meat until it became obvious that the carp were getting very scared of it.

One morning, towards the end of August, I was fishing alone. I had a rod cast right along the shallow margins to my left, only a couple of yards from the bank. This rod had often accounted for the only carp caught during a session, though anyone seeing it cast so close to the bank would have thought it idiotic. The other rod was fished about 25 yards out with a float and 5 pound line. The lake was quite shallow, averaging about 3 feet depth in the area I was fishing. At this time of the year the carp were prone to patrolling up and down the lake in twos and threes, passing my spot 25 yards from the bank. You could see the bow wave of approaching carp from 50 or 60 yards down the lake and I found out, by accident, that the approaching fish could be induced to go down in the baited swim. The trick was to wait with a catapult, loaded with three or four pieces of luncheon meat, until the carp were 6 or 7 yards from the swim, then shoot the bait samples to land near the float. It was great to see the bow waves diminish, turning into vortices as the carp pushed downward, following the slowly sinking luncheon meat. I had quite a few carp with this somewhat unconventional way of carp-fishing, the float invariably shooting under like lightning as the fish took in the bait.

This particular session things were not going well. The carp were bow-waving all right, and following the sinking luncheon meat down, but the float either trembled or shot down and back up again so fast it was almost impossible to respond. I missed one and pricked another, both fish creating a long, fast, bow wave over a hundred yards in length as they fled in panic from the area. It was the same story on the margin rod to the left as well. Two takes of a few inches of line; fast unhittable pulls, followed by frightened bow-waves. The luncheon-meat bonanza, having been responsible for the downfall of well over 100 carp during the time we used it, was now 'blown'. The choice of baits in 1971 was more restricted than now. Well that is not strictly true. The *choice* of baits was there, but confidence in using unusual baits was lacking. I remember using two small tins of sweetcorn in July 1971 on this same water and, not having a single run either session, I stopped using it! I have made some stupid mistakes in my time, but I reckon that must be the all-time high in the light of what happened later on as the Jolly Green Giant swept the country like a rabid plague. But what to use now the luncheon meat had lost effectiveness? I spent some time wandering around the local Woolies not quite knowing what sort of replacement I wanted except that it ought to be meat, rather than vegetable, in nature. Finally I settled for liver pâté and bought one of those plastic containers that look like a thick sausage. At home I opened the 'sausage' and the smell that greeted me was superb. Confident that this bait would work, I mixed a little, fine, groundbait and flour into the soft paste to stiffen it so that it could be moulded into small balls.

There was a different story to tell at the end of the next session. Fishing the same swim as the previous week provided an interesting comparison. The carp were late in starting to patrol this time, but about 11 a.m. the surface bow-waving began. I have never known a water where the carp are more prone to bow-waving than this lake and it can be so helpful at times. I was fishing in much the same way as the previous week, with a rod cast down the margins and the float rod tackle cast 25 yards out into the lake. On the margin rod the usual luncheon meat, on the float rod the liver pâté paste. I had only about half a pound of the pâté bait so I chose to use it in the most active rod position. Some had been shot in to bait the swim and there was enough left for my needs providing two swims were not baited. We only use small baits in the North. Even when we use No. 2 or 4 hooks the bait only just covers them. For the last month I had scaled right down to No. 8 or 10 hooks to keep the carp interested.

The first pair of carp came up the lake bow-waving towards my baited swim and I picked up the catapult, put three small balls of pâté in the sling, shooting them out as the fish drew near. Down went the carp leaving two big vortices on the surface, while I clutched the rod-butt in readiness. The float went down nice and easy a few minutes later. The strike connected and the next twenty minutes provided a fine scrap with the light test-curve rod and 5 pound line. I knew by the way the fish fought that it would go double figures before it was landed. There seemed to be just that bit more effort from the doubles in this water and rarely have I had one out in less than twenty minutes. The longest fight I have ever had here lasted for nearly three-quarters of an hour with the carp weighing 11 pounds 6 ounces. In spite of doing a 'Dave Steuart' by holding the rod well above the butt with the left hand when possible, my right arm felt as if it was dropping off by the time I landed that one!

This fish I was playing now fought well but did not make the repeatedly long runs that others have when brought into the 18 inch deep margins. The carp weighed exactly 11 pounds and I was very pleased indeed that it weighed so much. After two seasons' fishing here my friends and I had caught a fair number of carp by northern standards, but had only caught two 11-plus fish: one 11 pounds 6 ounces and one 11½ pounds. Funnily enough, as luck would have it, I was fortunate enough to get them both. That was why it was so pleasurable to get another 11 pounder, particularly with a new bait – felt like hugging myself I did!

Soon after, the margin rod to the left produced a quick bleep and a big bow wave as the carp ploughed off thoroughly scared. Feeling so pleased with the carp already caught I thought, 'What the hell, I'll put a bit of the pâté on that rod too.' So on it went and after casting, three small balls of my fast-dwindling supply were thrown in the same area. Back with the float rod, which required full attention, the odd carp passed through without going down to the bottom. . . . The margin rod indicator sang out, a slow confident, unmissable run and the carp made the clutch really scream as it powered-off out of the shallow water, leaving the disrupted margins rocking. As soon as the first run was over I screwed the clutch down and played the fish from the handle. The fight on 10 pound line and carp rod was a short, powerful affair and the fish weighed 10¼ pounds. Another milestone for me too, as this was the first time I had done the 'double-double' in a session. This water provided me with several threes, fours and one five-carp catch in a session, but never two *doubles*. The pleasure within reached even greater heights, while the pâté supply dwindled. My cup was full, however, and as a bow wave neared the float, the last pieces were shot out without regret. The bait was good and next week would see me with a larger supply . . . but it had not finished working for me yet. The sinking pâté attracted the approaching carp, the vortex clearly showing the fish had gone down – as did the float a few minutes later! This fish fought well too but only went 9 pounds. 'Only' is an understatement really, for the average carp here weighed about 6 pounds, being young fish just coming up to the peak growing period of their lives. That some were already in double figures spoke well of the growth potential of the water, as it had been stocked with fingerlings only six years before so far as I could ascertain from club officials.

That catch, which gave me so much happiness at the time, may seem small fry today. Though, more recently, I have fished a water where it is unusual to catch a fish under double figures, the catching of a double, while being more of a certainty, still gives great pleasure. The fish in this water are much harder to catch even though upper doubles and 20 pound fish are caught reasonably often. But my feeling of pride at landing one of the best carp in a lake remains the same whether the fish weighs 7 or 27 pounds. The problem facing an angler at any water, including Redmire, is how to catch the better fish the water produces. Providing he is able to do that at each water fished, he can hold his head high. Bear in mind, though, that the man who catches one carp that is a lake record is not necessarily a better angler than one who catches ten smaller carp from the same water – he is just more fortunate.

The slow, confident, butt-ringer type of bite seems to be fast disappearing in most waters. We can only guess at the reason and decide that pressure is the cause at the majority of waters. Often a new bait will ease the situation for a while, but before long we are back at square one again, fast pulls being the norm. The steady runs obviously come from fish that are passing through the baited area at normal cruising speed, tilting down to take the bait without pause, almost, as they cruise by. Runs of this nature require little study or analysis. They are the easiest bites to hit and we need only be thankful that we get them.

On the other hand the terrifically fast run that comes out of the blue takes some understanding. A fair-sized lake that I fish often produces some runs at long range that have to be seen to be believed. One split-second the silver paper is hanging still, the next it is dancing like crazy in the butt-ring, while the line rattles through the rings at incredible speed and the rod vibrates in the rests. There have been several attempts to describe why the carp should choose to take a bait in this way, but none really bear critical examination. One popular explanation suggests that the effect is due to greed on the fish's part, causing it to dash in, grab the bait, then swim away with it before another carp can pinch it. I do not know who first put forward this idea, but I am sure they spent too much time watching

Bob Ford with a 28¼ pounder

chickens and too little watching carp. The chicken analogy is doubtful anyway, since a chicken only runs from its neighbours if it finds a
food item that is too large to swallow at one go, running to find a
quiet spot to break up the piece. Anyone using a bait so large that a
double-figure carp cannot swallow it in one go does not deserve to
get any sort of a run. A carp has no external means of breaking up a
bait, so why should it swim away with it?

The other popular theory does not stand up to critical analysis
either. The explanation is that the fast run is caused by the carp
picking up a large bait like a potato and swimming fast with it,
hoping that the water pressure on the bait will shove it into the
mouth. This is more unacceptable than the first explanation for
several valid reasons. First of all, assuming that the fish did get such
a bait into its mouth, it seems most unlikely it would be able to get
the bait into its throat where the pharyngeal teeth could work to
break it up. Secondly, having got such a big bait into and completely
blocking the mouth cavity, the fish would be unable to eject the bait
again or breathe effectively. The gills are only 10 per cent efficient
when extracting oxygen from water entering in reverse flow and the
fish would suffocate in this predicament. Thirdly, as we saw at the
start of the chapter, the fish can create a tremendous vacuum within
its mouth, the effects of which are far in excess of that any puny
external water pressure might exert on a bait as the fish swims along.
There is no need for the fish to swim anywhere, the mechanism it
possesses inside the mouth is more than adequate, allowing it to
suck in any bait that is not too large to fit the pharyngeal area. A
fourth and very simple reason is that few anglers use potato for bait
these days – but carp still give fast runs on very small baits.

So what is the answer to lightning-fast runs? The only logical
explanation I can find is that the carp is afraid. The speed of the run,
with no initial warning either, suggests that the fish is accelerating
away at maximum speed in panic. It suggests that the carp has
picked up the bait without any indication reaching the angler then,
while chewing the bait, has pricked itself with the hook and charged
off in a panic-stricken run. Or, while chewing the bait with its
pharyngeal teeth, it might have felt the hook, spitting it out as a
piece of debris. The speed of ejection might cause the hook to
become lightly lodged in the mouth, again producing panic. My
reason for thinking this springs from the number of carp my friends
and I have lost with this sort of run while fishing at long range. The

loss has always been because the hook fell out, suggesting that it only had a light hold to start with. After losing three carp on the trot in this manner, I took to repeated striking, hoping the hook would find better hold. One morning I got a fast run while fishing at about 50 yards' range. The fish was heading up the lake and I followed the initial strike with two more as heavy as the 5 pound line would allow. A good 70 yards up the lake the run stopped. The fish created a huge boil on the surface and I began to pump it back. On the third 'pump' the line went slack and I reeled in – the hook had fallen out again. During that period I lost eight carp – three in one session was the worst – making me very despondent. Those weren't small carp, all were doubles and at least one may have fulfilled my ambition of landing a '20' on 5 pound line and Avon rod.

At first sight an experienced carp angler would say the hook fell out because the striking technique or tackle was wrong. I would accept this as fair comment except that so many others, using all manner of tackle combinations, have had the same experience. Recently I stopped using the Avon rod, instead favouring an Oliver's carp rod with 6 or 8 pound line. The results show what appears to be an improvement as I have landed every fish hooked at long range on this rig. I am in some doubt whether there is real improvement, or if I have just been luckier. Two of the long-range fish were hooked *outside* the mouth and one only lightly hooked just inside it. The hooks and terminal tackle were the same, No. 8 long-shank hooks with low profile cutting barb, and a plastic, large eye 'paternoster' rig to overcome the silk-weed. I am convinced that silk-weed is the real cause of the loss of so many carp. This lake has a tremendous amount of silk-weed and massive 'blooms' of filamentous algae. The line sinks into this clogging stuff between hook and rod, reducing sensitivity and allowing the carp to pick up the bait without any indication. Eventually either a full-blooded, panic-stricken run results or, as must happen so many times, the carp eats the bait and spits out the hook without the angler knowing. Floating cork or lightweight plastic paternoster rigs go some way towards eliminating the problem, but a tighter line to the bait would be better, except that tightening only sinks the line further into the weed. It might seem a bit negative to say there seems no way to improve bite indication at long range under the conditions mentioned. A 90 per cent hook-hold success rate is well above average for the long-range carp angler. However, I am sure that the fast runs

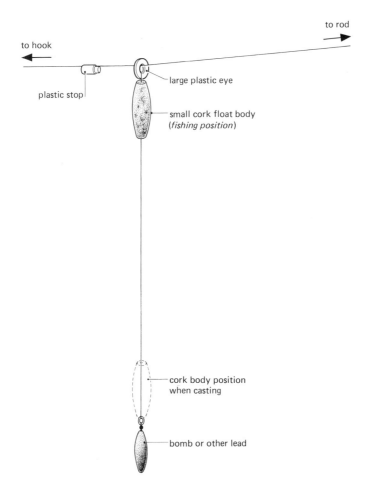

to rod

to hook

plastic stop

large plastic eye

small cork float body
(*fishing position*)

cork body position
when casting

bomb or other lead

Figure 4   Large eye plastic paternoster rig. The large plastic eye is made from Delrin or perspex and the plastic stop can be bought from a tackle dealer or made from plastic sleeving with a wooden or plastic plug. Length of line between eye and bomb is about 4 inches for soft silt and 12 inches for deep silkweed- or algae-covered bottoms

have nothing to do with chicken-like behaviour on the carp's part, or that the fish is trying to push a bait into its mouth with the water pressure assisting it. If we can rid our minds of inaccurate conclusions we might at least come nearer to solving the problem.

In 1975 I spent some time observing fingerling carp and roach feeding. The carp were between 2 and 5 inches long, the roach about $2\frac{1}{2}$ inches. All one need do was to throw a ball of Kit-e-Kat–groundbait mix into the edge of the lake and watch. Roach and carp came from all directions to this manna from heaven, the roach always beating the carp. It was interesting to watch the feeding patterns of each species. The roach, first there, would dart in, grab a mouthful and dart to one side to eat it. Then in again for some more. The carp arrived seconds later knocking out of the way any roach silly enough to be in their path. There was no darting about or running off with the carp. They went *into* the food carpet, sucked in a big mouthful and *lay there* chewing it. When they had finished that, in went another mouthful and so on until the bottom was clean. I then tried some small cubes of luncheon meat mixed with the Kit-e-Kat to see what would happen. The roach could not manage them at all and if a piece was too large for one of the smaller carp it spat it out, leaving it until one of the larger ones took it. I tried the same procedure in five different areas of the lake. Never did I see a carp pick up a piece of bait and *run with it*. . . .

Carp seem to retain a sort of rough shoaling instinct during the first few years of life. While never being tightly packed like roach or bream and still retaining a strong streak of individuality in their foraging, the carp drift about in a loose shoal looking for food. I once watched a small shoal of fish between $1\frac{1}{2}$ and 3 pounds drift into an area I had baited with meat-cubes intended for their betters. The baited swim was only a few yards from the bank in 3 feet of clear water, allowing good observation. There was no mad rush for the meat. The fish approached in an easy way, tilting down in orderly fashion to feed, colouring the water and blocking the view as more fish arrived to share the food. At no time did I see a carp emerge and belt off with others chasing it. . . .

When carp reach maturity they become much more individual and it is rare to see a 'shoal' of large carp under normal conditions. Sometimes on a hot day they will congregate at a particular part of the pond or lake and one must assume the conditions there suit their need at the time. Then at spawning time you will often see small groups of between three and five carp swimming together in a tight shoal. These groups are invariably comprised of one fat female in front, followed by males whose size can vary from 5 or 6 pounds up to big doubles. Carp will often feed between bouts of spawning activity, although during the act of spawning seem oblivious to everything. Several times I have stood in the margins and had spawning fish swim round my waders. I have watched these tight groups of carp feed many times on bait samples and never seen one dash off with a bait.

This is not proof that carp will not, at times, pick up a bait and swim at maximum speed away from their companions. But it is evidence that suggests this is very unlikely to happen under normal feeding conditions. It also supports the theory that fear, in the form of a fish already 'hooked', is the real cause of 'instant' fast runs. How one can detect the take of a carp that drifts into a swim 50 or more yards out in the lake, sucks in the bait and eats it without moving is a puzzle. But if bottom conditions allow it, the angler who is prepared to fish as tight as possible and hit what I term 'beep-and-hold' bites (where the indicator continues sounding but no line is taken) will find an increase in the number of well hooked fish.

The margin-patrolling carp will often whip line off the spool at a fair lick. These fish can sometimes be seen patrolling the edge of the lake, occasionally going down, without stopping in the process, to cause a puff of 'smoke' on the bottom. I have the distinct impression that most margin-patrollers at well-frequented waters half expect to be scared by an angler. Their cruising speed is slightly faster than when they swim farther out in the lake and their explosive take-off when hooked leaves little doubt that they know the margins spell danger. I have also noticed when carp are feeding reasonably close in that very often you get a quick 'beep' on the indicator before the run starts, giving fair warning to be ready for action. This was very noticeable, up to about 30 yards' range, in one clean-bedded Cheshire lake. I am pretty sure the initial beep was the shock wave caused by a hungry carp sucking in the bait and the effect travelled right up the line. I have been fortunate enough to see on several occasions the line, where it enters the water, jump when a beep has occurred. The speed of movement can only be due to a shock-wave effect – no fish could move that fast. So many times the short beep has been followed by a slow run a second or so later as the fish continues through the baited area, that it must be assumed the long-range feeding pattern is often similar to that of the margins.

I visualize the hookbait laying on the lake bed with odd bait samples scattered around it. A carp swims lazily through the area and sucks a piece of bait from the lake bed, continuing to drift through the area while chewing the bait. Then it turns round, swims back the opposite way, picking up another piece and so on, until it is the turn of the hook sample. When the hookbait is sucked in, the carp approaches the bait, tilts down slightly and sucks it in while still 3 or 4 inches away. This causes a sharp forward jerk on the line. As the fish continues drifting the slack is taken up and the long run comes seconds after the initial beep from the indicator. I have noticed, with this type of run, there is generally a brief pause when the carp is hooked. It is as if the fish has already been through the swim a number of times picking up bait, having no trouble. But suddenly that last piece of bait tries to stop it drifting forward so there is a pause, and a shake of the head which sends a thump up the line. Sometimes the fish, still not alarmed, will drift with the strike, making the angler think he has hooked only a small carp. Within a short time the carp finds all is not well and goes off on the first powerful run.

This 'puzzled' effect is very noticeable when light tackle rigs like an Avon rod and 5 pound line are used. I have often hooked carp on such a rod and pumped them in with little fight until the fish was a few yards from the bank – then off it went. The largest carp I have caught which reacted in this way was a common caught on a light rod and 6 pound line. It was hooked at something over 50 yards' range and came towards me as I recovered line. A large bed of lilies on each side of me began to look very menacing as the fish continued in. I began to stamp on the bank hoping the fish would turn, but it actually entered the gap in the lilies before panic set in. Only then did I know it was a big carp. As it set off the line snagged the outermost stalk of the lily bed and though it was dark I could see the pad pulled under as the fish accelerated into a tremendous run, finally rolling a long way off, lost in darkness. The situation seemed hopeless, 6 pound line snagged on a lily stem with a good carp on one end and a shaking angler on the other. The fish was pumped back – the very devil of a job with the line cutting into a lily stalk, until it touched the pad and off it went again, with me expecting the line to part any moment. Again I pumped the fish back, again it set off on the third run. Halfway through the third run the line pulled away from the margin pads. The line had cut through the stalk and the pad floated to the surface. The next time the fish was pumped in it was so tired it went into the net almost thankfully! It weighed 17 pounds exactly. You could question the use of 6 pound line near lily pads and would be right to do so. The two things that caused the choice were range and silk-weed. 6 pound line gave me the required range without using a big bomb. Anglers often have to pull for a break on much heavier lines when a 1 ounce lead sinks into the silk-weed. I expected the fish to 'wake up' before it reached the bank – it did not and I was very lucky the line went *through* the pads and not *round* one. Do not panic if you find yourself in a similar situation. Provided the fish is taking line all right, there is every chance the line will eventually cut through the stalk. Keep the rod tip reasonably high above the snagging point. This ensures the line will come out clean when the stalk is severed. You may also find the pumping action difficult. Line can be recovered quite well by giving the rod little upward jerks. But remember to go easy with the right arm.

Carp anglers generally seem to avoid floats – thinking, perhaps with reason, that the line from lead to float may scare the fish. I have caught some of my best carp on float tackle – in 'gin-clear' lakes too. Despite years of research no bite indicator can hope to be as sensitive as a correctly fished float. I could quote plenty of float-fishing instances where carp have been scared by the line. I could also quote many more examples, when fishing floating crust, of carp that have been scared by the line. Yet floating crust is an accepted way of catching carp, whereas until recently, when the particle boom and its often minute bite indication forced anglers to think again, the float appears to have been generally neglected. Floats can be deadly under certain conditions providing the range allows proper use. For fishing close in where the margins are 10 to 14 feet deep; for bubbler-fishing as mentioned in the bubbler chapters; for just-under-surface worm-fishing; for presenting both particle and other baits to carp that, for one reason or another, are giving infuriating twitches, some of which do not even register on the bite indicator or the line. We will look at deep-water indication first of all.

There was a deep sand-pit I fished about half a dozen times in 1971 and three or four times in 1972. Carp anglers in Sheffield are quite used to travelling 100-mile round trips to do their fishing and this water was 140 miles there and back. It is great setting off the night before full of hope and enthusiasm. But oh! the drudgery of the return journey the following day when weary and dejected, *another* blank recorded. The hot, tiring, drive home seems endless. My good friend and angling companion of many years standing, Eric Wainwright, was a tower of strength on such journeys. A blank always brought out his most sadistic sense of humour. My tired eyes have often burned with tears of laughter thanks to Eric's incisive wit. We did quite well during the visits we made, Eric, in particular, and my nephew Dave Mottram doing very well on a short holiday there. The distance and no night-fishing rule made things awkward and poor roads meant we had to set off about 1 a.m. to arrive and settle in for first light. We caught about seventy carp over the two seasons, but most were caught during the first three months we fished the water.

One swim I liked to fish provided thrills in two ways. The bank behind was near vertical, rising 30 feet or more and supplying a constant 'trickle' of falling debris as the rising temperature caused expansion of the soil. There was a ledge about 3 feet wide, all bare and exposed, that one fished from. The water lapped the bank and the margins fell off to around 14 feet deep in an almost vertical drop. I was fishing this swim one morning and was being constantly bothered with minute twitches, mere vibrations of the line. Periodically I would pull in the bait, which was being fished along the margin rather than out into the lake, to find the luncheon meat had been broken or had gone altogether. Small fish were blamed. There were a lot of long, thin tench in the water – fish more like trout in shape. We called them 'trench'. By nine o'clock I had become very annoyed with the continued twitching and, determined to find out what caused it, I rigged up a 'lift-method' sliding-float. If you have not used this rig before you may have difficulty getting it to work with 10 or 12 pound lines. For the method to work successfully the tackle requires a 'start' to pull the line through the small eye of the float. The illustrated tackle rig works effectively up to 30 yards and

Figure 5   Sliding float details. The Domhof knot forms an ideal stop-knot for a sliding float. Use nylon line of 3 to 4 pounds breaking strains and leave long ends until correct depth setting is found; then pull very tight and snip off to ¼ inch. Where the depth exceeds 10 feet, put additional turns on the knot to avoid slipping when wound through rod rings. Shotting weight is progressively increased as range and depth increase; usable maximum around 30 yards and 25 feet respectively

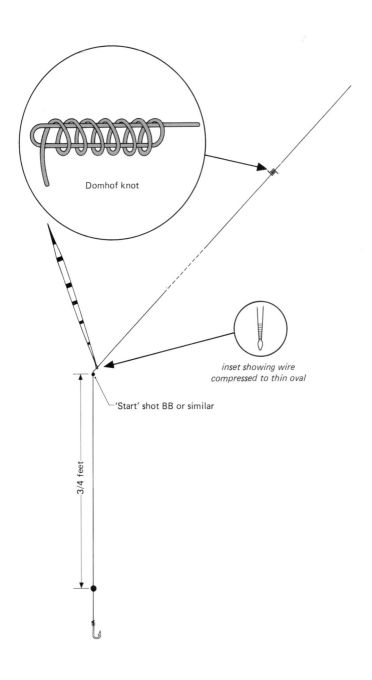

Domhof knot

inset showing wire
compressed to thin oval

'Start' shot BB or similar

3/4 feet

depths of 25 feet. Beyond that it becomes progressively more difficult, requiring more weight to pull the line along the surface, particularly in windy spells.

There were no problems like that in this swim. The float was a long porcupine quill with the wire squashed into a thin oval, although any float with a wire loop can be pressed into use. A Domhof stop-knot was adjusted slightly over depth at 15 feet. Two swan-shot were placed 4 inches from the hook and a stop-shot placed under the float. The first cast was made. When using this rig the float tends to bob up and down as the weight of the sinking shot pulls the thick line through the small eye. But when the shots hit the bottom, the float lays flat due to the over-depth setting. A couple of turns on the reel handle are needed to cock the float. All this had

A deep margin caught carp. Taken in 14 feet of water using a sliding float

been done and I had just sat back in my low chair when the float ups and lays itself flat again! The strike connected, the fish being a small 3 pound mirror that was quickly hauled out on the hefty gear. Re-baiting, I cast back to the same place, waited until the float lay flat and turned the reel handle to cock the float. The float cocked and promptly lay flat again. Thinking the shot had been pulled on to a ledge I tightened again. Once more the float lifted and fell over. I can be very stupid at times and a few more seconds passed before I realized that a fish must have either taken the bait on the drop, or on the second it reached the bottom. Again the strike connected and the fish came towards me easily for a few yards, then turned, making a powerful run, to the depths in the centre of the pit and taking 50 yards or more of line from the spool. After quite a struggle (there was a full-grown tree 15 yards out in the lake that had been completely submerged when the pit flooded) I landed a 'personal best' mirror weighing 13 pounds. Two casts and two carp. That must have been the quickest I have ever hooked and landed two carp. There were no more though. The tussle to keep the fish out of the sunken tree had put the rest down.

This 13 pound carp was above the best we had caught here and caused my friends to adopt sliding-float tactics too. The result was six more doubles, five of which fell to sliding-float tactics. The largest, of $13\frac{3}{4}$ pounds, was caught by Eric Wainwright. He hardly said a word all the way home; sat like a Cheshire cat, he did, with a contented smile on his face! The largest caught here by my circle of friends, it was almost the largest that season, fell to Gordon Chell. He made six visits, fuming inwardly at his failure to catch carp and cursing the endless 'trench' that took his bait. His seventh visit had us all looking to our laurels, for he landed a 15 pound 2 ounce mirror. To the northern carp angler that is still a big fish – in 1971 it was enormous. Unfortunately I do not know if this fish fell to sliding float tactics. I have records of date, line, hook, bait and time caught, but the method is not listed.

The sliding-float is also good for particle-bait-fishing in deep-margin lakes. On opening day 1975 I fished a very deep lake from midnight to mid morning. The swim was 13 feet deep only 4 yards from the edge, going even deeper farther out. A beta-light float would have been very handy before dawn, but not having one I had to manage with the indicators. Having arrived the previous evening I had had plenty of time to analyse the situation and decided to cast

(i) Dennis MacFetrich plays a 14 pound Waterways carp

(ii) Peter Evans sinks the net as Dennis applies more pressure. The carp is almost beaten

(iii) Dennis guides the beaten carp over the net. Both anglers crouch low to avoid scaring the carp

(iv) A big smile from Pete says it all!

along the margins to my left. When you fish close in from exposed banks the baited area should be 20 yards to one side or the other, regardless of depth. There was no cover here, just a steep bank down to water level. Nothing happened after the midnight start until just before dawn when the indicator of the left-hand rod began an intermittent bleeping. Crouching down by the side of the rod I felt the line for a while with my thumb and finger. Not feeling anything I reeled in and found the particle bait had gone. Re-baiting and casting again, I waited by the rod. This time I felt the sawing vibrations as the indicator bleeped. But by the time the bail-arm was shut and the strike made, the fish had spat out the hook. I am not keen on shutting the bail-arm when margin-fishing as a big carp can have the rod off the rests in a flash. It was rapidly getting lighter and by the time I had fitted a sliding-float it was light enough to see it when cast to the swim. Plumbing the swim the day before now paid off. The half-hitch float-stop was immediately tied at the correct depth. No time was wasted in having to cast two or three times into a hot swim to find the right setting. First cast into the baited swim. A few minutes' wait. The float lifted a little, settled back and slowly sank. A careful strike with the Oliver's carp rod to 5 pound line, two puzzled shakes of the head causing thumps on the rod end, and the fish ran out and down into the depths, taking an enormous amount of line from the spool. When the run stopped it took a long while to pump the fish back and, just as the float showed in front of me, the fish went off again on another long run. After some while, during which I began to think that I was into a really good carp, the fish began to tire and was quickly netted. It was a mirror in top condition, weighing 14 pounds. Just after I had released the fish four anglers clumsily stomped along the bank above me, making vibrations that even I could feel. What the carp felt goodness knows. Not surprisingly that carp was the only one caught on opening day.

Just one more example of deep-water float-fishing before moving on to other forms of float presentation. In June 1973 I began fishing a water where, for the first time in my angling life, there was a good chance of catching a 20 pound carp. Some very good anglers fished the water and the average catches showed that a lot of time had to be put in to catch a carp – most of which were doubles. My own start was little short of disaster. The first session I blanked; the second one I had a margin-fished rod whipped off the rests like a piece of straw, never to be seen again. I never did quite work out how it happened. I think the high wind must have tangled the line around the reel. After losing the rod my confidence went. I could do nothing right after that. Come August I crawled in among the trees of an awkward, overgrown bank to hide my failure from other anglers. I liked the swim and, though I had not fished it before, began to feel some confidence return. Three carp later my confidence was fully restored! It appeared that three carp in a session was something of a record in recent times. The local anglers told me it had only been done once – years before. However, the following week my good friend Rod Walker soon put that right by taking three carp, bigger than mine, from the same swim. Rod is a brilliant carp angler. His results, if published, would show him to be one of the best in the country. He fully deserved his success and I felt pleased for him.

The swim was about 10 foot deep, the hot-spot close to a large tree that had fallen into the lake – a cast of about 20 yards. The bank sloped gently into the lake, steepening about 4 feet out. The underwater slope was covered in a thick layer of cotton-wool-like algae that tended to clog the lines as they sank into it. This algae seemed to reduce the sensitivity of bite indication. The second time I fished the swim I had many twitches that set the indicator going without line being taken. During this session I landed two 13 pounders by holding the line with my fingers and feeling the fish chewing the bait. Had I realized sooner what was happening there may have been more than two carp at the end of that session.

The following week I thought about what might be taking place under water and decided that a different type of indicator, fished in conjunction with an underwater float, might help the situation. The float was a cork body from one of those plastic, antenna, floats and barely supported a swan-shot. It was rigged to slide up the line by passing the line through the hole the plastic spine had occupied. The usual half-hitch stop was set over-depth at about 12 feet. A swanshot and a BB, about 9 inches from the hook, provided just enough weight to overcome the buoyancy of the cork body. This indicator was similar to a tight-line/slack-line type I had experimented with years before, except that it only registered a tight-line bite. Now, what I hoped would happen, was that as the carp sucked in the bait to the pharyngeal teeth it would move about 4 or 5 inches of line, thus the whole tackle set-up would be displaced a little. The float, although sunk under the surface, would keep the line free of algae and move slightly to a new position when the carp took the bait. My rod-rest indicator was set to respond to a 1/32 inch movement. If it just beeped and stopped it was a small fish hitting the line in the margins; if the indicator continued sounding it was a fish at the bait. That was the reasoning behind the set-up and simulated test experiments at home suggested that it ought to work. Would it work in practice though?

Bob Ford was in the hot swim when I arrived and insisted on leaving it to me in spite of my protests to the contrary. His last words on leaving to fish a less productive area were: 'Get stuck in. I want to see you get your first 20.' Friends like that do not come every day and Bob knew as well as anyone that this swim was about the only one producing any carp. I rigged up the rods, fitting the underwater float to the one fishing the hot-spot, two feet from the sunken branches. There were slight qualms of confidence as I made the cast and set up the indicator, but it had worked in practice so....

Gradually the light faded and I kept a steady flow of bait samples, two or three every half-hour, going into the swim. It was just nicely dark when the new set-up started a prolonged beeping. The strike connected and, plunging the rod tip under water to pressure the fish away from the sunken branches, I heaved until the corks of the S/U bent. The fish came easily enough, fighting deep and strong in front of me without making any long runs. It was obviously a good one but wasted energy boring deep, until it rolled quietly, went down again for a short while, then came up blowing water and ready for the net. As I lifted the net I felt the front touch the fish's tail when its head was quite close to the net apex. Only then did I realize that at last here was a really good carp. It was a strange, quiet affair. Nothing like I would have expected. Calling softly to my friend Paul Stenson in the next swim, I asked if he could give me a hand for a minute. Paul arrived asking what was the matter not knowing I had a carp. Putting his hand in the net as it lay in the margins, he felt the fish's body: 'It's that 27,' he said. I was too amazed to speak. The fish has a small lump on the lower, right-hand flank and is well known, Paul having caught it in June of the same year at $27\frac{1}{2}$ pounds.

At 2 a.m. the indicator bleeped once more in a prolonged fashion and the hooked carp came in like a wet sack. A very peculiar one this, pumped with hardly a wriggle to the bank. I hesitated before netting it, as the dark shape breaking the lake surface told me it was no tiddler. The fish just flopped about on the surface so I stuck the net under it. As the net was lifted the bloody silly thing went berserk, saturating me! What a strange contrast between the two fish. Weighed next morning, after spending the night in my large sack, the big 'un went 26¼ pounds and the little 'un 10¼ pounds.

There are many times when a good positive indication of a take is given, and no special tackle arrangement is needed. When the going gets tough, as it often does at many lakes and ponds in late July and August, the float, combined with a general scaling down of line strength and hook size can often result in improved catches. This delicate approach to the problem, using a float to detect gentle takes, suggests that the carp are still feeding well, though the angler who insists on using a big bait/buzzer only approach may leave at the end of a session cursing twitching carp. The only important detail when using the lift-method for carp fishing is the placing of the shot. If shot is put too close to the hook the carp may feel it when it sucks in the bait. This may result in the carp spitting the lot out, thinking it has picked up some unwanted debris too. It then tries to pick the bait up again. The float then tends to bob about, or worse still, shoots under with the force of ejection when the carp blows out the bait, causing the angler to strike at 'nothing'. For this reason I have always placed the shot 4 or 5 inches from the hook. When the carp sucks in the bait it is able to take it right into the back of the mouth, leaving the shots outside. Bite indication on the float varies a little even with the lift method. This is perhaps due to the angle the fish approaches the bait. If it is between angler and float the float will invariably lift; if the fish sucks in the bait while facing the angler the float shoots under very fast and can sometimes be seen just below the surface. There is no hurry required, as a rule, when striking. I have sometimes been caught unawares, looking away from my tackle to see what caused a disturbance or something similar – only to look back and find my float laying flat or gone under. Fishing a float in this way and seeing how often a carp will gently suck in a bait makes you realize how many takes remain undetected with free-line/bite indicator methods. It makes nonsense of the accepted 'run' for which the carp angler is supposed to wait.

You can also use a float to present a bait when carp are 'humping' under the algal scum. One lake we fished had quite prolific algae at certain times of the year, making the water quite green. The prevailing westerly wind used to pile this up in one corner, making a thick surface layer of several square yards. A close look at the layer would reveal drowned flies and struggling nymphs trapped in it. Carp would often swim under the layer, picking off the goodies from the underside. I think it was Gordon Chell who first hit upon the idea of presenting a brandling through the surface layer. He used a small float with the worm suspended only inches below it. It looked ridiculous of course, but it worked because the thick covering reduced the light available, the carp locating the wriggling bodies by vibration rather than sight. This method became a standard procedure when the carp were humping in the algae.

We used the float-and-worm combination in another non-standard way that looked so silly a text-book carp angler would have died laughing. I am not sure which of us first tried it as we were always trying unusual methods when the carp were being difficult. However, the method was used when carp were still patrolling the shallows in small groups after spawning. A brandling or small lob-worm, impaled on a size 8 or 10 hook, was suspended 9 inches to a foot below the float. Any shot for casting weight was put directly under the float. In use it was just a matter of waiting until the carp swam into range and then a cast to drop the bait about 10 feet in front of the approaching group. The best chance of success came when the cast had been correctly judged and the float was centred in the carp's path. Too long or short a cast did not seem to be as effective. One of the best sessions I remember fishing like this was in early July. I counted fourteen carp on the shallows in four separate groups. One group consisted of just two carp, a male and female of about 8 pounds each that made a circular course out into the shallows and back to the fringe of horse-tail reeds to spawn. These fish were completely oblivious to the angler and his baits. The other three groups patrolled the shallows, swimming through the areas they had spawned in but not stopping to go through the spawning routine. There were four of us around the shallows at different points. We called softly to each other when carp were out of personal casting range, helping advise when a group were approaching. In this way we caught seven out of the twelve spawned carp before the rest became too agitated and left the shallows. Playing fish quietly increases the chance of more takes, but sooner or later the fish cotton on to what is happening and leave. The most amazing thing of all was the effectiveness of a worm dangling in open water a foot below a float. You would never expect any self-respecting carp to fall for such a simple dodge. Under normal conditions they would not even look at such a crude and obvious presentation. One is forced to conclude that the post-spawning behaviour had something to do with it. To see the float cocked in front of a group then to see it towed along behind them as they passed was almost unbelievable. Every fish was hooked properly, no foul-hooking at all. For some inexplicable reason they seemed compelled to take a worm dangling in front of their noses, though they would not move off course to take it. These particular fish were not interested in crust. But a friend and I once took six carp, which had just finished spawning, on crust. This was at a small pond 100 miles away. The carp had been going mad all night, crashing and splashing about like demented things. There have been other occasions, too, when I have caught carp just after spawning. The fish seem ravenous and it is well worthwhile hanging on the following day if the carp have been spawning all night. The activity seems to quieten down between about 8 and 10 a.m. and, though the carp are still swimming in the spawning area, they suddenly become receptive to almost anything you throw at them.

It could be argued that it is unsporting to take advantage of spawning fish. This is really a matter for the individual angler and his conscience. My own views regarding the northern half of the country are that the close season for carp is completely wrong. At most waters I have fished the carp spawn well after the season has opened. In any case the chances are that the eggs deposited by the carp will not survive. If they do it only requires a fraction of them to hatch to more than compensate for any natural loss of adults. A successful hatch of carp-fry can almost ruin a season's fishing in the smaller waters. The small carp attack any bait with a persistence that quickly leaves the hook bare. With all this in mind I try to catch any carp that will take the bait within the specified open season. I appreciate and understand that someone else might rather leave the fish undisturbed to their post-spawning patrolling.

In this chapter I have tried to highlight methods and approaches with actual fishing examples. It seems wrong to give advice without giving proof that the advice will work. To do this one must describe one's own fishing sessions. An angler must have some plan of action – even a bad plan is better than none at all. I have tried to detail the methods my friends and I have found the most reliable. There are many ways to catch carp: some require only that a baited hook is flung lakewards, while others require a more refined approach. I would not insult my readers' intelligence by quoting examples of the first, so I have chosen incidents where thought or experiment has produced the goods.

4 Winter carp-fishing

Since the formation of the Carpcatchers Club a quarter of a century ago there has been little real change in carp-fishing. It is true that carp-fishing is much more advanced now than it was then, and so it should be when you consider how many participate in the sport. Yet the advances that have come with the passing years are mainly technical; a wider choice of rods, lines and reels, etc. The approach to carp-fishing, the methods of presentation and the general attitude has remained much the same. The Carpcatchers were a very intelligent group of anglers who established most of the basic concepts of carp-angling at a time when carp were generally thought to be uncatchable. With Dick Walker at the helm, their approach was thorough and most aspects were either well covered or known about. Perhaps the one aspect that can be rightly attributed to a source other than the Carpcatchers is that of serious winter carp-fishing.

It is true that the Carpcatchers knew that carp were catchable below 58 °F but it is doubtful if they ever established that winter carp-fishing was a viable proposition. The general approach then appeared to be that carp were not worth bothering about after the first serious frosts arrived. There was a general belief, still prevalent today in some quarters, that in winter carp did a mysterious thing called 'going to mud'. Carp anglers today generally know that this belief is based more on supposition than fact. And what is more they catch many carp, often their best of the season, during the accepted winter months of November to March. Which shows winter fishing is not a waste of time. It is one thing knowing that something is possible, but it is another going out to prove it. The true pioneers of winter carp-fishing came a decade or so after the Carpcatchers had become an angling legend. It is because of people like Jim

Gibbinson, Mike Winter, Gerry Savage and others who wrote of their exploits, that significant advance was made. It was through reading of their catches that I first became interested in winter carp-angling. But before I relate my own experience you might find a letter I received from my good friend Kevin Roberts of York very revealing. I have known Kevin since he was a teenager and the one driving influence in his life in all that time has been carp. His letter concerns the winter period of 1975–6:

Dear George

Knowing of your interest in winter carp-fishing, you'll be pleased to hear that I've been knocking a few out recently. I'll give you a rundown on my winter efforts.

Because of the domestic upheaval caused by the arrival of our Son and Heir (who will hopefully carry my tackle when I am too old to do so!) I didn't fish between the end of October and the beginning of January. I did attempt to fish on one occasion in December, however, but was defeated by the weather. John Morrell and I got an all-too-rare invitation to fish Carp-lake which, as you know, is quite an easy water and can usually be relied upon to produce a few fish, even in the depths of winter. To our disappointment the lake was heavily frozen when we arrived and we were unable to break a hole through it. Our disappointment turned to despair when, on walking round the pond, we chanced on a group of five or six decent carp feeding in the extreme shallows, under the ice! Moving about quite rapidly too, they were, no sign of 'winter sluggishness'.

It was 10 January before I had the chance to fish again. A spell of unseasonably mild weather persuaded me to try my luck at Southfield where all my previous winter efforts had gone unrewarded, and I've never had more than five fish in any one season. I arrived at the water around 10.30 a.m. and just poked about for an hour or so wondering where to fish. The water looked as it usually does in winter – dull, lifeless and decidedly sullen and to be perfectly honest I didn't fancy my chances, despite the mild weather. I eventually set up my tackle in a swim which has a depth variation ranging from 4 feet to 10 feet and is fronted in the summer by a large weed bed, the remains of which now lurked, unseen, below the surface. Three rods were used baited with maggots and luncheon meat, with the reel pick-ups closed, twitcher-hitting style. Within minutes of casting I had a butt ringer on the rod closest to me but as I was fiddling with the indicator on one of the other rods I was unable to strike.

About 1 p.m. I had another run on the same rod and landed a small mirror of $5\frac{1}{2}$ pounds, one of the 'new' fish stocked a couple of years ago. An hour later I hit a 4 inch lift and, after being taken by surprise with the savageness and length of the fight, eventually landed a $12\frac{1}{4}$ pound mirror, a

Kevin Roberts with three Southfield winter doubles. 16 pounds 15 ounces (a personal best), 15 pounds 4 ounces and 14 pounds 10 ounces (the 16 pounder is thought to be a water record)

beautiful 'silver' fish in perfect condition. So much for being a good husband – I knew what I would be doing for the rest of the winter!

I returned to the same swim the next week-end and had two fish on the bank – 16¼ pound and 10½ pound – both taken in the early afternoon after a fruitless morning. The 16¼ set a new personal winter best, superseding the 14¼ pound fish I caught from Carplake twice in the same session in January 1973.

Then came the winter! Deep snow the next week-end and frozen solid the one after that! Needless to say I was very disappointed. The first week-end in February I had been invited back to Carplake and Bob Ford was coming up from Grimsby to join me. At the last minute the invitation was cancelled so we switched to Southfield. However, the winter refused to loosen its grip on our lakes and most of the water was frozen with the exception of a narrow band under the trees in the S.W. corner. We fished, or at least cast out a couple of baits apiece, but without result.

The pond was still frozen on my next visit but the ice was very thin so I was able to break a hole, which was later enlarged by a warm sun and light breeze in the hot-spot area. Caught three that day – a 5¾ pounder from the top end, where I fished until I thought my first choice of swim had recovered from my ice breaking activity, and 7 pound and 13¼ pound mirrors through my hole in the ice.

With the close season rapidly approaching I decided to intensify my efforts and managed three more trips in the last six days of February; Yorkshire fishing closes on 28 February. The first trip produced three fish – 16 pounds 15 ounces, 15¼ pounds, 14 pounds 10 ounces. The biggest fish was the same one as the 16 pound 14 ounce carp I caught in August 1973, a new personal best for the water and my winter best. Fished the same swim the next day and apart from 'bumping' a twitcher on the strike, on the first cast of the day, the swim was completely dead.

I made up for the blank on the final day of the season catching five – 14¼ pounds, 12 pounds 14 ounces, 12 pounds 6 ounces, 12 pounds and 7½ pounds. Just couldn't go wrong. As the man said, 'I just chucked me string in the 'ole and pulled 'em out!' As you know, I've never had more than five fish in any one *year* from this water, now five in one winter's day!

All the fish were in perfect condition and fought extremely hard. The 15¼ pounder took ten minutes to subdue. I used standard CTMs, 12 pound line, link legers and size 4 hooks throughout the winter. You'll probably think that 12 pound line is on the heavy side for winter fishing but there was a lot of dead weed and dying vegetation to contend with and the carp didn't seem to mind anyway.

These results really make nonsense of my previous efforts. Baits and tackle used were no different to those which I've used in summer. Luncheon meat (small pieces) maggots and sweetcorn all caught fish and the only ground baiting I did was putting a few samples in the swim while I was actually fishing. Why my efforts should suddenly be so well rewarded is a mystery to me. The lake was quieter than in summer but not that much. I can't even point to favourable weather conditions as the answer. I caught fish through the complete range of our typical winter weather, ranging from mild spring days to 'arctic' days with ice on the water. There was no rhyme nor reason to the type of bite given – butt ringers that would have undoubtedly been runs if left, slow lifts and really finicky twitches were all experienced with no apparent connection between the type of bite and water/weather conditions.

Anyway, George, I've given up trying to find answers and am just thankful that I managed to be in the right place at the right time with a swimful of hungry carp. Obviously the carp have always fed in winter, but my previous efforts have always been haunted by the many blank summer hours experienced at Southfield by friends and myself, and perhaps I haven't tried as often as I should have done. I'm beginning to think that the lake isn't really worth fishing in summer but I'll certainly be there again next winter – perhaps you'd like to join me for a session?

Regards

Kevin

When winter carp-fishing was first proposed as an extension of the carp season there were cries of: 'Special waters.' 'It's only possible in the south.' 'Like to see it done up here in the north,' and so on. I know, because I was one of those questioning that winter carp could be caught anywhere other than in a few, very special waters. If there are any carp anglers who still doubt that good catches can be made in winter or that winter fishing is not a proposition, then Kevin's letter ought to convince them that they are wrong. The York area is nearly as far north as serious carp-fishing goes – if carp can be caught up there they can be caught anywhere.

Following in the footsteps of the winter carp-fishing pioneers, I have tried to do my bit to popularize the winter scene. There is nothing revolutionary in my approach, since I have always been treading the path worn by those who led the way many years before. What I have to say has, in the main, been said before, though my meagre effort may have established that the carp in most waters usually weigh more in winter. If the evidence of this chapter is added to that of many other more successful winter carp anglers up and down the country, then winter carp-fishing is not only productive, it is also a good way of catching a personal best carp from a given water. Much of what I have to say about winter carp has been published in the excellent monthly magazine *Angling*. To those who are familiar with the argument, having read the widely spaced articles, I must apologize.

Since my views, which suggested that an angler had as good a chance of catching his 'personal best' in winter as in summer, were published my mail has always contained a small percentage of letters confirming or denying this. The majority of anglers who fish throughout the winter – not just the odd session – seem to find that, length for length, carp are heavier in winter. This measuring is not important unless you want to establish certain aspects through the season. Nor is it important if you just want to get on with catching carp regardless of theories – an understandable attitude. It becomes important when you want to say that carp are generally heavier at any given time. Some argue that bigger carp are caught in summer and there are more of them too. This is so simply because a lot more people fish in summer. It is surprising, though, that some will argue about summer/winter weights without having measured a single fish. As measurement is the only way of obtaining evidence – other than catching the same fish several times – it is difficult to discuss weight gain in terms of assumption. It is no use presenting a case for heavier summer carp if the case rests on fish that have not been caught from the same water. To obtain sound information you must look at the facts on a 'one angler, one water, one season' basis. Only by weighing and measuring your own and your friends' fish on this basis will you arrive at a sound conclusion. My own research suggests that most of the waters I have fished will supply their heaviest carp in winter.

In April 1972 I wrote a piece for the British Carp Study Group magazine, *The Carp*. I suggested, and gave evidence from the members' catches over the season, that there was a better than even chance of an angler catching his best carp in winter. Soon afterwards I received a letter from Jim Gregory, who is a biologist and Scientific Officer of the group, saying that he did not agree with my findings. He sent with the letter a long paper he had previously prepared on winter carp, containing a breakdown of over 5000 carp caught by Carp Study Group members and from press reports. This clearly showed that most big fish are caught in summer. I replied explaining that it was unfair to lump *all* reported carp under one heading, since more anglers fish in summer than winter and many only report their largest fish anyway. I asked Jim if he had tried looking at the figures on a one angler, one water, one season basis. A long while passed before I had a reply. When it came Jim had gone to the trouble of re-processing all the data as suggested and found that his results clearly showed that an angler fishing the same water all season had a better chance of catching his best carp *in winter*. These conclusions, Jim pointed out, were based on pitifully few winter reports. But to my mind if only a few reports established a definite pattern, more would consolidate and confirm it. Jim wrote an article for the group magazine confirming that, based on the one angler, one water, one season theory, winter seemed to produce better carp. The last time I saw Jim was in April 1975. He confirmed that the reports he was getting still showed the same trend. My own observations had continued to confirm this. But if you take only big carp from press reports etc., the majority of them caught in summer anyway, results are bound to be biased against winter fishing. Many good carp are caught in winter, most of which never get reported. The full-season carp man is not generally interested in either press or reporting schemes.

In the north our carp waters are often poorly stocked. We have to fish a bit harder to get results but there are some advantages. The unproductive waters are never over-crowded and we often catch the same carp several times in a season. This is very handy if, like me, you happen to be interested in seeing what weight is gained or lost throughout a season. My list of 'known' carp from various waters is growing all the time; in every case the fish has weighed more in winter. There are several fish on the list that have not turned up in winter yet. But as their summer weight pattern is the same as those caught winter and summer, it seems likely they too would be heavier in winter. One can only write in general terms of course. What applies to one particular carp might not apply to another. There are many reasons why a carp might weigh less in winter, and obviously the odd one may be caught that has a poorer weight for length than the summer average. When this happens there is always someone ready to leap in and confront you with conflicting evidence, thinking that your pronouncements are just theories. They are not theories at all, as anyone who carefully measures and weighs carp for three full seasons – as I did before writing my conclusions – will find out.

Many carp anglers seem almost apologetic because they haven't done any winter carp-fishing. Others become belligerent, saying that anyone who puts up with winter carp-fishing is a fanatic, as there are so many other species that offer a better chance of success. I would not argue with either, or try to alter their views in any way. Having, as a founder member, been involved in helping to run the Hallamshire Group for many years, I have learnt to respect a wide range of opinions from anglers I admire. If a man wishes to fish for pike, chub or zander in winter, there is no reason why he should become apologetic or belligerent when talking to a chap who prefers to fish for carp. Nor should he think the same chap is a fanatical or dedicated carp angler. So if you are keen to have a change of species in winter no winter carpman will say you are wrong – he is more likely to compliment you on your decision, 'cos it leaves more water for him!

There may come a time, though, when carp-fishing gets a hold of you and you find the short summer season is not enough. It is then that winter carp-fishing begins to look more attractive. If you are at that stage now this chapter may help convince you it is a worthwhile pastime. One thing I can guarantee. You will make some true friends during your winter sessions.

I started winter carp-fishing in 1970. I did try the odd winter session in 1967 and 1968, but even the most gullible would not accept these earlier attempts as 'winter carp-fishing'. As Jim Gibbinson says, winter carp-fishing is not simply trying a couple of sessions. You have to be ready to accept the challenge completely, experiencing a full winter period before any worthwhile conclusions can be reached. My winter carp-fishing began in 1970, for at the start of that season my friends and I began fishing in Cheshire, finding carp there were not as hard to catch as we had thought. When October came there was a parting of ways. For years we had always fished together, going for different species as the seasons changed. But I had carp-fever and continued to fish for them while my friends made the annual pike pilgrimage to the Fens. There was no bad feeling involved, we parted company with mutual respect for each others' desires.

The angling gods must have smiled upon me that first October, for I continued to catch at a similar rate to the earlier summer months. Sometimes one a session, sometimes none, while the last session of the month provided three. Since then I have always found October a rather patchy month, perhaps because of the poor weather and the exposed waters I have fished. Catching three right at the end of the month set me up for the first true winter month – November.

Whoever decided November should be the first winter month should try fishing in the north in October!

November seems quite good up to the second week as the carp are still moving well and giving reasonable runs. It is always hard to generalize about the sort of run you will get. The runs in November are little different from those of summer, and this covers a wide range of run patterns. As the month passes the carp becomes unsettled in its habitat. The earth is slowly tilting on its axis and the northern hemisphere gets less light and heat from the sun. The nights become longer and colder and the water temperature drops fairly rapidly. The aquatic and bankside vegetation also shows its dislike of the prevailing conditions. Weed beds die back; masses of leaves and bankside flora end up in the lake, causing a souring of the water and an oxygen reduction. These disrupting effects vary in degree depending on whether the lake is an open or tree-covered area, or whether it is deep or shallow. Given a choice of waters choose an open, deeper one at this time of year, as the effects of temperature and de-oxygenation are less. The small shallow waters that have a large vegetable 'input' are worst affected and it is not surprising that the carp go off feed.

When the weeds and external vegetation start to decompose, the bacterial action causing the decay uses up considerable oxygen in the process. The water temperature is still high enough in early November to allow some decay to take place, though as the month progresses and the temperature falls still lower, the bacterial action becomes less. But even without this action, sufficient leaves, which have their own distinctive sap content, may be enough to cause mild, unpleasant pollution. It depends on how much water there is in relation to the leaves that enter it.

Another unnatural effect caused by leaves must be considered when deciding on a winter carp water. The leaves have been on the tree for several months and will have picked up a considerable amount of industrial fall-out in that period. While summer rain will wash the leaves, much chemical content remains in the leaf mass and is soaked out gradually when the leaves sink. If you get a combination of high industry, small water and dense foliage around it, look elsewhere for a winter carp water. One similar small water I know rarely produces carp until well into December and is very unreliable too. After a dry summer, like 1975, the large leaves of the sycamore trees surrounding it carry a pretty high pollution content, making the water very sour. The 1975–6 winter period there was almost a complete write-off and I am sure industrial fall-out played its part. If you have to fish a small, tree-lined water, pay particular attention to the shallow places, or any inlet channels or 'bays' that are outside the main leaf-shed area. The shallows can be very productive in winter on a water where the prevailing wind blows from the shallows to the deeps. The wind blows a lot of the shed leaves to the deep end, leaving the shallows reasonably clear. Such a condition is important on the still, quiet winter days. I fished such a water for two seasons. On windless or light breeze days the carp would be on the shallows. You could almost guarantee it. If a good, stiff, prevailing wind was blowing from the west the carp would be facing it at the deeper end. A light wind blowing into the shallows from an easterly quarter always seemed to produce a run.

By mid December in the average season the water temperature has fallen and may have 'bottomed' once or twice. The colder the water gets, the less it is affected by sudden cold spells. Once the carp have become acclimatized to the cold water they start to feed again. There are always productive spells in between of course. One of the best days, run-wise, I have ever had came at the end of November. Much depends on being at the water on the right day. My own preference is a day when a moderate breeze is giving a nice rippling effect to the surface. The wind seems more important in winter than summer, and it is not too hard to see why. In summer there is an abundance of weed giving off oxygen during the daylight hours to sweeten the water and make fish inclined to feed. While fishing with the wind in your face is an old and reliable adage in summer, I have proved to my own satisfaction that carp can be caught without taking advantage of the wind direction. A 'hot' swim is much more reliable than the wind direction. In winter there is little weed to give off oxygen. While the water has a high content of oxygen in winter, the fish never being short, it is the *amount* of oxygen in relation to all the dead rubbish laying around that is important. A man could die in a room that contained plenty of oxygen if a small amount of lethal gas was released. To a point it is the same with the fish. There is little bacterial decay taking place because the temperature in December is too low to allow much. But the water is in a 'shut-down' state and many of the natural impurities are not being removed. The wind then, plays an even more important part in bringing up the oxygen level to a point where the carp are induced to feed. I have tried to find a factor that is conducive to getting a run in winter. The carp I have caught or seen caught have been taken under a wide range of conditions, from calm, bright, sunny days to gale force, torrential rain. One factor that stands out more than any other is the wind. I am sure it is a very important part of the winter scene, supplying movement to mix and oxygenate the water and induce torpid carp to feed.

I would not advise an angler that he must fish with the wind in his face in winter. A cold wind blowing over land finds any weakness in an angler's choice of winter clothing. When the same wind is travelling down the length of a lake it feels twice as cold! It is not of course, but the air picks up a little more moisture as it moves over the lake surface. It deposits this on the angler's clothing, making it a more efficient heat dispenser and the angler colder. This can be a problem on large exposed waters, making the angler uncomfortable and sapping his will to continue fishing. Many lakes and ponds offer the chance to fish with the wind in winter and retain some measure of comfort. It is possible to fish from one bank, casting towards the bank the wind is favouring. The angler is able to use an umbrella or bivouac for protection, while at the same time he is in a position to reach his rods quickly. If the angler has to fish with the wind in his face, an umbrella with a tilt device will give some protection. Rig the brolly wrong way round, with the top facing the lake and placed right on the edge of the bank. The rods can then be fished at one side of it, the butts and back-up indicators being in sight of the sheltering angler. This is very much a last resort but I have caught carp while fishing like this. In winter it is vital to be where the carp are. The feeding carp seem confined to a very small area with little or no over-spill to other parts of the lake. In summer they are more active, covering quite large areas during the average day. They are more likely to pass the angler's swim or bait in the process, giving some chance of a run. In winter this is less likely unless the water is very heavily stocked with carp. I know one water that produced fifteen winter carp in a few hours for a friend. He was not particularly interested in carp-fishing but just fancied giving winter carp-fishing a trial. I have never fished the water, though I was once a member of the club who had the fishing rights. There is no challenge in that sort of fishing and I would become quickly bored with it.

All my winter fishing has been at lakes and ponds that I have fished regularly in summer. This way I am able to feel the pulse of the water, seeing the gradual change as the season progresses and noting any change in feeding areas while the carp are still active. The areas that produced carp in summer can also produce them in winter. But switching waters from summer to winter does reduce the angler's chance of success. I am rather slow at getting the feel of a water. There always seem so many interesting things to weigh and consider that my fishing can suffer and three seasons may pass

Rod Walker with a well-conditioned 18¼ pound February mirror

before I feel I know the water. Knowing a water well is vital to winter success. Anglers who fish a water throughout the season always seem to fare best.

In December and January when water temperatures are low, a sudden cold snap can cause a lake to freeze over. If your winter fishing water is but a few miles away it is easy to decide whether a proposed outing is worthwhile. A lot of my winter carp-fishing is done in Cheshire. The Pennine range separates my home county of Yorkshire from Cheshire like a giant wall. The weather can be totally different on either side. In summer you can fish a full session on the Cheshire side in overcast rainy weather. The journey home over the high peaks may take you into the low clouds which may be so thick that you need to use dipped headlights at midday! On days like this you often find when reaching the 1700 foot high Mam Tor peak, that within a few yards the clouds are left behind, revealing the lush green Hope valley bathed in bright summer sunshine 1400 feet below. It has a special quality, this sudden transition, that never fails to impress me, bringing to mind Conan Doyle's *Lost World*. You can see for ten miles and in the distance stand the massive twin peaks of Win Hill and Lose Hill, each over 1500 feet high, standing like fortresses, set to guard the mighty Ladybower Reservoir. In winter the Pennine beauty is transformed into a treacherous bleakness. There can be rain on one side and frost on the other with four inches of snow on top. It is well to have plenty of petrol in the tank, for the Pennine passes become quickly blocked with snow and a detour can mean many additional miles to the journey. One never quite knows what to expect on the other side and several times the lake has been frozen over on arrival. It has been said the journey to and from a water has nothing to do with the fishing of it. The man who can travel through country like the Pennines, experiencing such a change without comment is, indeed, to be pitied.

Several times the shallow lake of my choice has been partially or completely frozen over, causing muttered curses. Strangely enough the ice layer will not stop carp from feeding. The first time I saw a small frozen pond I spent an absorbing two hours watching aquatic activity under the $1\frac{1}{2}$ inch thick ice of the shallows. Fortunately the ice had frozen like clear glass allowing really good observation and it was amazing how much activity was going on. It was mid November and the shallows were alive with many different forms of larval stages of life, plus a high percentage of water-boatmen. If a crack was made in the ice the resulting air-bubble would be explored by water-boatmen and other diving beetles that looked like corrixa. I could only presume that their repeated visits from the bottom to the trapped air-bubble replenished the air supply in underwater air chambers. I know little about the life-cycle of these beetles. But as it is rare to see them swimming on the surface in winter, I thought that some adults might spend much of winter in air-bell 'nests' near the lake bed.

On this particular day there was a big brown patch of suspended silt 10 yards out from the northerly bank in the 2 foot deep shallows. I could not see any carp swimming under the ice, but I was in no doubt as to what caused the brown staining – this area being a hot-spot for carp right through the season. On another occasion in February the same pond was half-frozen. Andrew Hughes and I were fishing the unfrozen part and we never had a run. Towards lunch-time the temperature rose slightly and a light, following breeze sprung up. The breeze skimmed over our high margin bank, leaving the margins untouched but rippling the central surface of the pond. Slowly the ice layer began to break up. By about 4 p.m. the ice had almost gone, just a thin fringe remaining along the length of the margins of the opposite bank. A carp rolled twice, close to the edge of the ice, causing me to bring in one rod to make adjustments so that I could reach the place – a cast of about 40 yards. During the next half-hour I had two runs, failing to connect with either. After spending the day without any sign of a carp or runs on our side of the pond, the first activity seen on the other side had produced two runs. There is no doubt that in winter moving carp are feeding carp. Instead of casting 40 yards to the fish I should have gone round to the other side to present the bait at close range. These sorts of incidents happen many times and cannot really be classed as 'mistakes' but rather as lack of experience. Were the same thing to happen again my bait would be presented on float tackle from the active bank. The one problem with small ponds is that an angler tends to become idle, staying in one position and just adding weight to reach the scene of activity. Sometimes it works and sometimes it does not.

For some inexplicable reason carp will often feed under an ice layer. Earlier I said that wind rippling the water was the one common factor on days when carp seemed prone to feed. Why carp should be motivated to feed when the surface is sealed, stopping any possible interchange of oxygen and obnoxious gases between water and atmosphere, is quite beyond reasonable explanation. There can be no shadow of doubt that carp feeding under the ice is not in any way unusual or restricted to one particular water. Too many reliable anglers have witnessed this activity in waters of varying character up and down the country. I have not had any success as yet when fishing through ice, though, as you read earlier, Kevin has broken ice to get at the carp. Fred Simson once hooked a good carp in a hole in the ice on the shallows. He tried to stop the fish going under the ice by plunging the rod tip under water. The fish ran under the ice and eventually did break the line. Fred told me that he played the carp for some time before the line cut into the ice and froze at that point, allowing the carp to break it. Catching a carp after breaking a hole in the ice must be very exciting and I hope that my turn will soon come.

Why do carp feed under the ice? There is little scientific information available on carp in a natural environment. The majority of it is about fish rearing and fishery management. There is a world of difference between the study of X pounds of flesh per acre per annum per ton of food and that of low-density-stocked fishing ponds or lakes. The fish culture experts suggest that when winter approaches and the temperature falls below 50°F the carp are less inclined to feed and eventually go torpid, neither feeding nor using much energy. The fish culturist will not find the winter carp angler agreeing because too many carp have been caught well below the temperature mentioned. But in carp fisheries, as opposed to carp farms, there are fewer fish per acre and more oxygen available. This, I am sure, is the key factor. It explains why carp stocked in thousands in a relatively small pond go off feed in winter, while those in the average lake will feed – sometimes under ice.

In my experience it is the exposed waters that produce carp in winter. I think that such waters have become well oxygenated by strong winds before freezing over. As soon as the carp becomes acclimatized to the change in temperature it is stimulated into feeding by the high oxygen level. Water is at its heaviest at 39·2°F. When all the lake has cooled to this point any further cooling causes the water to rise to the surface. If the air temperature falls low enough the water at the surface will freeze at about 32°F, depending on the purity of the water. I did some temperature checks in a 5 feet deep swim through a 1 inch ice layer when the air temperature was approximately at freezing point. There was an apparent increase in water temperature of about 1 degree per foot of depth. The lake bed was warmest at 36·5 °F. It would have been nice to compare the temperature at 8 feet. By my calculations it should have come close to the critical mark of 39·2 °F. Obviously my simple experiment has limitations as the lake was only 5 feet deep at the points I could measure from. But it does show that the lake bed is far warmer than the surface appearance would suggest. Provided there is sufficient oxygen, in relation to whatever other impurities the water may contain, the carp will begin to feed again once they have become acclimatized. This is fact, not theory. It must be so or otherwise it would not be possible to see carp feeding, or catch them in surface ice conditions.

I may have laboured the point but to take a carp with ice on the surface must be one of the greatest achievements for a true winter carp angler. My aim has been to show that it is possible. Apart from breaking a hole in the ice to make a swim, another reliable period is when natural conditions cause the ice to break up. The following is an account of such a day.

My good friend and fishing companion, Fred Simson, and I were fishing a shallow lake in January, the morning after the lake had all but frozen over. There was a narrow strip of water along the northern margins which provided us with some sort of fishing. Fred had a run from a bait cast right to the edge of the ice but did not connect with the fish. Soon after a south-easterly breeze began to blow, stiffening gradually to a light wind. The wind blew up and slightly across the lake towards our fishing position. As it strengthened, the thin ice layer broke loose from the southern and eastern banks to drift across the lake. We had to take our tackle from the water before the mass of floating ice reached our margins, grinding and crunching as it scraped its way obliquely along the edge of the bank.

Fred decided to stay where he was, waiting until the ice had drifted past on its journey towards the distant westerly shallows. It did not take long because we were fishing within 50 yards of the easterly bank that formed the dam wall of the lake. By the time I had collected my tackle together and begun the walk to the south-eastern corner swim I fancied, the ice cleared Fred's swim completely, allowing him to cast farther out than before. I arrived at my chosen spot and began to set up my tackle. As I sat making adjustments to the terminal tackle, Fred struck and hooked a carp. I was dumb-struck at the short time between the ice moving and the carp being hooked. I walked round to net, weigh and measure the fish. It was a 7 pound mirror in good condition.

Fred and I have acquired a good sense of combined humour over the many sessions we have shared, always being ready to chide each other with good-natured banter. I asked Fred: 'Can I come round and sit on your knee, Mister, so that you can show me how to catch a nice carp like that – but *rather* bigger please?' His reply to my polite and reasonable request was quite unprintable. So I slunk back to my, as yet, unfished swim.

The time passed slowly while the wind veered easterly and the shivers began. I had several twitches on the ledgered bait which I was fishing about 25 yards out in 4 feet of water. The margin rod produced nothing, so I concentrated on the line of the ledger rod where it entered the water. The line twitched and lifted. Not waiting to see if the indicator sounded I struck and the light Avon rod arched over. At first it seemed as if the terminal tackle had snagged, for there were no vibrations coming up the line. Then the fish began one of the slowest and most ponderous runs up and across the lake that I have ever witnessed, taking a great deal of line off the spool before the pressure stopped it. The fish was pumped back with little fight, like a dead weight, and netted. I have always advocated winter carp-fishing as a means of catching a personal best from a given water. You could have knocked me down with a feather when we weighed this fish. It went 15 pounds – the best I had caught at the time and a lake record by $2\frac{1}{2}$ pounds.

January is perhaps the hardest month for the winter carp addict. Yet, like December and February it sometimes produces very good fish for the persistent angler. The week before I caught my personal best, Fred raised his from 11 pounds to $13\frac{1}{2}$ pounds with a fish from a different water. When you consider that his previous best was also a December-caught fish and my previous best of 14 pounds was caught in February, both from waters we regularly fish in summer too – there has to be some reason why the better fish are often caught in winter. My friend Andrew Hughes also had a personal best of $14\frac{1}{2}$ pounds in December. He upped this to 16 pounds in January a couple of seasons later and then to $16\frac{1}{2}$ pounds the following January. There are many other similar instances.

There are many difficulties in winter carp-fishing, one of them the number of blanks suffered at poorly stocked club waters. The fish that are caught are often the larger ones. These fish seem to require more food and seem inclined to feed when smaller fish are less active. My conclusions are based mainly on results from two waters. It takes so long to collect first-hand fishing information that three or four years might pass before you can really decide what has emerged. Fred, Andrew and I obtained our results from fishing two waters over a three-year period. If our conclusions are correct it would be interesting to see what Redmire might produce fished in winter on a regular basis. It is on the western side of England as were our productive Cheshire waters, and it is farther south. Redmire is not all that big, so location is fairly easy and it is relatively well stocked. There is a good chance that many of the 'troublesome' 20 pounders – old fish that have been caught several times since the period Dick Walker fished there – would be less inclined to feed, leaving the field clear for the few potential record-breakers the water might still contain. No English carp is going to reach or maintain a weight of 50 or 60 pounds by feeding only six months out of twelve! The angler who fished Redmire through the winter might catch few fish. But the angling world might be surprised at the size of them. It is not an easy task I know, but the prize is one of the biggest in angling. This is not 'sour-grapes' on my part and I have no wish to criticize those who fish Redmire. To an outsider it seems that an awful long time has passed since Dick caught the big one. The record has trembled once since then – would more winter effort crack it, I wonder?

In February there is a slight increase in the tempo of life. The sun begins to climb higher in the sky and there are often one or two nice spring-like periods during this month. The water temperature begins to lift a few degrees. The water is still in a stable condition, with minimal bacterial activity taking place and, provided the wind can supply oxygenation, carp will move and give runs. February perhaps offers the angler the best chance of taking his heaviest carp or a fish with its highest weight for length ratio.

I think this is because the carp are in peak condition. Assuming the fish is still growing, it begins to accumulate fat and tissue in late autumn. Eggs and milt also begin to form in February and these factors help ensure the high weight for length ratio. Some of the best fish in quite a wide range of waters have been caught between mid January and late February. By 'best fish' I do not claim you will catch a 20 plus from a lake that has no history of supplying 20s regularly. If the better fish in your particular lake are say 10, 15 or 20 pounds, and infrequently caught in summer, then January and February will offer you a better than even chance of contacting them. There are several reasons why one carp will grow bigger than another while subject to the same environmental conditions. The main reason is that the larger fish feed more frequently. This is why mid January onwards offers such a good opportunity to catch these fish. Like any other branch of angling time and effort is needed. It would be a fortunate angler who nailed the water record first winter out, yet the possibility is always there. Odd sessions rarely produce unless you are very well acquainted with the water and with carp movements throughout the year. Those who put the time in with regular, if short, sessions usually have the best tales to relate as the season ends.

I have always found March a bit of an 'up-and-downer', though I admit that this is perhaps due to the type of waters I have fished. If you are fortunate to have a choice of lakes, or a choice of shallows and fairly deep water in one lake, March might be the time to move venue or look for other feeding areas. Many of the shallow lakes suffer an algal 'eruption' in March, commonly known as the 'bottom coming up'. If you look at a shallow lake bed early in the spring, you can see a considerable amount of moss-like growth beginning to appear on the sedimentary remains. The colour can vary from dark brown to green in different lakes depending on minerals or conditions. As the temperature and light starts to increase in March or April this algal carpet becomes unstable and pieces begin to break loose, rising to the surface in increasing numbers. When observing these rising mats of algal growth, one can see many minute bubbles escape when a piece tears free from the lake bed. It is obvious that gas accumulation causes the piece to rise and some of the tiny bubbles are marsh gas or methane. A few may be oxygen bubbles that have been synthesized within the algal mass.

This re-cycling of the lake bed deposits plays an important part in re-distributing mineral and organic deposits to all areas of the lake, as I briefly mentioned in the Bubbler chapter. Much of the sedimentary deposits in a lake or pond find their way into the deeper depressions and would remain in isolated areas were it not for this eruption. When the pieces rise to the surface they leave a fine trail of minute particles of suspended matter. On days of maximum eruption I have seen the water become so cloudy between early morning and lunch-time that it has been impossible to see the bottom in only 2 feet of water. There are always sub-surface currents in a so-called 'still-water', ensuring that the minute particles are well distributed throughout the entire area of the lake bed. This action must be nature's way of supplying fertilizer in readiness for the new season's crop of vegetable growth. The floating algal scum invariably ends up against one bank or another, usually that favoured by the prevailing wind. Resulting wind action gradually breaks it up until, once more, the material re-enters the nutrient cycle of the lake.

The fish go quickly off feed when this happens, although it is hard to bear such things philosophically after a 40 mile journey to reach the lake. Knowing that the lake will benefit from the action does help relieve the feelings of bitterness. In my experience these eruptions reach their peak about noon or early afternoon. The carp will often feed in the early morning until the rising debris and resultant pollution sends them off feed. My best March session was just before the water became clouded by increasing amounts of rising scum which put an end to the fishing. Three carp, of average size for the water, were adequate compensation for the journey.

It is time now for another letter from one of my friends. I received this, just as the 1975–6 season had ended, from Bob Chambers, who lives in Middlesex. Bob wrote to say he had just finished his most successful season ever and you will see that winter fishing played no mean part in supplying the success. From Kevin in the north to Bob in the south, those interested in winter fishing can see there is little difference in the results when the angler knows his waters well.

Dear George,

Knowing your keen interest in all aspects of winter carp, here are my results for this last winter and, for what they are worth, my opinions and conclusions on winter carping.

I spent the winter on the water where I had had most success during the summer. I reasoned that as my bait had been acceptable during the summer and I had amassed a certain amount of knowledge regarding that water, I would be some sort of a 'nut' to switch to an unknown water for the remainder of the season.

The water is an old, square, gravel pit of about 4 acres and deeper than most carp waters with about 10 to 12 feet under the rod tip in most places and depths up to about 20 feet. No emergent weed other than a small reed bed which marks the start of one of the two bars that this water contains. There is a good head of double-figure carp.

My 'set-up' remained much as it was for the summer. I chose to use a pair of stepped-up rods as I consider them the best 'tool' to hit the type of takes I expected. The bait was a skinned paste which I fished in smaller and softer balls than in the summer. Hooks were barbless, size 4 or 6. I ledgered with ½ or ¾ ounce leads on a fairly long link. The reel line was of 8 pounds breaking strain. My rods were set high with closed bale-arms and a varying amount of drop to 'squeezy-bottle' bobbins. Self-contained indicators were used.

Being a shift-worker, I was able to fish on different days of the week and at various times to try to establish 'hot spells' or feeding patterns. This proved to be difficult and, as far as I was concerned, no definite pattern emerged until March. My intention was to keep in touch with the few carp anglers who would also be fishing the water, mainly at weekends. Their results would be a useful yard-stick from which I could judge my own results and vice versa. I live close enough to the water to make short sessions economical and enable me to fish, should I feel so inclined, two sessions in a day.

For various reasons, my 'campaign' did not get under way until 16 November. An evening session on this day produced a leather carp of 14 pounds and a 'wildie' of 3 pounds 8 ounces. The leather was in excellent condition and fought very strongly. This fine condition and strong fight was to be duplicated in every carp I caught during the winter. Gone was the bulging, spawn-bound look of some fish caught in June and July. Gone also was the flabby, listless look of fish that had recently shed their spawn. Instead, what remained was what I can only describe as a creature 'in the pink' of its condition. Sleek, yet strong and packed with muscle.

Four more sessions in November produced seven fish including two doubles. One double came during a morning session, the other during an evening session. This latter fish was a mirror of exactly 12 pounds. Beyond any doubt at all, it was the 11 pounds 7 ounce fish I had taken from this water in August. 9 ounces' gain in body weight in fourteen weeks.

December produced three fish, one of them was a double, in three sessions. This double, a common of 11 pounds was absolutely immaculate. Not a scale missing, no splits in its tail or fins and the body shape was perfect.

My last December session was on the 11th, as I had to 'prepare' myself for the forthcoming festivities. (Yes, George, I know there were still two weeks to go but I had to *practise*, didn't I?)

The festivities lasted longer than I anticipated and it wasn't until 3 p.m. on 1 January that I staggered up to the lake to be greeted by the good news that one of the regulars, John Baker, had taken a common of 14 pounds that morning. Fishing until 10 p.m. with a splitting headache, I missed four good takes and, vowing 'never to touch the stuff again', I staggered home.

Due to that inconvenience called 'work', I only managed four more sessions in January. One of these, an evening one, proved to be the highlight of the winter. I started fishing at 4.30 p.m. At 6 p.m. I hit a jerky lift on my right hand rod and netted a common of 10 pounds 11 ounces. An hour later, a steady lift of the bobbin on the same rod resulted in the landing of the 'twin' of the first fish except this common weighed in at 2 ounces more. A winter double gives me a thrill. Two doubles in one winter session makes me very happy and when they are both *commons*: 'Out of sight, man!'

This was the half-way stage in the nineteen weeks that make the accepted winter season. It seems an opportune moment to reflect on what had passed. As regards results, I was well pleased: fourteen fish had been caught, six of which had been doubles. I had fished seventy-eight hours, spread over ten sessions. At this stage there was no connection between the weather and the fish caught. I had taken the majority of the fish during the first few hours of darkness, which tended to bear out a lot of what I had read about winter carping. But isn't this the period when most winter carp anglers are fishing? Many was the time when, during the morning sessions, I had the water to myself. It would be in the evening that other carp anglers would join me. I was happier fishing in the evening. It was more convenient. What was encouraging was the amount of action I was getting. Only two of the ten sessions had been absolute blanks with no other signs nor indications of feeding carp. During the other eight sessions I had either caught carp or had had twitches.

January ended with two blanks and February started with another two blanks. The two February sessions were fished when the weather was mild, overcast and a west or south-west breeze was blowing. Ideal conditions?

Feeling a bit disheartened, I left the water for a while and fished several very enjoyable sessions in the company of fellow BCSG member Derek Stritton. We both caught carp up to 8 pounds from a small, well-stocked water.

On the last day of February, full of optimism, I returned to my usual haunt and at 11.30 a.m. I landed a leather of 12 pounds 6 ounces. Once again the condition of this fish was something to marvel at. The fight it gave was equal to that of bigger fish I had caught from the water during the summer.

March came in with a long spell of settled weather. The nights were still cold and clear with heavy frosts. The days were sunny and cold with an east wind that sprang up at around 9.30 a.m., blew steadily all day and dropped away in the evening. It became apparent that action could be expected at any time roughly between 9.30 a.m. and 1 p.m. The afternoons were dead. However, once the light failed, takes could be expected up to about 9 p.m.

During this settled spell I was fishing a morning session. At about 1 p.m. I was packing up my tackle when the bobbin on the one rod still in use slammed up to the rod and the reel started to spin at an incredible rate of knots. I grabbed the rod and struck into what was obviously a double. I later wished I hadn't struck so hard because when this fish, a common in the region of 12 or 13 pounds, was actually over the net, the hook pulled out.

Bob Chambers with a November carp. 'Best reported carp of the season' from the lake and a personal best – 17 pounds 3 ounces

Instead of just lifting the net I gazed stupidly at the fish which slowly righted itself and drifted away. I was sick! Nevertheless, that incident kept alive my faith in the morning 'hot spell'.

Three days later Ricky Gibbinson from Southend joined me for a day on the water. The weather was as it had been for the last week. To say that Rick was pessimistic is putting it mildly. My boundless optimism failed to rub off on to him. We fished side by side in a large pitch because, as Rick put it, 'We won't be bothered by fish and can have a good chat.' When the east wind, a 'facer' commenced at about 9.30 a.m., this really put the cap on it. All I could hear from Rick were mutterings such as: 'Diabolical.' . . . 'No chance.' . . . 'Should have stayed at home.'

I replied with snippets such as: 'Wait and see, old son.' . . . 'They'll soon be 'aving it.' . . . 'On your toes, Rick mate, on your toes.'

At 9.45 a.m. the indicator of my right hand rod sounded and the bobbin started a leisurely ascent to the rod. I was able to strike without haste. As I was bringing in the fish, a common of 7 pounds 12 ounces, Ricky, ostentatiously studying his watch, remarked: 'Fifteen minutes late, it really won't do.' Ten minutes later on the same rod, I had an identical take, did everything right but missed the fish. Ricky by now had ceased his caustic comments and was on the alert. His change of attitude was rewarded at 11 a.m. when he struck a small lift of one of his bobbins and landed a leather of 10 pounds 2 ounces. Knowing my affection for this type of king carp, Ricky apologized profusely for disturbing this fish and continued in a similar vein until I threatened to exclude him from the afternoon meal of hot stew (and whatever else was in the tins).

The afternoon was fishless but as dusk fell I exhorted Ricky to ready himself for the second feeding spell.

'Never,' was his reply. 'We've had our share for today.'

However, the pattern ran true to form and at 6 p.m. Ricky struck a very small lift and the answering curve in his rod indicated that he had hooked a much larger fish. Time and again this fish tried for the submerged branches of a large willow on Ricky's right. It then decided that the middle of the lake was a better bet and reached there in about ten seconds flat! Ricky was able to tire the fish at some range and, minutes later, I was able to net this beautifully conditioned, dark-coloured, 15 pounds 12 ounce mirror. I don't know who was more pleased with the day's results. I had taken the baby of the three fish but all my promises had, for once, come true.

Luckily, the weather held good for two more days and I fished another morning session. Although I was fishless another of the winter regulars, BCSG member Len Barker, took a mirror of 12 pounds. I returned to the water that evening and fished the swim that Len had vacated. My poaching paid off in the form of a common of 11 pounds 14 ounces taken at 9.15 p.m.

Unfortunately, the weather then changed completely. The wind swung around to west or south-west and the temperature rose. The skies became overcast and we were back with 'perfect' winter carp conditions. Despite fishing four sessions, morning and evening, I was fishless until the morning of 12 March when, at 9.40 a.m., I hit a small lift which turned out to be a common of 14 pounds. This was the strongest fish I had caught all season. It is impossible to be disappointed with such a fish, particularly at that time of the year, but there were times during its fight when I was sure it would weigh a good deal more.

For the next couple of days, the wind swung all over the place. Three more fishless sessions and the dreaded 14th was upon us. In the morning Len Barker took a 10 pounds 12 ounce mirror and at 1 p.m. I caught a mirror of 8 pounds 8 ounces. I returned to the lake for the last evening but nothing was caught.

Conclusions? Any reached, George, apply to me at that water. It was a very profitable winter in terms of fish caught – twenty-eight winter carp, nine of which were doubles. Short, hard-fished sessions were, in my opinion, far more beneficial than marathon sessions. In most cases the takes were short and fast. I don't feel an angler, unless he is exceptional, is in a position to hit too many of these at the end of ten or more winter hours beside a water.

I found that winter carping had a different appeal from that of the summer. Pressure on the water is less and an angler has to be content with his own company for most of the time. Midway through the winter, I invested in a set of thermal underwear and a one piece fishing suit. I blessed that investment many times.

Confidence in the water, the bait and the set-up is, I feel, of paramount importance.

A last word on 'ideal' winter carp conditions. There is no such animal in my book. Long settled spells of weather, wet or dry, cold or mild, windy or still, are, I believe, the times to fish as hard and as often as possible.

Best wishes,
Bob Chambers.

I have not yet discussed fighting abilities, but as Kevin and Bob have both given their accounts I need only outline my own impressions.

Some carp certainly go well in winter in spite of the lower metabolic rate which is said to make them sluggish. I can think of several very thrilling scraps that had my heart pumping like mad as the fish went every bit as hard as in summer. We all get the odd sluggish fish, even in summer. Winter is the same except for the different ways in which the fish fight. The 15 pounder mentioned earlier is one example; a long, slow run taking line without any real speed or scrap developing. Another is the carp which sets off slowly, gradually speeding up and becoming more powerful as the fight progresses. One gets the impression that it takes some while before the carp realizes anything is wrong. The other sort of sluggishness peculiar to winter, is when a carp is hooked in the margins and comes to the net with hardly a movement, finally going mad as the mesh of the landing net closes round it. The number of feeding fish in an area may determine how a carp fights. Slow fights occur most often when only a single fish is taken in a session. If two or more are caught the fish are usually quicker off the mark. Perhaps when several fish are feeding near each other they are stimulated by this group feeding and their metabolic rate is raised. The biologists claim that low water temperatures produce low metabolic rates and the fish become very sluggish. The only problem with this claim is that too many winter carp anglers have found the reverse to be true with the hooked fish going like the proverbial rocket!

Winter feeding spells are difficult to categorize. Many of the shallow waters I have fished seem to provide the most runs between 11 a.m. and 3 p.m. Fishing on into darkness rarely produces anything of significance, though I have had odd runs after dark. These waters were usually dead at night from August onwards, although I do not know why. A few years ago I did a breakdown of several seasons' carp catches. This covered a wide range of fairly shallow waters. Lakes that had a night-fishing ban were omitted and the list includes only those places that were regularly fished night and day. Here is the breakdown:

Time	Number of Carp
midnight to 4 a.m.	16
4 a.m. to 8 a.m.	32
8 a.m. to 12 noon	74
12 noon to 4 p.m.	29
4 p.m. to 8 p.m.	19
8 p.m. to midnight	14

These figures, based mainly on summer-caught fish, give little incentive to fish long, cold, winter nights! Taking the 8 a.m. to 4 p.m. period, we can see that 103 carp were caught. If this is extended from 4 a.m. to 4 p.m. the total caught is 135, making evening and night fishing, even in summer, look somewhat poor by comparison.

However, it would be wrong to conclude that 11 a.m. to 3 p.m. is the best time for winter carping just because this has been the most productive time for myself and my friends. Others have fallen into the trap of assuming their experiences must echo everyone else's. Much seems to depend upon individual waters, and only by making your own observations can you arrive at the best time to expect runs. This applies to both summer and winter. I know from experience that the most productive period on the above list (8 a.m. to 12 noon) does not apply to a deeper water I have been fishing for the last three seasons. This is quite definitely a 'night water', producing more carp from late evening to dark and again from 2 a.m. to 6 a.m. than at any other period. If I were to offer any sound advice about feeding times it would be to ignore what other people say about *their* waters and to concentrate on what *your* water reveals.

I have not made a habit of night-fishing in winter, though I do manage the odd all-nighter now and again. It is perhaps because I was already forty years old before I began winter carp-fishing. Some swear they feel as young at forty as they did at twenty; all I can say is that I never see many forty-year-olds fishing all night in summer – let alone winter. There is no need to put in long sessions if you have calculated the feeding times correctly and live reasonably close to the water. If long travelling distances are involved it is often financially more economical to fish long sessions, which take in not one but two feeding sessions.

The correct clothing can make long sessions more bearable. I have had a pair of arctic-issue ex-government trousers for many years and I used to think that they were ideal for winter fishing. Admittedly they now have a very liberal coating of grease from fatty baits and fish slime around the knees, which does not help the insulative qualities. I have recently bought a John Partridge one piece thermally insulated suit that has proved ideal in cold, wet conditions. Otherwise I have plumped for several layers of thin clothing in preference to one thick one. Several layers of thin, loose clothes not only keep you warmer, they allow you more freedom of movement. My normal dress for winter night-fishing is woollen 'long-johns' (ridiculous but warm!); a pair of old crimplene trousers and a pair of close-woven trousers over them, both loose fitting. On top of that lot I wear a pair of lightweight nylon, proofed over-trousers. Footwear is two pairs of socks, one long enough to reach the knees, and a pair of felt-insulated 'woodsman' rubber boots. Upper body protection is: vest, shirt and close-woven woollen polo-neck pullover; woollen cardigan with pockets, topped by a blanket-lined, proofed-nylon fishing jacket. The jacket should preferably have a hood under which a balaclava can be worn in really windy spells. I find fingerless mittens best for protecting the hands. You do not have to take them off to bait up or cast. When a run occurs you are able to strike and play the fish without fumbling about for the reel handle.

While trousers and pullovers are within the price range of most anglers, coats are more expensive. Always buy a coat of sufficient size to allow for the layers of clothing underneath. To have warm, loose-fitting clothes topped with a tight-fitting coat is self-defeating. It is the air trapped between each layer that really keeps you warm. A tight coat removes much of this, causing all the clothes to be pressed in close contact with the body and leads to excessive conduction. The law of conduction is that 'hot' flows to 'cold'. The problem facing the winter angler is that of trying to stop heat escaping from his body. Loose-fitting, layered clothing goes some of the way, while a regular intake of hot soup supplies fuel to keep the 'boiler' going. You must be prepared to approach long, winter sessions seriously. Exposure is an insidious enemy that can often affect you as you are driving home afterwards. I once dozed off while driving on the motorway after a long, cold session. I was lucky and lived to tell the tale.

In summing up winter carp-fishing I can only repeat what I have been saying for several years: the number of good-quality carp that turn up is amazing. Some waters respond better to winter fishing than others. The reason is usually that the angler cannot find the fish. Large waters can be a problem any time, but in winter they become nearly impossible unless the angler is familiar with their fish movements. So many winter carp have been caught throughout the country during the last five years that we must assume carp feed in all waters. A series of mild winters is perhaps the reason winter fishing has been good. It is hard to claim that lack of success at any water is because the fish are not feeding when you consider the range of conditions under which winter carp have been caught. There is no substitute for knowledge gained from fishing a particular water and for confidence in approach. Newcomers to winter fishing should take heart from my experiences when I began. Despite reading that others were catching carp in winter, I still lacked confidence in my own ability to catch. The first winter run is a tremendous morale-booster. And when you land your first carp you just wonder why you ever thought the task was all that difficult.

My own results are not as good as those of many of my friends but I am satisfied nevertheless. When the first barrier of putting a winter carp on the bank had been overcome, it became important to me to try and catch carp in every month of the coarse season. Why, I do not really know, but the target was reached after three seasons. This might appear a long time. If I had lived nearer the waters and been able to put in more effort, the target might have been reached sooner. It is a question of what time and effort you are prepared to put in, and in this respect winter fishing has given me ample reward for the time put in. One has to feel the satisfaction of seeing a personal best on the bank to appreciate fully winter fishing. The satisfaction of taking a personal best, one of them a water record, two winters in succession from two different waters is beyond description.

5 Woldale

The fine old chestnuts once stood proud,
In days so long since past.
Still standing now with crutches, propped;
One season soon their last.

G.S.

Far From The Madding Crowd is the title of a book by Thomas
Hardy. Yet somehow the title always brings to mind the wonderful
relaxed days I have spent at Woldale during the last few years. My
good friend Bob Ford has been kind enough to invite me as a guest
several years running for the odd weekend or a few days midweek. I
have always left with regret, looking forward to a future visit.

Not that we ever catch a great deal. The carp are not all that easy
to tempt. Perhaps the lake is not fished enough and the carp, being
used to foraging for natural food, do not respond to standard carp
fishing techniques. Whatever the reason, many good carp anglers
spend a few days there each year without, to my knowledge, ever
really getting to grips with the place. The original lake record was set
up by Maurice Ingham in 1950 with a 17 pound mirror. Maurice
followed this with several 16 pound plus fish and Dick Walker and
Fred J. Taylor each had fish over 16 pounds. Bob Ford had a 15
pound carp a few years ago but the only angler I know of to break
the 17 pound lake record is Rod Hutchinson with a 23 pound
mirror. I am told these larger fish are not of the same strain as those
that Ingham, Walker and Taylor caught. It has been my earnest
desire at each visit to catch a long, lean carp weighing $17\frac{1}{4}$ pounds or
so, fish I have seen at odd times and am sure are the carp caught by
Maurice, Dick and Fred. One day it might happen, and if it does I
will feel immensely proud of my capture.

For those who have read of Woldale in angling books by the

above authors and not had sufficient description to satisfy, let me describe the lake and the beauty of its surroundings that have left such a lasting memory upon me that I can recall almost every moment spent there.

There are two lakes at Woldale joined together by a small brook. The top lake contains the carp and a number of roach, tench and perch. The bottom one has pike, tench, perch, roach and a preponderance of bream. Both lakes are set in 30 or so acres of private land which forms a small nature reserve. There are so many things to see, so many distractions. Small wonder I never catch many carp, for the place enchants me the moment I enter the reserve! Within this small area of land there are rabbits. hares, partridge, pheasant, grass snakes, grebe, squirrels, owls, woodpeckers and a host of small birds. There are carnivores too – fox, badger, stoat and weasel. One of the fondest memories I have is that of seeing a hawk stoop twice, trying each time to catch a small bird. It missed as the intended meal peeled off right into the security of a big thick hawthorn. The hawk peeled left at the last possible moment, wings all a-quiver with the rush of air screaming through turbulent feathers. Then there was the time when I was privileged to see a hawk pulling out of a stoop right overhead as I sat fishing; the vicious hiss of air when the dive is checked is a thrill beyond description and living testimony to the terminal velocity these winged predators can reach. Money cannot buy these experiences and would that we could all share them ... 'far from the madding crowd' ... how much city-dwellers like me miss in a single year.

The carp lake at Woldale is quite small – about 3 acres and roughly triangular in shape. It is at the bottom of a natural depression in the surrounding land, the lake being formed by a dam built across a small feeder brook that flows roughly west to east. The dam forms the eastern bank, which falls away into a densely wooded valley.

Stretching the whole length of the southerly bank, which is quite steep in places, are big sycamore and beech trees. At the start of the northern bank, where the corner joins the dam, are patches of alder trees growing half in the water. A little farther along this bank is the famous chestnut tree swim – the scene of many a tussle that ended with the carp making the sanctuary of the trees. Two of the magnificent old chestnut trees sag towards the lake in their dying years. They remain upright only because the lower branches act like crutches, supporting an ever-increasing load. What an ignominious end for such splendid trees. What a store of events they must have witnessed in their long years; the big carp that have wallowed under the spread of their mighty branches; the thousands of animals that have scampered past their massive trunks; and the birds and squirrels that have trod their crowns. What tales they could tell of life and, perhaps ... death. If only trees were able to talk – I for one would be an enraptured listener!

The bank behind the chestnut trees rises very steeply and is covered with big beech trees. Below these trees the earth has a thick covering of dry, dead leaves that never seem to be in the stage of damp decay one expects of leaf-mould. During the day there is a regular pitter-patter of falling beech-nuts and debris as squirrels and birds, lost from sight in the leafy fastness, feed in safety and contentment. A path runs along the edge of the lake here and walking along it you pass through a wooden swing-gate till suddenly, the full, intense light of a summer's day makes the pupil contract sharply as you leave the trees behind. Here the northern bank has a more open and gentle slope and the lake edge is fringed with the tall, sword-like, leaves of the sweet flag. It is here that many carp can be seen moving in the late afternoon if you stand well back from the water on the higher ground. The sweet flag continues right into the narrow shallows that form the western apex of the triangular lake. The shallows are badly silted with heavy colonization of sweet flag, whose thick stems and roots spread in the rich silt. Many of the carp spend much of summer feeding in this sanctuary. There is an overall quietness so rarely witnessed in this high-speed world. It is perhaps best characterized by the perpetual wide spectrum hum from the noise of countless thousands of insect wings beating their busy way through the heat of a summer's day. Also by the quietness of night, when the screaming yowl of the vixen carries a long way.... Huddled in a blanket, alone in the night, a shiver runs down the spine – in spite of rapid progress man's ancient fears are still near the surface.

In late July 1974 I spent a weekend with Bob and another friend, Barrie Varney ('Baz' to all his friends) who, like Bob, has caught many big carp. We gave Baz the first choice of swim after a tour of inspection as this was his first visit. He chose the shallows where many carp could be seen bow-waving, appearing deceptively easy to catch. I spent my first weekend at Woldale in the same swim and had only a small common to show at the end of it. How the heart beats faster as large carp swim right over your baits. How disillusioned you become when they continue to ignore them. If the carp would bolt in fright now and again at least you would know they were *aware* of the baits, but to have a series of baits totally ignored is very frustrating indeed.

I chose to fish the chestnut tree swim for various reasons. It had that air of mystery that I like and, though no carp were showing there at present, I knew from chatting to Bob that the carp usually moved down under the chestnuts as evening approached. This was only my second visit and I leaned heavily on Bob for general advice on fishing the swim. He said that when a carp was hooked it in-

'Still standing now with crutches, propped' – the chestnut tree swim at Woldale

variably went like a rocket for the sunken tree branches. The only two people he knew who had some measure of success in the swim were Peter Mohan and Rod Hutchinson. Baits had to be placed as close to the sunken branches as possible. Then, should a carp be hooked the drill was to strike and 'walk' the fish away from danger, moving to the left until the first alder tree a few yards away prevented further movement. The fish was played from this position which had the advantage that if the rod was held low, maximum side-strain away from the snags could be applied. I set up the bivouac so that there was room to walk between it and the lake, fishing both rods slightly to the right of it as bushes behind limited the space available. Then after setting up my tackle carefully and mentally rehearsing the low sweeping strike to the left, I went to have a natter with Bob, for as yet it was only late afternoon.

Bob was fishing in his favourite swim where the line of chestnuts end and the open northern bank begins. I had to marvel at Bob's aplomb, for 18 inches to his left was a wasp's nest built in what was once a rat hole. Now I know quite a bit about wasps – it stems from the days when I used to take their nests and use the plump grubs to catch chub, trout and roach. I know that there is always a main 'flight path' into the nest. The approaching wasps line themselves up with the surrounding vegetation before descending down the flight path to the nest entrance. They do this to ensure they always find the right hole, for sometimes the entrance is in the most awkward place. I think the vegetation is used for initial guidance to the hole and if any small branches or tall grass in the immediate vicinity is bent or removed, the wasps are in trouble. The smooth practised descent becomes erratic. In-coming wasps collide with outgoing ones as flight paths become intermixed. Until the new approach is learned there can be fifty to a hundred puzzled wasps buzzing around the confines of the nest site, and puzzled wasps have a quick temper!

It was not that any vegetation had been removed. The three rods poked through narrow channels in the flag leaves and were set too low to interfere with the landing approach. It was Bob himself that blocked the flight path! When I first arrived he appeared to be sitting in a shimmering haze of wasps! The following day the situation was under control once again, the wasps had modified the approach, learning to use Bob for initial descent guidance: what confusion each time he left and re-entered the swim. Bob never got stung but goodness me, bet those wasps were awfully glad when he packed up that weekend!

By 7 p.m. I was nicely settled in my swim. Both baits had been cast and bait samples had been introduced into the swim. I had decided to fish one bait close to where the chestnut tree branches sagged into the water and had cast it within six inches of the branches. I used my trusty $2\frac{1}{2}$ pound test-curve built-cane rod that has a very powerful 'feel' to it, coupled with 12 pound breaking-strain line and a strong No. 2 hook. I felt confident the tackle was up to the job, for the same rig had dealt effectively with 20 pound fish in another 'tree' swim the previous year. The other rod – an Oliver's 11 foot carp rod with 10 pound line and No. 6 hook – was cast farther out into open water some yards to the left of the snags. Subtle ripples and small rocking eddies began to disturb the surface of the lake as the evening sun dropped below the tall trees at the south-western corner of the lake. Some carp had arrived ... things were looking good.

Soon after, Rod Hutchinson arrived at the lake to carry out some experiments. Rod had been fishing Redmire, spending the time between rota weeks at Woldale trying to solve some of the Redmire problems. This particular evening he had come to test some new floats. He went to the dam head to rig up a rod, as the light was already failing. The continual swish of casting and the plop of float, plus the muttered curses drifting across to my swim, told me that things were not going well. However, after a while Rod sorted things out and managed to complete the testing of various floats before the light failed completely. Testing ideas before fishing is the hallmark of a good angler. You do not get to Rod Hutchinson's standard of angling without a fertile mind and many years of successful carp-catching. His tally of big carp puts him in a class of his own, well above the level of we lesser mortals. He is the only angler I know who has a separate photo album for 20 pound carp – and there are plenty in it too! The only northern angler to equal Rod's ability is Kevin Clifford, who burst upon the angling scene in 1975, with a record catch of more than twenty carp in his first season at Redmire.

When the light had gone Rod came round and we had a long chat about carp-fishing and the swim I was fishing. Rod confirmed what Bob had told. The carp went straight for the tree branch snags the moment they were hooked. He told me to pressure them from the off and that I would be lucky if I managed to land one out of three.

Rod was speaking from personal experience too, for he had hooked six carp in this swim and landed only two. By this time, much of my former confidence was evaporating like the morning mist in the rays of the rising sun. If Rod had difficulty with the swim my efforts could only end in fiasco! Not that I had any past history of losing carp through breakage or snags, though I have lost quite a few through failing to set the hook correctly on the strike. During the last four seasons I had been broken only twice. In that time I had caught a fair number of carp on lines as fine as 3 pounds breaking-strain and considered breakage a thing of the past. My ego, already deflated by the conversation, was soon to be completely flattened.

Rod left just before midnight, the quiet of Woldale at night being broken as his old Volkswagen, which had done an incredible mileage, climbed out of the valley and headed towards Grimsby. As the sound of the car faded into the distance, I began to rehearse mentally the procedure I would follow if I hooked a fish. A hard, low strike to the left ... keep on full pressure while walking left, away from the snags ... keep rod tip low – even in the water – until fish is well clear of danger area. I was still trying to prepare myself for action when at midnight the indicator of the left-hand rod, the one fishing in open water 10 yards away from the snags, sang out its transistorized warning.

Two quick strides saw me hovering over the rod, ready to strike. But the silver paper tell-tale on the line between rod rings remained stationary. I paused for vital seconds, not knowing if a carp had the bait or if a line bite had set the indicator going ... then the silver paper began to lift. It was hardly an inch higher before I had the bale-arm shut and put in the low, powerful strike. Everything went to plan; the strike, the walk to the left, the rod down low, but on my second step I knew I had failed, for all went solid as the carp hit the snags.

During the next half hour I had plenty of time to re-live the event as I tried the usual procedures for freeing snagged carp. Of one thing I am sure: no one could have put in the strike, or pressured the fish away from danger any faster than I did. This part had gone like clockwork once the silver paper moved. And this rod had been fishing several yards to the left of the snags. How could the fish have made the snags, yet only moved the silver paper at the last moment? There was only one way it could have happened. The carp must have picked up the bait without the indicator registering then, while chewing the bait felt the hook and panicked, fleeing towards the snags and causing a slack-line bite. Eventually the line had caught somewhere, triggering the indicator and finally lifting the silver paper, possibly as it hit the first of the branches. That had to be the explanation for I had given no line from the spool. It was the only way the fish could have gained enough line to make the snags.

All this and more passed through my mind as I tried to free the fish. If I put pressure on it came to the surface, making the peculiar slurping noises that a carp makes when its mouth is above the water. The sound suggested it was only just inside the snags. If only I had struck immediately instead of waiting. To make matters worse the fish had crossed the line of the other rod and each time pressure was applied it triggered the other indicator. What a complete and utter mess I had made of it all. All I needed now was a run on the other rod – that really would put the lid on things! I decided to pull for a break. Allowing the snagged fish too much slack line would, more than likely, result in additional line being tangled in the snags. It would be better if the break was as near to the hook as possible.

Gradually I backed away from the lake with rod tip pointing at the snags and finger hard down on the reel spool. It is incredible how much pull a good 10 pound line will take before it breaks, but finally it did, with a sharp crack that echoed around the quiet lake like a rifle shot. That carp proved to be the only chance of the weekend. We fished hard but no more runs came our way.

During the following weeks Bob invited me back to Woldale for a few days' fishing in August. Unfortunately he could not spend much time with me but promised to call in for a few hours when possible. As I motored over to Woldale the one thing on my mind was the chestnut tree swim. I was still smarting from my failure in July and determined that I would have a carp out of that swim – or bust in the attempt.

I had taken two of my young sons with me, on what was to be a four-day session. The eldest one was still recuperating from an appendicitis operation; Woldale would be a good convalescence for him. Both sons take a keen interest in anything that squirms, crawls, runs, swims or flies – they both expect me to have the knowledge of a zoological encyclopaedia, constantly perplexing me with a wide range of questions about the entire fauna of the British Isles! It is not all one-sided though, and often I too learn from their simple, uncluttered observations as they study the things small boys love like frogs, toads and spiders.

When we arrived Bob was waiting for us. The first task was an inspection of the lake. The inspection finished, I chose a site for our small green tent, reasonably close to the swim I intended to fish, but hidden under the trees so that the aesthetic beauty of the place was not spoiled. With the tent up, ground sheet and sleeping bags installed for the two lads, I set about organizing my own bivvy and tackling up the two rods. I had three full days and nights before me – surely long enough to find an answer?

Bob left, just after dark, to go to work. He works an unusual shift system that, from the angling point of view, has both advantages and disadvantages. The major advantage is that he is often able to fish for three days midweek, when there is the least pressure on a water. The disadvantage is that only rarely can he share a weekend's fishing with friends. It was very dark and gloomy under the heavy-leaved chestnut trees, though out on the surface of the lake there was still sufficient light to see the swirl as a fish broke the glassy smoothness. There had been a north-westerly wind blowing down the valley ruffling the water earlier in the day. This is about the only direction that the wind can touch the water in summer, for the high banks and thickly wooded areas that surround the lake protect it from winds from other directions. I like to see a good blow rippling the water surface in summer, especially during the day on shallow lakes. The wind keeps the temperature down and helps to oxygenate and mix the semi-stagnant water. Although I had not fished Woldale often enough to be certain, I felt that if the deeper end of the lake was to produce carp – particularly the chestnut swim – a wind blowing down the lake would be vital. The wind had been blowing, almost to order, and as dusk approached it dropped off to leave a flat calm. These were ideal conditions for summer carp – it was up to me to make the most of them.

At ten o'clock there was an excited outburst on the dam head where my two boys had been catching small roach and perch on maggot. Andrew, the younger one, suddenly appeared in an absolute frenzy of excitement. It transpired that Richard had accidentally caught a bat with the hook while casting. Fearing he may receive a nasty bite – for some bats have several rows of small sharp teeth – I called softly to him to bring it round for me to unhook. A few minutes later he arrived with a tiny Pipistrelle bat held gently in the palm of his hand. He had released the hook from the leathery part of the wing himself and the bat appeared undamaged. Both the lads were fascinated by bats, and had asked many questions about them. Now we were able to examine in detail this minute creature before releasing it, unharmed by the experience. Never mind if the disturbance had cost me a carp, it was a fair exchange for the pleasure of seeing two pairs of shining, eager eyes, and hearing the bubbling questions from my offspring. Woldale had already cast its spell over me in the few hours I had been there. If I was not careful I would forget my resolve to land a double-figure carp from the difficult chestnut tree swim!

Pip-pip-pip-pip-pip-pip! The stuttering sound of the indicator aroused me from my reverie! Leaping towards the rods, I found the silver paper of the left-hand rod had disappeared. Placing the back of my hand under the rod, I could feel line ripping off the spool at an alarming speed. No time to lose, must strike quickly or the fish will be in the snags! The strike connected and the rod tip wrenched round towards the snags. But I crammed on pressure and found myself tight against the alder bush without remembering walking there. The carp boiled on the surface about 2 yards short of the dreaded branches; the side-strain had beaten it – he was coming towards me! Quickly I wound down and pumped the rod back to gain a few precious yards of line before the next run . . . and then the line went limp.

All carp anglers learn to live with the shock of losing a good carp. Sometimes it is easier to bear the loss when a critical look at the sequence shows that the mistake is yours. But here all had gone right: the strike, the low side-strain, the three or four paces along the bank, and then the line had parted at a time when the fish was coming towards me. A check of the terminal tackle in the light of the torch revealed the BB shot-ledger was still in place, and I estimated that the line had parted about 3 inches above the hook. The last 2 inches of line had a peculiar crinkled look about it that was not there when it was cast into the swim some hours before. It was now 4 a.m. I sat wondering about the break and, not finding any ready answer, I cut the line at the shot. Carefully storing it for examination in daylight, I tied on another hook, baited and re-cast.

As soon as it was light enough to see clearly, I took out the piece of line and examined it with the 8× lens I carry. There were a number of odd-looking flattened depressions in the last $1\frac{1}{2}$ inches. I had never seen a line damaged like this before. A few more minutes' puzzling and then I had the answer. The carp had chewed through the line with its pharyngeal teeth. When you have the answer to a problem it all seems so easy and you wonder why you did not think of it sooner. There had been several times when friends had complained of line being bitten by carp and, though this was the first time it had happened to me, I ought to have realized sooner the significance of that peculiar crinkled effect.

The chestnut tree swim always seemed dead during the day. There were no signs of carp in it and I have never had a run during daylight. During the day there are always plenty of carp on the shallows at Woldale, one can see them to-ing and fro-ing around the 'bays' formed by the emergent sword-like leaves. The vast majority are small carp just short of double figures, but occasionally an obvious double will show. I have yet to see a really big fish on the shallows. No doubt they often go there, perhaps at a particular time of year, but the only big carp I have seen – fish in the 15 plus bracket – seem to spend more time in the deeper water. I enjoy catching carp of any size but prefer to set myself an above-average target. If the average carp a water produces is 5 pounds and I land one of 6 pounds, I go home highly delighted. At Woldale I wanted a double-figure fish to be satisfied. So far the carp had denied me that pleasure.

The day had been calm and hot, conditions which, if my theory was correct, did not guarantee much chance of sport in my swim. In the morning a few carp had rolled along the southern edge of the lake and I had taken a rod round. There the water was quite coloured with several denser smoky patches when bubblers worked along the bottom. Fixing a small Arlesey bomb close to the hook with brandlings for bait, I spent half an hour bubbler-chasing before catching a $5\frac{1}{2}$ pound common that fought very well. Some time later a carp of enormous length slowly rose to the surface on an even keel, laying there, seemingly chewing something about 15 yards from the bank. I had enough time to retrieve my tackle, re-bait with fresh worms and make a cast before he sank, just as slowly, down into the coloured water. A few minutes passed before the line, hanging limp, twitched a few times where it entered the water. Grasping the rod butt, the old familiar tremble in my body, I waited until the line began a slow steady lift as it tightened between rod tip and bait. A strike, a huge swirl, a bow wave and the fish had gone. The hook had

My friend the robin begging for another piece of Bacon Grill

failed to find a hold. Either I was cursed or these larger Woldale carp live charmed lives. By now there was a despairing note creeping into my thoughts, marring somewhat, the beauty of the surroundings.

The evening slowly advanced. We had eaten a vast meal of potatoes, greens and meat balls. To see my two boys ravenously clear a plate piled high with food then ask for crisps or biscuits gave me great satisfaction. The fresh air was doing their appetites a power of good. The meal was cooked in a pressure cooker, the best method I have found for preparing a large meal. Tins of meat and peas or carrots are put in the cooker with lids opened. Then peeled potatoes are put into the removable sections that fit inside the pressure cooker. My cooker has three removable sections. By removing one, the tinned food can be fitted in its place, leaving the other two sections to accommodate the potatoes. The cooker is then put on the primus stove with the 10 pound pressure weight in place. Ten minutes after the steam begins to issue from the escape valve the meal is cooked. Only one utensil has been used. The cooker can be removed and it will act as an excellent oven, keeping all the food within piping hot, until you prepare gravy, or boil a kettle. A good meal can work wonders for a despondent outlook.

As dusk approached vast numbers of bats emerged to begin feasting on the prodigious range of flying insects available. I have never seen so many bats in such a small area, proof indeed of the rich feeding available. To watch the fantastic manoeuvrability of this highly developed animal belies its rather ancient-looking construction, reminiscent of the clumsy age of the pterosaur and pterodactyl millions of years ago. Later, long after I had seen the lads safely tucked up in the tent, I was laying on my camp bed under the bivvy when a bat entered through the open front, did a circuit round the inside, and left the same way. It was far too dark to see the bat and I followed its progress by the flap of its leathery wings and the waft of air on my face as it passed a few inches above my head. I have noticed also that bats will often dive close to an angler's head when he sits at dusk on the bankside. I could not understand why until I shone a torch above my head. There, captured in the beam of light, were dozens of flies, dancing up and down in the rising column of heat escaping from my body. All these little 'happenings' help to relieve the hours of waiting, adding interest to any fishing trip and sometimes softening the bitter pill of failure.

The night passed without a single bleep from my transistorized alarms, providing further evidence that a lack of wind on the water caused this swim to be dead. There was a good deal of activity on the bank though. A constant coming and going of rats and much pitter-pattering of heavier feet in the dry, dead leaves behind me. Several times the dark shadow of an animal far larger than any rat scampered past the open front of the bivvy. Perhaps a fox on his nightly prowls who, finding his normal route partially blocked with this peculiar contraption, had sat for ages in the darkness before deciding it was safe to pass. In the early hours before dawn, several carp rolled near the southern bank and leapt clear of the water twice causing a tremendous crash that cleaved the quiet like a knife, sending ripples across the lake to lap the undercut bank in front of me. In the grey light of dawn a large hare lolloped down the path looking so ungainly at low speed. It stopped, less than 6 feet from me, then sat upright, eyeing this strange thing with interest, ears cocked forward and nose a-twitching. The hare sat for a good five minutes while I, hardly daring to breathe, wondered if it would come even closer. But eventually, either through lack of interest or courage, it dropped down on all fours, lolloped back up the path and disappeared from view. I sat very still hoping that I would have the same experience that Bob had had one morning while fishing this swim. That morning a hare had approached him in the same way. It had gone away but about ten minutes later two hares had returned to look at this strange thing sitting at the lake side. Bob is convinced that the first hare had never seen anything so amazing before, and had purposely gone to fetch its mate to look too before the strange apparition disappeared. Perhaps the hare had become rather blasé since then, having seen many strange things around the lake edge, or perhaps the mate had been taken by a fox. Although I sat motionless for a long time, camera at the ready, the hares did not return.

In the afternoon my friend David Moss-Allison called in for a chat. Dave was a member of the syndicate and had fished Woldale quite a few times. When I had finished moaning about 'bad luck' and 'jinxes' affecting my results he told me that there had been relatively few carp caught all season. Only a handful of doubles had been taken and even the smaller carp were difficult to catch. Our conversation then turned to the design and use of bite indicators.

Dave had recently been 'bitten' by the bite indicator design bug. This is a subject on which I can bore anyone, having undergone the same pre-occupation years ago. Since the sixties many designs have been made in an effort to improve reliability. Dave was an avid and intelligent listener, grasping the more profound points of design with ease and asking questions that showed a depth of understanding which belied the limited time he had been involved in their construction. It always gives me great pleasure to pass on, what seems to me, sound information. To see that information put into practice, as Dave did, doubles the pleasure of giving it. We discussed the various reasons behind the design of the latest indicator I had developed for use in the chestnut tree swim. Then I showed Dave how to achieve maximum sensitivity for winter carp-fishing by using an indicator 'remote' from the rod. The afternoon passed quickly and soon it was time for Dave to leave and for me to start preparing the evening meal for my ravenous offspring. This was my last night and the wind I had hoped for had been blowing down the lake all day. With it had come a lifting of spirit. Surely the swim would fish tonight ... please let my last night be successful.

By 11 p.m. the sky had clouded over and the night had turned into blackness. The rods, only two yards away, were completely invisible. I could not see a single detail to guide my hand, having to grope until my fingers touched some part of the rod before I could grasp the butt. I had never fished through a night as black as this, it could not possibly have been any darker. There was also a complete lack of movement from the animals around me. Even the familiar flap of bat wings overhead was missing. The silence was absolute and for some reason the expression 'quiet as the grave' crossed my mind.

For a long while I pondered my decision to continue fishing the chestnut tree swim when all my instincts told me that the southern bank offered a better chance of success. Carp had been rolling there during the last two mornings and the colour in the water left no doubt in the mind that they were also feeding. 'Why stick here in this gloomy swim that so far has brought only failure?' My thoughts rambled into the night until at last I knew why I fished the swim. It was nothing more than injured pride that kept me here. Losing two fish in this awkward swim had annoyed me. I never considered myself an expert carp angler, yet usually, by sheer determination, I would catch the fish I was after, even if it took me twice as long as the expert.

The indicator of the left-hand rod sang out, startling me from my dreams. With adrenalin-boosted movement I plunged out into the blackness, guided towards the rods by the red glow of the light-emitting diode in the left-hand indicator. My right hand found the butt first time, while, above the insistent note of the indicator, my ears could detect the rattle of line fairly sizzling through the rod rings. No need to feel if line was being taken, it was – and at a fantastic rate! I shut the bale-arm, put in the low strike away from the snags, then blundered left until my head hit the leaves of the alder bush. It was just a matter of how much line the fish had taken, for the rod was now hard round, tip pulling towards the sunken branches as I hung on to the butt. As before the low side-strain told and the fish was turned. Yards of line, vital to success, were pumped back on to the reel spool. I began to feel hopeful as the fight progressed in complete silence. For years now, except when fishing very close in, I had played fish from the reel handle, so even the clutch was silenced.

After two or three minutes the fish began to tire. Slowly the pressure told and it came nearer to the bank. The only noise came from the reel spool. When the fish pulled hard there was a soft rustle as taut nylon bit down through the lower coils. It was uncanny, almost dream-like, and then the silence was broken as the carp rolled for the first time, smacking the surface with its tail. Away up the lake in the shallows a startled moorhen gave a cry of alarm. Suddenly I felt very cold and the first touch of fear crept through my body.

The carp set off with renewed energy after the first roll. Each second I played the fish I became more afraid. Of what I do not know. But the hair at the back of my neck was bristling while my body shivered. Something felt wrong and all I wanted was to land the carp as soon as possible. Applying greater pressure than I would normally I pumped the fish towards the bank, lifting the net when I judged from the sound it was over it. The first time I missed and touched the fish, having to give more line as it tore away from the bank. The second attempt was more successful and, feeling the weight of the fish, I put the rod down and hoisted it ashore. By now I was in a near panic. Desperately I tried to calm myself as I unhooked the fish and put it in a sack, dumping it unceremoniously in the water. Quickly re-baiting the hook, I flung the bait out into the lake, not caring if it landed in the baited swim or not. Diving into the bivvy I hurled myself on to the camp bed and pulled a blanket over my head. I lay there shivering, waiting for dawn to end this stygian blackness and bring relief to my shattered nerves.

I am not normally of a nervous disposition. Until this experience at Woldale I cannot honestly say that I have ever been really frightened. Like many beginners to night fishing I have had my share of nervous jumps when a rat has run over my wader or a sudden near-by noise has startled me. But after years of night fishing one becomes used to these things, learning to enjoy them and taking pride in identifying the creatures that make the noises. The explosive plop of the vole in the margins when a movement scares him; the scamper of a rat through dry leaves; the quiet rustle of a mouse in the bramble patch behind; the eerie whistle of pinioned wings, followed by the sh-sh-sh-sh-splosh! as webbed feet plane the water and the solid body of a mallard flights in after dark; the quick yap! yap! of a tawny owl which has landed silently in the tree above your head – you grow to love these things and they become part of the night fishing scene. I have spent many nights alone at various ponds and lakes and never felt afraid. Perhaps the incredible darkness had caused my panic.

I tried to reason out the cause but that did not help at all and I was terrified that one of the indicators would sound again. 'Why had I cast the bait back in?' 'Wouldn't it have been better to have wound in both rods when the carp was caught?' 'Conditioned reaction no doubt, to bait and re-cast after landing a carp.' ... 'Don't let another run develop ... don't think I could respond to it anyway.' ... 'I'm not moving from here to pull in the rods either ... they can stay where they are!'

After what seemed an eternity, the black night gradually lightened until dawn revealed the sack, still in the shallow water at the edge of the lake where I had dumped it. It wasn't a nightmare after all! Here was proof of that – the sack with rope fastened to the neck, the bank stick driven into the ground to hold it. 'Hope the carp's all right; wonder why it hasn't pulled the sack into deeper water, as they normally do.' 'Wonder how much it weighs!'

The terror of the night momentarily forgotten, I jumped up and hoisted out the sack to look at this carp. I hoisted it ashore and, rolling down the big sack, gazed at a nice mirror. It was short and deep, looking as if it might just go to double figures. It was 22 inches long and weighed $10\frac{1}{2}$ pounds. Success at last! My resolve to catch a double from this difficult swim had been fulfilled. Third time lucky!

(The reader might think the above account of that last night at Woldale has been dramatized as a climax to mark the end of the session. He is, of course, entitled to his own opinion. I have tried to describe what happened as truthfully as possible, only regretting that my pen is not able to convey my feelings more accurately. The experience has not stopped me night fishing, nor has it reduced the attraction of Woldale. Yet ... if the same thing happened again, well....)

Each carp I had hooked in the chestnut swim had made a bee-line for the sunken snags: the first one must have been nearly in them before the silver paper began to lift. The second one was stopped 2 yards short of them. The third one, although it was too dark to see anything, obviously ran it very close; the direction of pull on the rod

Author's son Richard holds Dad's Woldale common

and the line pumped back before the rod could be lifted from the side-strain position to upright, suggested that the fish was only yards short. It was as if the carp were trained and knew that the sunken branches offered a means of escape. I had never witnessed this before.

I have never subscribed to the theory that a hooked carp will deliberately swim towards a sunken obstacle to snag the angler. It is quite impossible to imagine a carp thinking: 'Blast it! Slipped up there with that piece ... got a No. 2 in my top lip now ... let's see, will it be the tree branch snags or that big rough boulder out yonder?' ... 'Think I'll make it the branches.' Carp can be pretty cute at times, but no fish has enough grey matter to reason in such a way. Before my Woldale experiences I had found that most carp near snags had accelerated in the direction they were facing when hooked. If this was towards the snags and I was using light tackle the fish was usually lost. If it was away from the snags it was usually landed. I like to use light gear whenever possible but 12 pound line and a $2\frac{1}{2}$ pound test-curve rod provide tremendous power in 'tree swims'. Together with the correct strike this tackle sways the odds in favour of the angler. A long, powerful, heaving strike helps pull the fish's head away from the snags before it makes its first mad dash. Once it runs away from a snag it has no chance of escape on such tackle, unless the angler makes a mistake. Carp often reach a snag because the reel clutch is set to give line. Normally the experienced carp angler need use the clutch only for margin fishing. If the total of lost carp per season could be analysed throughout the country, I am sure that misuse of the slipping clutch would account for a high proportion.

So why should all these Woldale carp head straight for the snags when only one out of seven had gone for the snags at another lake the year before? Most anglers who have fished the Woldale swim have had similar experiences. The only suitable explanation I can give is based upon the age of the average carp that live there. There is little doubt that many of them are quite 'old' in fish terms. Perhaps those that inhabit the chestnut tree swim have been hooked several times during their life span, learning in the process that the sunken branches offer a way of escape. It seems more reasonable to me that a thirty- or forty-year-old carp would learn rather than think that the snags offered a means of freedom. If a carp could think so well we would never hook it in the first place. There is a vast difference between a conditioned reflex and premeditated thought. It is a question of whether a hooked carp deliberately seeks out snags or runs into them by chance. These carp at Woldale appear to have learned a good way to avoid capture: those in other lakes may not have had sufficient conditioning as yet.

Also of interest was the complete failure of that Woldale hot-spot, right at the very edge of the snags where sagging branches and water met. Apart from a couple of half-hearted twitches the bait remained untouched. I had rigged a special indicator for that rod too, one that would respond to a mere tightening of the line, giving a 'beep' when the carp took the bait in its mouth. The indicator had been tried with great success on twitching fish in another tight swim and I had high hopes for it at Woldale. But lack of runs prevented any useful conclusions being made. Had I fished both rods in the hot-spot – or in this instance cold-spot – there may not have been any runs at all. It always pays to diversify the effort.

The following August I was on my way to Woldale again. Again I would be night fishing alone and could not help wondering if my nerves would stand the test after the episode the previous year. This time I was going to concentrate on the southern bank where the carp had been rolling the previous year. I do not think my nerves would have allowed me to fish the gloomy chestnut tree swim but in any event, the swim was now unfishable. Sometime during the spring, maybe just after the buds had split and the large leaves had unfurled, a wind had blown from just the right angle, putting the final stress on the rotting crutches. The two magnificent trees had collapsed into the lake, completely blocking the swim. As I stood on the bank surveying the tangled mess my mind went back to the few precious hours I had spent fishing there. It would never be the same again, it was so much lighter now. With the collapse had gone the dark, brooding mystery of the swim. Despite my frightening experiences there I felt regret and sadness at the change.

The visit did not work out as planned. There were several reasons for my lack of success, one of which was my choice of swim. Things had altered since the previous year and I would have been better fishing elsewhere. But I had formed certain opinions about the southern bank and wanted to put them to the test. It did not work out as expected, though I did catch a very nice common from the swim and saw one of the 20 plus carp pass through. With a touch of luck things might have been different.

While fishing there two sturdy gamekeepers, who also bailiffed the fishery, turned up. We got into conversation after they had checked my permission to be there. They were mainly interested in how many ducks I had seen flighting in at dusk and were at a loss to understand why anyone should want to fish for carp. We talked of this and that for a while. Then for some reason the conversation turned to the chestnut tree swim. Perhaps I mentioned the fishing had been ruined there now the trees had fallen in the lake.

'Oh, yes,' said the larger of the two, 'funny spot that.... There was a youth drowned under the chestnuts a few years back....'

6 Reflections on a pot of gold

I am not in the position to write about the capture of a really big carp from personal experience, so I have asked a guest writer, who I have long admired as a carp angler, to relate his experiences with a monster fish. That a man can catch carp weighing 43 pounds $14\frac{1}{2}$ ounces and 38 pounds, and yet still enjoy catching 5 pound wildies highlights a depth of character not readily found in the average angler. My own fishing outlook is always geared to the water being fished. I get satisfaction from catching carp that are veritable 'monsters' for the water. These fish need not be huge yet it has become fashionable to ridicule such fish, by a variety of silly names, because they are not over the 'magic' 20 pounds. My guest is in a position to show that there is very much more to carp-fishing than mere size. Having caught the second largest carp in England gives a man the right to discuss carp-fishing as few can. Therefore I am privileged and honoured that my guest, Chris Yates, consented to write this story for me.

Reflections on a pot of gold by *Chris Yates*

Twenty years ago, when I was eight, I saw my first carp. For twenty years now I have been under the 'carp-spell'. I was having a walk round a local heath pond with my father and, in a willow-shaded corner, we came upon an old man sitting on a basket, fishing. In answer to our questions about his luck that day he lifted out his keep-net. Lying in the mesh was a gigantic golden fish. To this day I remember it vividly; the bluish back, tail and dorsal, the reddish under-fins and those glistening gold scales. For days afterwards I was haunted by its image. It did not seem possible that the small, muddy pond I knew so well could have produced such a creature and I used to spend hours gazing into its green depths, expectant yet half terrified that I would see it again. And now, all these years later, though the carp in that pond were all wiped out in the freeze-up of 1963 and though the pond itself is now no more than a cracked dusty hollow, those feelings are just as fresh and strong. Great bronze fish with blue backs continue to glide through my dreams. As long as the dream is there I will always go carp-fishing. Call me a romantic or an idealist if you will but, for me, that dream, that sensation that is really just a slightly poetic element of one of man's old hunting instincts, is the essence of my fishing. And the monster that all carp men hope for, including me, is not as important as the dream. I enjoy my fishing. I take it very seriously too. But I love it too much to let the monster spoil it. After all, you are more likely *not* to catch the monster than catch it. If you are like a lot of today's carp anglers who only think in terms of monsters, then the end of each season will see you very dissatisfied and frustrated with the failure of the preceding months. Though I cannot say I am never frustrated – some carp can be very obstinate – I have never been dissatisfied.

I hope I do not give the impression of being complacent. Just because I am not going all-out for the biggest carp that swims does not mean I am lying back on my bed-chair watching the world slide by. For a start I have no bed-chair and, even if I had, I would hope not to be on it when a carp took the bait. I always think it is a bit unexciting and unimaginative to have caught a carp that just happened to stumble on my bait after it had been out for hours and hours. That method is certainly not very skilful. No, I like to work for my fish; I like to stalk a visible quarry; creep up on him and cast for him, knowing that a single wrong move will lose the fish. That, in my view, is the ultimate in carp-fishing, though once again, if the attitude is wrong a lot of the true enjoyment is lost.

At the risk of overstating my point, I would like to relate my experience with two big carp. I hope that the conclusions I drew after their capture will make clearer my belief that quality is more important than quantity.

In June 1972 I had my first week at Redmire. Though I failed to get one of the big ones I could not have hoped for a better opening. Within four days I had made a discovery that I had fully expected to take four months; the discovery of a bait to crack Redmire. And

Chris Yates with his Pot of Gold

crack Redmire it did. Everyone in the syndicate started catching carp on it. On my second week I got my first Redmire '20' and on the third I hooked a carp so huge that both Rod Hutchinson and I, seeing the fish wallowing in the net, knew was very close to the record. As it turned out, I missed the '44' mark by $1\frac{1}{2}$ ounces, but I could hardly feel upset. I called that fish my 'pot of gold' (it was like a brass pig!). There was some justice in its capture for though I did not catch as many carp as some of the Redmire group did on 'my' bait, I did catch the heaviest. The bait was sweetcorn and people have been catching carp on it ever since.

A 40 pounder is a monster in anyone's eyes and it might have seemed that I had reached the zenith of my carp fishing. Yet far from curing my obsession it just seemed to inspire me. All I wanted was to carry on fishing, not just for another monster but for any carp that would put a good bend in a rod. As it turned out I hooked a fish that made me think, for a while, that I really had broken the record.

It was after the first frosts of autumn and things had been so quiet at Redmire that I was planning on a different venue for my last October session. Then Rod phoned me in the middle of the week. He was almost speechless, having just seen a carp at Redmire that made even 40 pounders look puny. He hardly mentioned that he'd just caught a 22 pound mirror. 'Things are looking good,' he said, 'I think you'd be barmy not to come down!' I had some work to finish so it was not until the Friday of that week that I could go down.

Rod had no more fish to report and the pool looked bleak and cold; grey ripples down to the dam and bare trees. Yet while I was setting up stall I saw a fish bubbling. I cast for it and caught it and though it only went 14 pounds I thought it a good start. Next morning another patch of bubbles rose. With ultra-light tackle (in Redmire a 10 hook, 6 pound line and tiny link is ultra-light) I cast into them and in fifteen minutes had a 24 pound mirror rolling into the net. It was overcast, not too cold and we were hopeful. Yet nothing else happened. The sky cleared towards evening, the wind dropped and a pale quarter-moon appeared above the black trees. Though there were no signs of feeding fish I suddenly had a strong feeling something was going to happen. I hoped that if it did happen, it happened before seven-thirty for at that time we had a dinner engagement with a young married couple we had befriended in a near-by village. Just before last light I quickly moved round to the corner of the dam with the ultra-light gear and, putting on a small quill float, I dropped the sweetcorn right under the rod tip so that it was just touching bottom in 6 feet of water. I was absolutely positive that a fish was going to oblige.

Just as it was becoming difficult to see, two large bubbles rose near the float. By now it was six o'clock; nearly dark. The float lifted, very slowly, then disappeared. I struck gently. Something went round in a tight circle below me and seemed confused, for a moment, as to what had happened. I stood up and applied a bit more pressure thinking I had hooked a baby. There was no movement on the surface and I could not budge the fish from the bottom. It was not a baby. Suddenly the carp began to take line. It was only a couple of short spurts to begin with but then he really began to move, charging straight out up the deep centre channel. I was giving the light line as much as it could take and the rod, specifically sold as a 'barbel rod', was bent double. Rod came running up out of the gloom.

'Stop playing around with it, if he goes any further he'll ground himself in the shallows!' That is how it seemed and yet I could not stop the fish's flight.

'I'm not playing around Rod, he just will not stop!' Suddenly I remembered that the line did not go on for ever, there was only 150 yards. In the fading light I glanced at the spool on my Ambidex reel. The metal was beginning to show, the spool was nearly stripped. I ran across the dam, my fingers jammed over the clutch. As I ran to the left, the rod began to bend to the right; I remember feeling it twisting like an enormous screw in my hand. Far out over the dark water we heard a tremendous splash as the carp swung round and rolled on the top. Then there was another splash and the bend began to go out of the rod. The carp had turned and was heading back down the pool, coming straight towards us.

I wound and wound. He had surfaced somewhere near the island, up towards the shallows and that meant I had a tremendous length of line to recover. But it was all right, the fish was coming in at medium speed and, though my left hand was going like a piston, I was maintaining contact. I took a quick look up to the rod point and to my horror noticed the tip was beginning to swing to the left towards the old willow, 30 yards away. Under the water there was a mass of big dead branches, snags that cost me my first 20 the previous July. I shouted to Rod to get round there quick and make a commotion and off he shot, vaulting the stile and crashing up the bank. I winced as the carp kept travelling to the left, swerving faster now. Soon, I guessed, he must hit the branches, then there would be no hope – the line would snap instantly. 'Throw something!' I yelled. There were a few splashes that must have been well aimed. The carp swung out from the left-hand bank – he was coming in again.

Playing a big carp from the dam at Redmire was a definite advantage. I could move from one side to the other, keeping in direct contact. Wherever the carp went at the dam end of the pool I could cover it and counter its movements. Now that we had overcome its attempt to get in the willow snags I moved to the centre of the dam and pumped it through the deep water until it was right beneath the rod tip, about 11 feet down. The net was positioned and I began to lift. Rod flicked on a small torch and in its light we saw the white quill-float, tangled with a bunch of dead weed, break surface. The rod was bent right over. The float came to a dead stop a foot above the surface. I kept maximum pressure on but the carp would not rise an inch. Again Rod thought I was playing around. He looked up at the quivering bend above him and knew this was no game. On 6 pound line he had beaten a 22 pounder inside five minutes. After quarter of an hour my fish was just taking a breather before charging out once more, heading for snags on the west bank. By the time I had got him back half an hour had passed and we still could not lift him up to the net. I wound right down so that the tip was in the water and then heaved. Rod shone the torch and we both peered into the depths. We could see the float, the bunch of weed and the line quivering down below us. But of a carp we could see nothing. Again he suddenly turned and recommenced battle, heading powerfully up the pool, untiring, unstoppable.

It was quite dark. The moon was turning orange behind me and the stars were bright. I kept looking up at them, trying to find a contrasting peace to the turbulence below. I was forcing myself to keep calm and not lose this fish through a nervous, uncontrolled manoeuvre. An hour had passed and we were both convinced that, whether the carp was *the* monster or not, it just had to be of record proportions. It was still fighting relentlessly, charging up and down the pool, coming in now and then but never coming to the surface. There was a way, though, to get this fish. It was risky but just possible. Though there was deep water at the dam centre, on each side it was quite shallow, especially at the eastern end. The danger was that there were bad snags at both places. On the western end there was a tangle of dead branches; on the east there was a platform jutting out into the water, the weed filter for an old pressure pump. Of the two the west was marginally the worst. The plan was to draw the carp into the shallow water where, if it hugged the bottom or not, we could at least get the net to it. But as soon as I began to try and steer the fish to my right it turned sharp left and went flying towards the snaggy corner, almost as if it had heard us discussing our plan! I raced after it, the rod held out over the bushes that grow up along the dam rail. The fish was going fast, right next to the stonework, and I felt the line 'ping-pinging' through trailing twigs and brambles. It was a miracle that it did not get caught. At the last possible second I turned it and it swung out away from danger. I still could not coax it right out of the corner and it circled round and round, threateningly close to the sunken branches.

I began to notice how cold I was. There would be a frost before dawn and my hands were numb. As the fish turned and turned again I put my left hand in my pocket and huffed on my right. Suddenly I saw Rod had taken off his waders and jeans and had the net held ready.

'I'm going in for it!' he said.

'What! It's freezing, it'll kill you,' I said.

But, courageous lad that he is, he began lowering himself off the dam wall into 3 feet of ice-cold water. I strained the tackle again, the net was ready. He seemed to be coming, though again there was no movement on the surface. Just when we thought we must have him – whoosh! Away he went again, sailing out towards the deeps, the clutch screaming once more. We followed. This time I got right over into the eastern corner before tightening up and pumping him in. As he neared us we watched big, inky ripples spreading out not 20 feet away. He rolled, gurgled, swayed this way and that. Rod climbed out to the end of the platform and I began to ease the fish towards him. I remember him as a black figure, crouched above the dark water, leaning out with the net as a black wave came slowly up to him. This must be it, I thought, the record is nearly ours. There was a flurry of action. Something was wrong, there was a tremendous splash then the clutch began to scream again. But the line! It was running against something! It was caught round the landing net on the S link that holds the cord to the arms. For a horrible second I thought that was the end, yet somehow Rod managed to free it. The rod was swept up, the carp was stopped and once more he began to come unwillingly to the net. This time there was no mistake. I saw Rod lift. There was a tremendous thrashing and I could see the net-handle bending. The carp was *still* fighting! I dropped the rod and leaned out. The net was passed up and I dragged it over the rail and laid it on the dam. We flicked the torch on.

'Well,' I said, 'it's certainly very long.'

'Yes,' replied Rod, 'but it's no record.'

Had that carp made good one of his numerous chances to escape, then to this day both Rod and I would be convinced I had lost a record. But I cannot say I was disappointed when the pointer on the spring balance stopped at a mere 24½ pounds. The battle was won, against all the odds. The carp was certainly the longest I have ever caught; getting on for 3 feet. It was solid, like a length of carved wood and with great muscles at the base of the fins. It was a king-common, yet the nearest thing to a 20 pound 'wildie' I will ever see. That was the reason, I am sure, that it fought so hard. It was built for fighting! In fact it was still fighting when we tried to photograph it the next morning after a night in a sack. It was like a wrestling match and we really did not get a good shot of it. There was no long last look when I released it. It leapt out of my arms, crashed into the water and belted off like a torpedo!

The fight itself took two hours – the moon had set by the time we had landed the fish and we were very late for our dinner engagement. Rod had got so cold and wet he had to go in his tank-suit and waders!

Of those two carp the 24 pounder was far and away more memorable than the headline-making 40. At the time of writing, four years after the event, I have had five more carp over 25 pounds. Yet the fish of that October night remains the most important. It did not matter at all that we had not landed a record, we were just overjoyed that we had landed that carp. The atmosphere of that autumn evening, the long taut struggle, the surges of emotion, the fear and joy, all these elements made up a never-to-be-forgotten event.

So, you see, size does not matter. I take great pleasure nowadays fishing for wildies with an old Hardy sea-trout rod (1935), 5 pound line and a centre-pin reel. I still like fishing for the monsters as well, but both aspects of the sport have equal amounts to offer. When I think back to the carp that started all this, the 'monster from the willow', I recall the dream that goes with it. A dream of calm, green pools with mysterious depths. I agree the fish is all-important, for it is the motive force. While the best fish I have landed was not really huge neither was the carp that began my obsession. In fact it could not have weighed more than 5 pounds!

Postscript
While this book was at the printers, Chris Yates finally caught his monster. On 16 June 1980, at 9.30 p.m., he landed a new British record carp weighing 51 pounds 6 ounces.

Part Two

7 The carp: birth, growth, longevity and death

Carp have always fascinated me. Like any other angler I progressed from the minnows and sticklebacks of childhood to roach, chub, tench and barbel. But, looking back over forty years of angling, it seems that fate has shaped and moulded my experiences in such a way that the carp was destined to end my search for the ultimate angling quarry.

To some lucky anglers the carp is just another fish. To me it is much more than that. Since my first encounter with the species in 1965 I have become more and more involved in studying it as a fish as well as a quarry. In all that time scarcely a day has passed without my thoughts grappling with some problem of carp-fishing. This study has opened up a whole new range of questions. The carp has become a sort of figure-head in my life; helping me to write with greater ease than I ever thought possible; teaching me to use my eyes; and taxing my meagre brain beyond its normal capacity. I owe the carp a debt of gratitude for all the hours of interest it has provided to lighten the burden of everyday working life. I hope that in some small way the following two chapters will settle the debt.

The origins of wild carp are surrounded in mystery. *Cyprinus carpio*, the common wild carp as we know it, appears to originate from eastern Europe or China and to have spread outwards. We are not so much concerned with this hazy antiquity, since the fish that really holds our attention is far removed in time and shape. The average 'wildy' rarely reaches a size to excite the imagination and, until 'king' carp came on the scene, a 10 pound carp would have been classed as 'massive'. There still exists a certain 'fogginess' regarding the different varieties of carp, even though the subject has been flogged by almost every writer. The novice has some excuse for his confusion between 'wild' carp and 'king' carp. But only last season I found myself explaining the differences to an experienced carp angler. With this in mind then, let me try to describe the background of the two types.

'Wild' carp, which have scales all over their body, are the original species, *Cyprinus carpio*. These fish once played an important part in day-to-day food supplies. Most old monasteries had a stew-pond where fish were reared for the table. A fish pond was a highly prized asset until refrigeration and improved transport facilities made sea-fish available to all. Since then the stew-pond has declined, though some old stews still exist and contain progeny of the carp they were stocked with hundreds of years ago.

The carp, which was introduced into England around 1500, was popular with stew-pond owners because it grew to a reasonable size, was hardy and could be stocked in good numbers in a small pond. As it is more or less omnivorous, feeding it and turning it into tasty food for human consumption presented few problems. These stew-pond fish were what we today call 'wildies'. These fish are long and lean in shape, looking more like barbel than a bream in shape. A good wildy weighs 5 pounds. There are a few waters up and down the country where wild carp exist up to and beyond double figures. But generally a fish in excess of 5 pounds is a specimen.

Anyone breeding and rearing fish soon notices that some fingerlings grow much faster than others, and long ago the continental fish-breeders realized the potential of this faster growth. If some carp grew faster than others on the same food, then why not retain these fast growers and breed from them? The parent fish would surely produce a higher percentage of faster-growing offspring, which in turn would reach market weight quicker than the average batch of fish. At this point the 'king carp' enters the scene. Man has now begun to breed carp selectively instead of allowing nature to take its course. Before this the so-called 'wild' carp bred true, retaining its fully scaled pattern because natural dispersion virtually assured that there could be no in-breeding. But now fish were being selected by man, whose sole objective was to improve the fast growing abilities. This upset the natural genetic balance, resulting in partially-scaled mirrors and leathers as well as the original fully-scaled wild type.

This combination of natural and controlled breeding has resulted in the king carp. The original wild carp and this new 'contrived' carp are biologically sufficiently alike to be classed under the same name

Cyprinus carpio, and are called 'variations' or 'strains' of the original fish.

The king carp is now well established in many countries throughout the world. Housewives, preparing fish to eat, found the leather

The top fish – a mirror carp – is 24 inches long and weighs 13¾ pounds. The centre fish – a wild carp – is 23¼ inches long and weighs 7½ pounds. The bottom fish – a 'king' common – is 22 inches long and weighs 7¼ pounds. This gives some idea of the wide difference in weight for length between different strains and varieties

variety a boon because there were few scales to remove. Anglers and fish cultivation experts were overjoyed with the short time it took to grow double-figure carp. Had not the king carp become so widespread, carp-fishing would not be what it is today. The leather carp offer no identification problem, being almost totally devoid of scales, apart from a few each side of the dorsal-fin. It is easily recognized as a king carp. Mirror carp too leave no doubt, in spite of the wide range of scaling patterns, which vary from a near-leather with just a few small scales here and there, to scale patches all over – the 'scattered mirror'. There is the 'linear-scaled' mirror, where all the scales on each side of the body are arranged in a neat row along the lateral line. And finally there is the 'fully-scaled' mirror that is completely covered with the large, mirror-like scales and can be an exceedingly good-looking fish – particularly if it weighs 20 plus! In my experience the big fully-scaled mirror is rather rare, though I have caught several small ones. Let's hope I catch 'em when they have grown a bit!

So we are now left with the common scaled variety and here we run into difficulty. There is no way to be sure that a fully scaled carp is a wild carp or a king carp. This does not matter until you claim to have caught a 'double' wildy. A 12 pound wildy must easily be the equivalent of a '30 plus' king carp so you can see that you must be sure of your facts if the claim is to carry any validity. You must be absolutely certain that the water you caught the fish from contains only true wild carp and that there has been no 'king' stock introduced at any time. Checking with club officials can go some way towards establishing this, but it does not rule out the odd king carp being popped in by some well-meaning angler. Although wild carp are long and lean, while king carp are generally shorter and deeper in the body, I have seen quite a few old king carp, going back in condition, that have displayed a similar body shape to a wildy. When such fish have the common scaling pattern it becomes very hard to decide which variety you have caught.

It is easy to write about cultivated carp, as there is a whole mass of scientific data available. But there is much less data available about carp living in the wild – the angler's quarry. The angler must be ready to form his own opinions from his fishing experiences and use the fish-culture expert's data as a guideline only. The study of 'tame' fish-farm carp and carp living in the wild are poles apart.

The original 'wild' carp breeds true to form and, apart from a

Barrie Varney expertly holds a good example of the leather variety (caught by the author)

slight difference in maximum size of fish from a given water, does not vary at all in appearance. Not so with king carp! The differences in appearance are enormous due to the genetic mix-up caused by selective breeding. This can be very handy. The observant angler can begin to recognize individual fish from scaling patterns, and even the fully scaled common loses its anonymity when you have seen it on the bank a few times. Each one has its own distinguishing marks or body shape which can be of tremendous help in piecing together the fascinating life-story of the carp. Where to begin the story though? With ten years of input the memory cells are crying for release and will pour out information willy-nilly if not controlled. Best start at the beginning with the egg.

Those who have watched carp spawn can hardly have failed to be impressed with the complete abandon with which they do it. In the north the carp are often late in spawning and sometimes the fishing season is well under way before they start. I have been very lucky in being able to observe carp spawning in a variety of waters. In waters where there is a lack of emergent weed and reeds, the carp will spawn on the branches of trees where they sag into the water. They seem to prefer to deposit their sticky eggs on hard-stemmed material, rather than the soft milfoil types of weed. Willow trees, in particular, are much favoured and in two successive seasons I watched carp playing follow my leader over sagging, water-immersed branches and roots. To see the energetic way these fish flung themselves over the low branches was an education indeed. When they were caught later it was easy to see how they had received their cuts, scratches and missing scales. At another lake the shallows allowed excellent observation in water around 2 feet deep. Here some carp chose emergent horse-tail reeds and spawned with their backs protruding above the surface. It was possible to stand within a few inches of their chosen spawning area and watch them complete a circular route over the shallows before they returned to the spot to lay side by side, quivering, as the eggs and milt were deposited. This sequence would be repeated over and over again by the same group of fish.

Another group I watched had been spawning all night in a small bed of amphibious bistort just to the left of my pitch. When it came light I was able to see these fish swim past my feet on their way to the tough-stemmed bistort. The group comprised a very rotund female that looked under double figures and four attendant males, the

Kevin Clifford with a super example of a 20-plus linear-scaled mirror

largest about 11 or 12 pounds and the smallest about 4 pounds. The explosive laying of eggs contrasted sharply to that of the group which had spawned in the horse-tail reeds. This group would swim into the underwater stems and then virtually explode into activity in a mad spawning flurry. With head and shoulders above water, the two mating fish threshed the water to foam, showering the area – including me – with water droplets. As far as I could tell, it was always the largest male who attended the female during this activity, though the 'back-up' males may have been shedding milt at the same time under the surface. Twice I saw the male butt the female round until she was turned back into the bistort for another thrash!

A female carp can deposit a prodigious number of eggs. Fish in the 15–16 pound range produce more than two million eggs; larger fish even more. The mortality rate must be high, for if only 0·00001% were to survive any water would become over-populated in a few years. The eggs are very small in relation to the parent fish,

Mick Dougill with a 16 pound plus scattered mirror

averaging about 1 mm in diameter. They stick to branch or weed stems and, provided water temperature is suitable, take less than a week to hatch. Fortunately, in England, few of these eggs or fry survive because the climate is too unsettled. I say 'fortunately' because most English carp waters have insufficient food to produce or support a large head of big carp. Large numbers of small carp can eat an enormous amount of food, much of it immature larval forms that would provide a good food source for the larger carp if allowed to grow. Carp $2\frac{1}{2}$ to 3 inches long have a voracious appetite as any aquarist knows. You can put a mixed netful of aquatic fauna into a tank and watch the fish hunt them down, one by one. Snails up to a quarter of an inch in diameter, bloodworm, nymphs, water-boatmen, shrimps and even caddis grubs in tough, sand-covered cases are rooted out and devoured. This supply of natural food must provide some sort of growth hormone, because carp fingerlings fed on high-protein flakes do not grow as fast as those fed on flakes and natural food.

Carp continue to patrol their spawning areas long after all spawning activity has ceased. This 'post-spawning' activity can continue up to August in some waters. It has been said that carp will eat their own eggs and fry. They may do accidentally, but how they manage to select and eat the small eggs is hard to imagine. The fry are more of a proposition, yet they have the ability to swim for safety. Somehow the thought of a big carp, selectively feeding on eggs the size of a full stop, appears ludicrous to me and in any case I have never seen post-spawners linger in the places they have deposited their eggs. I have seen roach and perch fry – which hatch before carp fry – leap above the weeds when post-spawning fish have swum through. Artificially bred fish might eat eggs but in the wild it is different. The behaviour of a natural post-spawning carp group suggests the fish are trying, in a limited way, to protect their eggs or progeny from the predations of the more advanced fry of other species.

Once the eggs are hatched and safely over the early fry stage, the tiny king carp grow very fast in a good environment, quickly outstripping the fry of any other species present. This is very important from the carp's point of view. In any summer fish population there is a predominance of small fish hunting tiny items of food. The quicker an individual fish or species can grow, the greater its ability to dominate the available food supply and the sooner it can move on to larger food items. The king carp, provided that it survives the fry stage, has this fast-growing ability. I have seen king carp fingerlings measuring from 2 to 5 inches long in late August, the result of a successful spawning on 30 May. If you should think that 5 inches does not seem all that impressive, I would point out that roach fingerlings in the same water were only averaging half this size despite hatching six weeks before the carp. This fast growth is one reason why fingerling carp introduced to most waters will do well at the expense of other species. Tench in particular appear to come off second best in the carp waters I have fished.

The actual growth rate of king carp is variable. Claims vary from the ridiculous to the sublime. Yet to some extent anyway, they may all be true. I mentioned earlier the inbreeding and cross-breeding that has gone into producing the various king carp varieties and strains. It is possible, under controlled conditions, to breed selectively a given variety by placing the right parent pair together. But unselective spawning in the wild can result in an infinite variety of scaling and growth-rate capability. Even in controlled breeding this growth ability can only be assessed in general terms. This is the result of a genetic upheaval that makes ERNI – the 'Electronic Random Number Indicator' used to select premium bond numbers – look as crude as Marconi's first spark-gap transmitter. The subject of genetics is very complex, involving things like chromosomes and genes, deoxyribonucleic acid and ribonucleic acid which are component parts of the parental egg–sperm fertilization process. I do not pretend to understand the complexity of the processes that go on inside a fertilized egg, but I do know the genetic combination can produce infinite variety.

When egg and sperm unite the growth rate of the eventual offspring can vary enormously.

In some individuals it is very poor and massive in others, even in a batch of fingerlings from the same parents. For people like me it is not easy to grasp the significance of all this. But I have been lucky in that I have had an interest in scale reading for many years and this has helped my understanding. I have examined scales from average fish on up to 44 pounds. At best scale reading is an imprecise science relying, to some degree, on experience instead of an applied scientific procedure. There is plenty of scope within the radial striae – the concentric rings around the scale – for an enquiring mind to find discrepancies in the accepted way of reading scales.

I once wrote an article for *Angling* on carp scale interpretation. I had been studying the subject intensely for some time and, at last, it was beginning to slot into place. I started the article with a poem:

> There's a tale in the scale the wise man said:
> A tale in the scale to see.
> Of what has passed and what is now,
> And what has yet to be.
>
> A tale in the scale that tells, my friends,
> Of the secret that is life.
> It tells of youth of growth and age;
> It tells of birth and strife.

Wordsworth would no doubt turn in his grave if faced with such doggerel, but then, I had no 'host of golden daffodils' to inspire me – just a lot of annuli that Wordsworth himself would have been hard put to immortalize!

In the early years before sexual maturity the so-called 'checks', which are supposed to be areas of retarded or reduced growth due to shortage of food and the lower temperatures of winter, are unreliable as a method of estimating the fish's age. It is impossible to estimate growth rate or potential growth rate if you do not know how old the fish is. While carp in some waters show quite well-defined checks throughout the growing period, the majority appear to me to show vague 'zonations' during this early part of life and it takes a resolute man to give precise judgement. There have been some wild claims for growth during the four to five years it takes the average carp to reach sexual maturity. A carp must eat to grow, and accepting that unlimited food is available, it is still doubtful that a fish in England could eat and convert enough food to make valid some of the claims. I have not seen a wide enough selection of immature carp scales to give a really firm generalization of weight gain during this period. But the hundreds I have seen, plus the calculations made from mature carp, would suggest that 3 to 5 pounds at four to five years of age might be a reasonable average growth in many waters.

After a carp becomes mature and begins to spawn each year there is a well-defined check left on the scale. Though some still insist on calling this particular check a 'winter band' my own investigation suggests that these checks are spawning checks caused by the considerable reabsorption of the scale material during the post-spawning period.

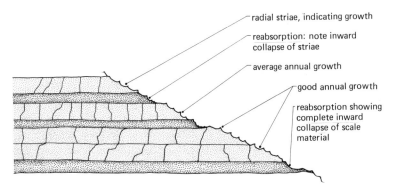

radial striae, indicating growth

reabsorption: note inward collapse of striae

average annual growth

good annual growth

reabsorption showing complete inward collapse of scale material

Figure 6 Fish scale cross-section, showing growth after sexual maturity. Drawing at approximately 1200 times magnification showing apparent inward collapse and vertical collapse of cellular scale material at reabsorption areas

I have prepared cross-sections of scales and looked at the areas of reabsorption at high magnification. In line with the well-defined checks, and running right through the scale to join the same annuli on the opposite side, runs a line of what appears to have been cellular growth that has suffered massive collapse. If my interpretation is correct – and the scales of several other species which I have looked at show similar reabsorption areas – then carp are still losing body weight for a considerable time after spawning has finished. This loss of weight is occurring during the summer when carp are normally thought to be putting on weight due to the mass of food available.

We have got the average carp nicely into sexual maturity now, covering the period from egg to first spawning. A point that I have stressed, and will continue to do throughout this chapter, is individuality. If I was discussing roach or chub or bream or any fish not selectively bred this would not be so important. But there is a long way to go with the life-story of the king carp yet. The individuality of each fish will now begin to play an increasing part in the tale.

The onset of sexual maturity of the carp also brings the probability of considerable weight loss. Before sexual maturity, the average carp, if my scale interpretations are correct, has stopped growing only during periods of famine or temperature or environmental extremes. Until the first spawning there is no positive scale indication of weight loss. But after shedding eggs or milt the carp is in need of certain vital minerals and some of these are taken from the cellular layers of the scale material. Scales are made of bone, something after the fashion of our own fingernails. The new material at the outside edge, that which has grown just before spawning, appears to be able to feed back elements like calcium to the fish's body should it be required. This facility is called 'reabsorption' and is a negative factor in carp growth or weight gain, since a carp that is

Dave Booth with a magnificent example of a 20-plus fully scaled mirror

A 15 pound 13 ounce common. This fish received accidental damage in the area above my fingers in 1973. Here it is shown in 1975 and it can be seen that there are three areas where scales have not regrown. (See page 184)

reabsorbing cannot be increasing weight because it is living off its own body.

The many scales from mature carp that I have examined suggest that spawning affects the individual in a number of ways. In a small percentage of fish spawning acts as a severe deterrent to growth and these fish have a struggle to make double figures in what growing period is left. (More on this growing period later.) Other carp seem little affected by spawning and, although the scales show a well-defined spawning check, the fish continues growing at an ever-increasing rate after the temporary spawning setback. The bigger the fish the more food it can process, providing the food is available. At the top end of the growth scale are a small percentage of fish that might not spawn at all. These fish seem to have massive growth potential even in average waters. Sexually mature carp have to go through the wasteful spawning routine and the ensuing post-spawning period. A sterile carp will be utilizing what food it eats to support a much lower maintenance requirement, leaving more for growth. If such fish have also inherited a good growth rate they will obviously grow better than spawning carp in the same water. The best example I have seen of a possible non-spawner is an eight-year-old carp weighing $19\frac{3}{4}$ pounds. Dependent upon the number of years this sort of individual continues growing and upon what food is available throughout the period, the terminal weight may well be in considerable excess of the average for that water.

The reabsorption checks on carp scales give one a fairly definite way of age estimation – they are certainly more well defined than the checks of pre-spawning growth. Thus at last we can see and count reasonably solid annual checks in growth. (Operculae and otoliths are better for age determination but the fish has to be killed.) There is a lot of information locked within the radial striae of a scale. It contains the fish's growth record since birth and, reading between the lines – or striae in this instance – it is possible to unlock some of the less-readily-appreciated information. To do this, though, may require not only an interest in scale reading, but also an active part in the big-fish angling scene, allowing one to relate more accurately to the environment the fish have been under since introduction.

One topic of interest to most carp anglers is the annual growth rate. This varies enormously from water to water and is usually expressed in 'pounds per year'. A fish of 15 pounds with ten annual checks could be interpreted as having an annual growth rate of $1\frac{1}{2}$ pounds per year. Quite a few people take this figure literally, thinking that, machine-like, the fish has gone on laying down $1\frac{1}{2}$ pounds of bone and tissue each year. The scale record shows that this is not so and that, as the carp grows larger, the corresponding yearly increase in weight is greater too. Let us assume we have a scale with evenly spaced checks from centre to outer edge. Now assume we are able to remove all of the first year's growth from the top section and calculate the total area. Then we remove the second year's growth and so on, calculating the total area of each. We would find the areas involved increasing at a rate of growth determined by the individual's own growth characteristics. In any given fish, weight increase will always be greater during the second half of the growing period, when more than two-thirds of the terminal weight may be acquired.

Where the annual checks show a gradual reduction in their spacing towards the outer edge of the scale, the assumption is that the fish is not maintaining a given growth rate. But is this so? A fish that is *maintaining* a given growth rate, as opposed to *increasing* it, would surely show this by laying down less material between each annual check. The distance between checks would be smaller if the growth rate was to remain the same, occupying the equivalent area of previous years. A carp making a 2 pound weight gain in the fifth year of growth would appear to have grown much more than it would for the same weight gain in the tenth year. A scale cross-section reveals that where there is an increase in diameter there is also an increase in thickness too. A cross-section also confirms that where there is evidence of above-normal growth, shown by wider than average annual spacing, there is also a corresponding increase in the thickness of the new material grown that year. The inference is that the weight increase in such a year will be relatively enormous compared to normal growth.

It has been said that fish grow and increase in weight by the cube of their linear dimensions, the mathematical expression suggested being: $\frac{W}{L^3} L^3$. Thus a fish 5 inches long weighing 2 ounces would weigh 1 pound when it was 10 inches long. Over the years I have accumulated a mass of information from fishing in several counties and a wide range of environments. The fish examined have weighed between a fraction of an ounce to over 26 pounds, and varied in age from a few months to over fifteen years. Now I've been convinced that one ought to be able to calculate, roughly, the weight of a fish at any previous period in its life by measuring the annual scale checks. Using the $\frac{W}{L^3} L^3$ expression to relate growth measured from a scale to an approximate weight for a given age, I found the results unacceptably low. They did not fit the specific examples of age–weight relationship I had noted.

I am no mathematician, but when a problem such as this exists,

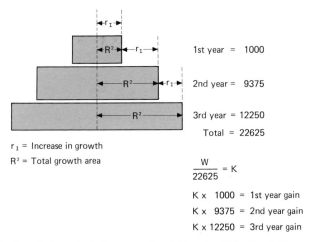

	1st year = 1000
	2nd year = 9375
	3rd year = 12250
	Total = 22625

r_I = Increase in growth

R^2 = Total growth area

$$\frac{W}{22625} = K$$

K x   1000   = 1st year gain

K x   9375   = 2nd year gain

K x 12250 = 3rd year gain

Figure 7   Details for calculating annual weight gain. Weight gain figures are calculated by measuring the annual checks seen when reading a scale in the normal way. Enlarging the scale in a photographic enlarger or projector allows a more accurate measurement. The drawing here is not representative of any particular carp and has been shown in cross-sectional form so that the relationship between $R^2 r_I$ can be appreciated. Note how the thickness of each year's growth varies with an increase or decrease in r_I

I will keep at it until a reasonable answer emerges. It took several weeks before an expression emerged that more accurately fitted the age/weight average I was looking for. The expression is: $\frac{W}{R^2 r_I}$. The radius, R, of each scale check is measured. The figure is then squared and then multiplied by the increase in growth, r_I. As the new growth is directly related to the thickness, the expression is more efficient than the previous one. The reason for this is, I believe, that $\frac{W}{L^3}$ treats a fish scale like a cube when, in fact, it is a truncated pyramid. By using $\frac{W}{R^2 r_I}$ $R^2 r_I$ a more realistic constant emerges. Weight gain figures for each check then compare favourably with average weights of specific fish. A mathematician may be able to produce a more 'streamlined' method than mine. But I doubt the results would be any more accurate without having specific annual weights from a cross-section of individual carp throughout their entire growing period. So bearing in mind that king carp exhibit enormous variety in their growth rates, let us have a look at some calculated weights from carp of different age groups.

Yearly weight increases in carp (as calculated)

2 years old, weight 9 ounces

age (years)	weight (lb oz)		weight gain (lb oz)		remarks
1	–	$\frac{1}{2}$	–	$\frac{1}{2}$	A 17 times increase in weight during
2	–	9	–	$8\frac{1}{2}$	the second year

4+ years old, weight 5 pounds 4 ounces

age (years)	weight (lb oz)		weight gain (lb oz)		remarks
1	–	6	–	6	Note how the calculation reveals a
2	1	8	1	2	significant drop in weight gain during
3	2	6	–	14	the third year of growth. This may be
4	3	10	1	4	due to food shortage
4+	5	4	1	10	

7+ years old, weight 10 pounds 12 ounces

age (years)	weight (lb oz)		weight gain (lb oz)		remarks
1	–	$2\frac{1}{2}$	–	$2\frac{1}{2}$	This average-water fish has excellent
2	1	0	–	$13\frac{1}{2}$	weight gain up to the fifth year. The
3	3	$10\frac{1}{2}$	2	$10\frac{1}{2}$	fish scale showed heavy reabsorption
4	5	15	2	$4\frac{1}{2}$	(spawning) in the years following and
5	8	$2\frac{1}{2}$	2	$3\frac{1}{2}$	this has had a severe effect on the
6	8	15	–	$12\frac{1}{2}$	weight gain
7	9	13	–	14	
7+	10	12	–	15	

8+ years old, weight 19 pounds 12 ounces

age (years)	weight (lb oz)		weight gain (lb oz)		remarks
1	–	$1\frac{1}{2}$	–	$1\frac{1}{2}$	I found this fish very exciting. The
2	–	5	–	$3\frac{1}{2}$	scale suggested that it had not
3	1	1	–	12	spawned at all and because of this has
4	2	8	1	7	made terrific growth in 8+ years.
5	4	14	2	6	Unfortunately this fish died through
6	7	$0\frac{1}{2}$	2	$2\frac{1}{2}$	an accident, which is a pity, because it
7	11	7	4	$6\frac{1}{2}$	was nearly 5 pounds heavier than was
8	15	$11\frac{1}{2}$	4	$4\frac{1}{2}$	the British record carp at the same
8+	19	12	4	$0\frac{1}{2}$	age

11+ years old, weight 22 pounds

age	weight		weight gain		
(years)	(lb	oz)	(lb	oz)	remarks
1	–	3	–	3	This fish made a rather poor start
2	–	8	–	5	according to the weight gain figures
3	1	0	–	8	calculated. After the sixth year the
4	1	9	–	9	fish really began to cram on weight.
5	2	2	–	9	Note, however, the drop in annual
6	3	6	1	4	gain in the eighth year and the 11+
7	6	0	2	10	year, which in this November-caught
8	8	6	2	6	fish is about half a year's growth. This
9	12	0	3	10	and other similar examples perhaps
10	15	11	3	11	reflect a shortage of available food in
11	20	2	4	7	that particular year of growth
11+	22	0	1	14	

15+ years old, weight 44 pounds (the present record carp, caught September 1952)

age	weight		weight gain		
(years)	(lb	oz)	(lb	oz)	remarks
1	–	3	–	3	There is a certain magic that sur-
2	1	6	1	3	rounds a record fish. The magic here
3	2	6	1	0	lies not in the annual weight gain
4	3	14	1	8	figures, for apart from the thirteenth
5	5	15	2	1	and fourteenth years there are none
6	7	2	1	3	better than the two previous fish. Nor
7	8	8	1	6	does it lie in the environment for here
8	11	0	2	8	again in the sixth, seventh, twelfth
9	14	9	3	9	and fifteenth years there is a reduc-
10	18	14	4	5	tion of annual gain. The magic centres
11	23	2	4	4	on the long growing period and the
12	26	3	3	1	generally high weight gain made each
13	31	8	5	5	year throughout that period
14	37	8	6	0	
15	41	12	4	4	
15+	44	0	2	4	

The measurements for this last calculation were taken from the scale photograph in Dick Walker's *Still-water Angling.* Recent work on actual scales from the record carp has given slightly different results to the above calculations. This is because my interpretation of the scales is marginally different from those shown on the photograph. The information concerning this will be published in the book under preparation by Kevin Clifford and Len Arbery.

There is no doubt in my mind that carp require more than a good environment to reach record proportions. The major requirement for anyone who wants to catch record carp lies in first obtaining the right strain of carp and then finding a suitable environment. There are so many poor strains of carp around that fulfilling the first requirement would be the harder of the two tasks. I am quite convinced that while Redmire holds the record and has been 'glorified' by all, including me, the real answer is in the stock and not the water they grew in. There must be a number of 'Redmires' in this country but to prove it you will have to get the right strain of carp.

Some carp show bursts of really exceptional growth between annual checks. This take-off in growth rate appears to be generally confined to the period of life, just after sexual maturity, at about six or seven years of age. How much weight is gained at this time depends on how big the fish is when the super-growth begins. There seems no reason why the right individual will not be able to make an annual gain of 10 pounds in a very good environment providing the growth burst comes in later years, rather than those prior to spawning.

Dawn flash shot of a 17 pound common. Note line-damaged areas on upper operculum which sometimes become infected with algae

The evidence is that carp have only a limited time to reach their maximum weight. This is another talking point with carp anglers and it appears there is general misunderstanding of the way carp grow. Carp anglers are usually well read and any lack of understanding is usually due to lack of information on the subject. I have put a lot of thought into how carp grow; how long it takes to reach maximum size; and how long they live. The following is my personal opinion at the time of writing. It may well be modified by the future accumulation of further evidence.

A 50 pound carp would easily break the existing English record. Yet available evidence suggests that such a fish would grow to this size in the same time another fish in the same water would take to reach 20 pounds. Why? Because we are back to that word *individuality* again. For some reason the '50' inherited a better growth rate than the '20'. And it is no use going on about rich or poor waters because the same relationship exists in any water. There are always a few fish that grow bigger than average and fish like these end up 'big' compared to the rest. In any given successful spawning of a good strain of carp there must exist a small percentage of potential record-breakers. Whether they attain their potential – and nature is not keen on extremes – depends upon them first being hardy enough to survive the initial period of growth until they reach a size where they can *really eat.* (The maintenance level of a small fish is much bigger than a large one and its diet is more restricted.) Once the fish has reached reasonable proportions the entire food supply of the lake becomes obtainable. The major growth-limiting factors are: how much food is there available? How conducive are the conditions to stimulating long feeding sessions? What growth potential has the fish inherited? How many years will it grow for?

A fish is ideally suited to its environment. Being virtually weightless in water and having no precise temperature to maintain means that little energy is required to keep it alive. Because so little energy is required to maintain the correct function of its organs much of the food it consumes is channelled directly to its rate of growth. It also means that a fish can survive for long periods with little weight loss if, for some reason, the fish stops eating. (This assumes that the fish is relatively inactive and is not suffering severe parasitic infestation.) Where carp are still growing and actively spawning, my weight-for-length measurements suggest that there is some weight loss during about six weeks following spawning. I do not imply that this is the case in every water, but it certainly seems so in some of the waters I have fished. The fish will obviously lose considerable weight when shedding eggs and milt. This relatively sudden loss is followed by a gradual reduction of body condition due to the long swimming and seemingly short feeding sessions of this period.

There appears to be two main periods when a carp will grow. For the average fish these seem to be in April–May, when fishing results in syndicate waters not subject to close-season laws can often be exceptionally good. While some of the food consumed in this period will be used for egg and sperm production in sexually mature fish, the overall effect is weight gain *plus* growth where there is a surplus of food. For sexually immature fish the surplus is used entirely for growth. During this late spring period more natural 'mature' food is available than at any other period of the year. The water still has some stability and is not yet subject to the summer temperature or decay extremes that can affect oxygen levels and upset feeding spells. The many forms of aquatic larvae and nymphs which are now fully grown provide a rich food supply at a time when good feeding is required.

The second main period of growth appears to be from late July onwards, although this growth may not necessarily mean a big increase in weight. At this time of the year carp often appear long and lean leading one to think that food is used for growth in length and depth. Later on, from October onwards, I suspect the carp begin to fill out more. There, food is used to lay down fat and tissue reserves and actual growth falls off. This food causes a direct increase in weight as increasingly smaller amounts of it are now needed to keep the fish's body mechanism ticking over. This weight gain, as opposed to growth, seems to continue during the winter months. Carp caught during this period invariably have a better weight for length ratio than at any other time of the year, apart from immediately prior to spawning. This pattern applies only to carp that are still growing. It has been suggested to me that work done on carp growth indicates that short bursts of growth are followed by a short corresponding increase in weight. Thus the condition factor of the fish fluctuates in sympathy; first low, then high. Sexually immature fish may well follow this regular fluctuation. But growing, sexually mature, carp do not. If they did one would only rarely see the long, lean fish that are so common in many waters from mid-July to late September. It is not that such fish come from 'hungry' waters either, for the better fish are making '2 pounds per year' and are always better proportioned in winter.

We have seen how the average carp grows throughout the year and now we will turn to the question of how many years it will continue to grow.

The growth record is left in the scale, giving reasonable, if questionable evidence. However, if we do not split hairs by arguing about whether a given check is annual or environmental in nature, then we can make some progress. When I first began my scale-reading studies, back in 1967, I was very fortunate to have the advice and guidance of Dr David Cragg-Hine. David patiently steered me around some of the pitfalls awaiting the unwary newcomer to scale reading. Since that time I have studied scales from stunted fish living in very poor waters; from fish living in 'average' waters and from fish living in 'rich' waters like Redmire. My own fishing and that of my friends has provided evidence enough to support what I have to say about terminal growth – the number of years a carp takes to become fully grown. There must be some advantage in a situation whereby you catch or see caught a 'known' fish; weigh it, measure it, and read a scale at say ten-years plus; then find three seasons later the same fish is still being caught at the same weight, and at the same length. This must be more accurate than reading a scale sent through the post without location, environment, length and, in some cases, not even weight information! My own personally collected evidence indicates that carp only grow for a period of between ten to fifteen years and that the number of years a carp is growing has little bearing on what its terminal weight will be.

If two individuals are both growing at the same annual rate, but one grows for ten years whilst the other grows for fifteen years, the latter will be the bigger fish. It is here we come to the significant difference in growth ability between individual carp. The evidence in the scales suggests that some carp stop growing at the age of ten. It also suggests that no carp will grow for more than fifteen years. This evidence has been collected the hard way by catching carp. This evidence also includes a number of 'known' carp that have not appreciably grown or increased weight over a period of three or more seasons, all of which adds validity to the theory.

Some carp anglers seem to think that carp go on growing for the whole of their lives. They go to some length, in letters and articles in the angling press, to explain how growth rate can be affected by

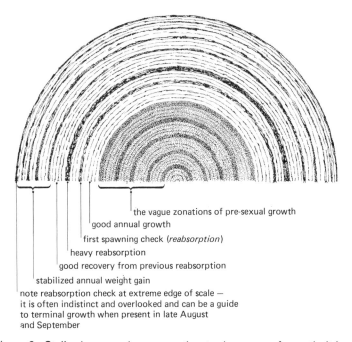

the vague zonations of pre-sexual growth
good annual growth
first spawning check (*reabsorption*)
heavy reabsorption
good recovery from previous reabsorption
stabilized annual weight gain
note reabsorption check at extreme edge of scale —
it is often indistinct and overlooked and can be a guide
to terminal growth when present in late August
and September

Figure 8 Stylized carp scale representing twelve years of growth. It is not possible to show all the variety of checks seen in carp scales since each fish displays its own individual growth pattern. For instance, I have seen evidence in the scales of some carp which suggests that they have spawned twice in one season and there is a little visual evidence to support this possibility. Scales exhibiting this feature require very careful interpretation

catching an individual fish too often. One such piece I recall involved a carp that had been caught at 14 pounds and subsequently caught during the following season. The third season it was caught again. In the second capture it weighed around 13 pounds and on the third capture it was back to its original weight of 14 pounds. This evidence was then interpreted as meaning that the fish had taken three seasons to recover from its initial capture.

I can say with some emphasis that the wrong conclusions have been drawn from the evidence.

Here is evidence suggesting that the fish had reached terminal growth sometime before its first capture. When a carp is fully grown its terminal weight might be 5 or 50 pounds, depending on the individual fish. When terminal growth has been reached, the maxi-

An example of a carp scale

mum weight of the fish in the following years will be governed by the food supply available in any particular year. There is a waxing and waning of food within the aquatic environment in just the same way as that noted and well documented in easily studied land animals – the predator–prey relationship of foxes, hawks and owls, for example. A similar relationship exists between fully grown carp and the amount of food available in any given year. The only difference is that in many waters the predator (carp) population is stable because carp do not easily reproduce. Thus, in years of excess food supply any growing carp will make good growth, while terminal growth carp will put on more weight. The reverse situation exists in the lean years, when a stable population will show evidence of the lack of food by less growth or reduced weight.

Unfortunately one cannot easily predict what conditions promote a 'good' year food-wise in an aquatic environment, because the conditions that promote it may occur from one to three years in advance. The vast range of aquatic insect fauna requires this time span to grow to maturity before repeating the life-cycle. But there is no doubt that in most waters carp are subject to these weight fluctuations. Later I will list 'known' carp that have become fully grown at weights as low as 12 pounds, fish that reached this terminal growth a long time ago and are still going strong. They are not growing any more but fluctuating in weight by as much as 4 pounds. This leads us nicely on to how long a carp will live in the wild in a decent environment.

As I said at the start of the chapter, carp in the wild are surrounded in mystery. Because of this various legends have sprung up concerning what age a carp will live to. There is no hearsay or legend in what I have to say about the subject of longevity – just an accumulation of evidence and facts that have been gathered over some ten years of general interest in the subject. That my interpretation of the information might be as wrong as the next man's is taken for granted.

Legend has it that a carp will live for 150 years. The scientist is more conservative, suggesting up to fifteen years while allowing there are a few known examples well in excess of this norm. Now, I do not know of any animal that takes fifteen years to reach full maturity only to lay down and die at the end of it; it just does not make sense. The general evidence available for all forms of higher

How insignificant it looks! But huge carp have lived and died within the tranquil depths of this lake, for it is Redmire Pool seen from the dam end

animals shows that the longer they take to reach full maturity the longer is their total life-span. It might be that some carp will grow for longer than fifteen years, though I have not seen any evidence to support this from my own investigations. The largest authentic carp caught on rod and line in England was found to be fifteen years of age. This fish, caught by Dick Walker in September 1952, weighed 44 pounds on arrival at London Zoo; had it been weighed accurately when caught the record may well have been 46–47 pounds. I saw this fish in 1960 and it still looked magnificent – perhaps majestic would be a better word – when compared with the sundry other large carp present in the aquarium. The fish lived in captivity for many years but I will not quote the number in case anyone should accuse me of citing it as evidence of longevity. I have no need of this fish for evidence in that direction, because many of the 20 plus fish that are still swimming free in Redmire today are carp that can be identified from photographic evidence to be contemporaries of that record fish. These positively identified carp have not grown in the intervening period and their weight has remained reasonably consistent within the limits I have already laid down.

In any book on carp-fishing it is necessary to mention Redmire fairly often. This is not because the facts of carp growth there are of use when applied to the more average waters most of us fish. Redmire is unique in this respect because of the way it was stocked and the time that passed before it was fished. It is because Redmire is the pinnacle of carp growth as we know it, having supported more big carp than any other English water. Now it may seem that I have strayed a little from my theme with all this talk of Redmire and the fish it contains, but my reason for bringing Redmire into this section on longevity is simple. When the evidence I had collected regarding the life-span of carp in average waters was published in letter form in *Angling* it turned out that similar longevity also existed in Redmire. Now I put it to you for consideration: if carp live for a long time after attaining their terminal weight in the average waters you or I fish *and* in Redmire too, would you not expect that the same condition might apply to most waters in England?

So how long will a carp live in the wild?

Here we run into difficulty because we must rely on scanty facts and the evidence of regular contact with old fish. I would not dare insult my reader by presenting lightly held off-hand views regarding the average carp's life-span. Therefore I trust that you will accept my estimate as a genuine attempt to give an answer to the question.

After a carp has reached terminal growth there is no longer any growth record left upon the scale. A decade or more can pass without the casual observer knowing that the carp is actually older than a scale reading would suggest. The more observant angler, however, soon begins to recognize individual fish and, providing they are still growing, is able to follow their progress up to terminal growth. My friends, Barry Varney and Kevin Clifford, are almost infallible at recognizing previously caught carp and seem to have photographic memories for the scale patterns, etc. It is when such known fish have been caught over a period of several years at a steadily improving weight, then for three or four seasons at a reasonably stable weight, that terminal growth is finally established. From this point onwards growth in length has finished but weight will continue to fluctuate. There are other major clues which indicate terminal growth has been reached. The most common are if the measurement of a known fish shows no increase over a period of several seasons and when a scale from such a fish shows reabsorption at the extreme edge. I have noticed that scales from carp in this stage of life often have a definable reabsorption check at the extreme edge. This has been interpreted variously as a lack of food or the final spawning check or even illness from which the fish has recovered since it reached terminal growth.

There are many more subtle and less well-defined clues. These are torn and tatty fins that have not grown back to their original contours since being damaged. Common carp often have missing scales that have been replaced with a superficial layer of dark skin instead of a new scale. (Unless you have some history of the fish this is not too reliable because a small percentage of common carp appear to have a few scales missing as part of their genetic inheritance.) There may also be peculiar filamentous algae-like growths on the operculae or head region which appear to be rooted in the underlying bone and are perhaps caused by line damage while playing the fish. Old fish seem unable to grow new tissue on these damaged areas before they become affected, or infected, by this parasitic growth. Some waters are more prone to this phenomenon than others. And finally there is the long thin fish which displays any (or all!) of the aforementioned damaged areas.

I believe that there are three well-defined phases in the life-cycle of the average carp. The first phase is from early life to full maturity when the fish reaches terminal growth. Those which survive the rigours of underwater life for a period of between ten and fifteen years to obtain maximum growth are obviously strong, healthy fish and able to enter the second phase. This second phase covers a period that can last twenty years, perhaps longer with undisturbed fish. In the third phase – the dying phase – the carp gradually, over a period of years, begins to lose body weight and begins to look thin, having a poor weight-for-length ratio too. The low energy requirement of the fish suggests that it may take several years to die. But eventually, perhaps forty or more years after the developing eye first detected light through the translucent egg shell, the big body sinks into the silt of the lake bed, returning to the lake cycle in death many of the vital elements taken from it during life.

In writing at length about the carp's life-cycle I have tried to present the reader with the evidence I have accumulated over the years and let him decide for himself as to its validity. We have seen the carp through life with only passing reference to the main essential that supports it: food. Before we turn to what food is available and in what quantity, I want to present a list of known fish that have helped provide much of the evidence for my theories on growth and life-span. I have personally seen and measured quite a number of the carp in the list, though a percentage are from reliable friends. Apart from the fish listed here, I know of many others that provide further evidence to support what I have said. Not having all the details of capture, year, month, etc. I have not included them though they cover a range of fish up to more than 40 pounds.

Year	Month	Weight (lb oz)		Remarks

Carp No. 1

Year	Month	lb	oz	Remarks
1968	August	8	0	Winter weight well in excess of the
1969	January	9	15	high summer period

Carp No. 2

Year	Month	lb	oz	Remarks
1972	September	9	4	A young growing fish showing a
1972	November	10	0	weight increase. Scale shows: 7+
				years, 22 inches long

Year	Month	Weight (lb oz)		Remarks

Carp No. 3

1972	December	11	4	Fish showing a high winter weight
1973	June	10	0	followed by low summer weight –
				spawning loss?

Carp No. 4

1975	August	11	7	Fish showing higher back-end
1975	November	12	0	weight

Carp No. 5

1975	November	11	0	A clear indication of winter weight
1976	February	12	2	gain

Carp No. 6

1973	November	13	8	A terminal growth 'free-wheeler'.
1974	June	12	13	No growth in evidence during this
1974	August	12	6	period. Length 24 inches. Age 12+
1974	September	12	12	years. See text concerning
				free-wheelers

Carp No. 7

1972	February	14	0	A terminal growth free-wheeler.
1972	July	12	4	This fish may not have spawned
1972	September	12	8	since July 1972, hence the steady
1973	January	13	8	increase in weight. See page 188
1974	June	15	0	regarding low July 1972 weight.
1975	January	16	8	Length 25 inches. Age unknown
1975	June	16	8	

Carp No. 8

1976	August	15	1	Suspected terminal growth fish.
1976	September	15	1	Further catches required. Age 12+
				years. Length 25 inches

Carp No. 9

1973	September	15	4	A terminal growth free-wheeler
1975	June	15	5	showing remarkable weight stability.
1975	July	15	13	Scale shows 10+ years. Length 25
				inches

Year	Month	Weight (lb oz)		Remarks

Carp No. 10

1971	June	16	0	This fish grew an inch between this
1971	August	16	12	period; only 12 ounces gain, weight
				should increase in autumn and
				winter

Carp No. 11

1973	August	16	14	Obviously at terminal growth. No
1976	February	16	15	length or scale information.
				Exceptionally stable weight

Carp No. 12

1973	August	16	12	A fish showing higher winter weight
1974	February	18	4	with fall-off the following summer.
1974	July	17	8	No scale information. Length 28
1974	August	17	1	inches (February). Thought to be
				still growing

Carp No. 13

1973	June	19	12	A young fish with good growth rate.
1973	August	19	4	Scale shows 8+ years. Length $26\frac{1}{2}$
				inches (June)

Carp No. 14

1973	July	22	8	A growing fish that has continued to
1973	September	24	12	put on weight in spite of being
1975	July	25	4	caught regularly. Weight is
1975	September	26	12	influenced by feeding habits and
1975	October	26	8	food available. No scale
				information. Length 30 inches to 32
				inches in period

Carp No. 15

1972	October	26	4	A very generous fish this, having
1973	June	27	8	supplied more personal bests to
1973	September	26	4	anglers than any other fish I have
1974	June	27	0	known. Caught at least twenty-five
1974	August	25	12	times in the period, this fish, plus
1974	September	27	2	carp No. 14 perhaps knocks out of
1975	July	28	4	sight the theory that being caught
1975	September	27	4	causes weight loss. No scale
1976	June	27	0	information. Length $28\frac{1}{2}$ inches. A
1976	June	27	4	free-wheeler at terminal growth for
				a number of years

A few points in the remarks above need explanation.

Terminal growth free-wheelers are carp that have reached maximum growth and have begun to 'free-wheel' around a mean weight. The weight of these fish in any given year seems to be governed by what food is available. Thus in good years the 'wheel' will gain momentum, causing an increase in weight, whilst in a poor year it will be free-wheeling, losing weight and with it, 'momentum'.

Carp no.7 is thought to be quite old and it lives in a small exposed pond. I have thought for some time that carp might not spawn after they have reached a certain age, though they may still go through the spawning ritual with fish that do. If this is so, one would expect a weight increase where a fish no longer had to go through the wasteful egg or milt production. In such conditions the weight increase might be expected to be more pronounced in a female. The low summer weight of this fish could be evidence of a food shortage. When I caught the fish in February, 1972 it was in good condition. But during that winter period I came to suspect that a percentage of the larger carp might be feeding on the odd dying roach seen flapping on the surface. There were no pike in the water and while I was never fortunate enough to see a carp actually take one of the small roach, several disappeared in a quiet vortex. I passed these suspicions on to my friend Andrew Hughes, who lived locally. He decided to try a dead roach during the summer recess from training college. He caught the same fish twice, once in July and once in September. Tackle used was standard free-line carp gear with a small dead roach, lip-hooked. He told me that both runs were slow, confident butt-ringers; quite a change from the normal 'twitcher' type we usually experienced here.

Scales have been studied from most of the fish in the list. Unfortunately it is often difficult to obtain a good scale from a fish that might be twenty to thirty years old. Many fish in the list are near-linear or scattered mirror type varieties. Scales along the lateral line are subject to natural loss because of the massive muscle forces along this part of the body when the fish is handled, etc. It is not then surprising that many of the scales taken have been cast at some time in the period mentioned. Cast scales offer little information of value.

The *terminal weight* that a carp will attain in any water is governed, as we have seen, by how many years the fish is growing and how much weight is gained each year. There is another little-discussed factor that rarely receives any attention. Many of the carp that have been available to suppliers in this country are bred from 'table-fish' parents. The main market of the fish breeder for many years was that of providing continental housewives with a carp of a few pounds in weight. Thus strains of carp have been selectively bred with certain characteristics in mind, the primary one being that, from the breeders' point of view, the fish reach table weight as soon as possible. The fish-breeder or rearer is not interested in 20 pound fish – they would not be a viable proposition. While it is a good bet that fingerlings that reach saleable weight in the shortest time are also likely to make double figures, there is no real guarantee that the genetic code inherited will allow a long enough growing period for really big fish. Because of this there is the distinct possibility that many strains of carp are not really tailored to the anglers' needs and would never make the coveted 20 pound weight, however good the environment. More recently, the attention of some fish-breeders has turned towards the angler with the breeding of carp specifically for stocking fishing ponds or lakes.

I have included all the 'known' carp under one heading in this chapter to avoid confusion. Some of the information relates to winter-caught fish and should be looked at in conjunction with the chapter on winter fishing. Rather than separate the winter and summer fish I have left them together to avoid breaking the continuity and to allow easy reference to the weight fluctuations that occur throughout the seasons.

Having dealt with the actual weight of fish it is, perhaps, appropriate to deal with how they should be weighed by the angler.

When you have caught your fish the first priority is to weigh it accurately. Do not put it off until later because your fish will be losing weight all the time. It is understandable that you may want to retain the fish in a sack to obtain a really good photograph in daylight conditions; flash shots are always difficult with close-ups of fish and have a tendency to be 'burnt out'; colour can suffer too. However, regardless of these considerations, you must weigh your fish first. I have established that weight loss after approximately eight hours in a sack is around the following order. Carp weighing 10 to 12 pounds lose about 4 to 6 ounces. Fish of 14 to 17 pounds lose about 6 to 8 ounces. Fish of 20 pounds plus lose 12 ounces to 1 pound.

Some fish are possibly more prone to weight loss than others but all will lose some weight. The loss is caused by the fish emptying the intestines and by mucus production. Mucus (fish slime) is secreted by the fish as a protective covering for the body. In the close confines of the sack the mucus is constantly being rubbed off and so the fish must produce more. While doing so it is constantly losing weight. The larger the fish the greater the body area and the greater the loss. It has been said that carp lose weight when confined, worrying or fretting at being restricted in a sack. I have difficulty in trying to relate a mental condition into a positive weight loss and feel that the mechanical one of bodily contact with a rough sack is a better explanation.

When weighing a fish please handle it carefully and weigh it as accurately as possible. If there is any doubt as to its weight always err on the low side – this way you will keep your friends! And please, when photographing, none of those irresponsible shots holding the fish above your head. Respect the carp, for if it is a mature fish it might be older than you.

8 The carp: food supplies and sense organs

One often hears talk of 'hungry waters' where the carp are easy to catch because there are too many fish and not enough food to support them. It is unlikely that there is any real food shortage in waters where carp grow to double figures. If carp in a particular water manage to grow only to the mid-teens in weight, it is quite possible they would grow no larger in any other water. Stocking a water of unknown potential with an excessive number of big carp to make instant carp fisheries can result in steady weight loss and mortality in the weaker fish until an equilibrium is reached between stock density and food supply. Let us take an average water where fingerling carp of random strain have been introduced. Let us also assume that these fish have reached double figures in weight. If they are to grow on to 20 pounds plus they should attain double figures in their sixth or seventh year. Failure to do this indicates stock of inferior growth rate or too many fish for the food available. The stocking policies of some clubs and syndicates are completely crazy. Only recently I was told of a club that had drained their pond and cleaned out the silt and weed. Within six months the water was stocked with a thousand fingerlings and is shortly to receive as many big, mature carp as can be obtained. No thought for the enormous amount of food that disappeared up the sludge pump pipe or allowing food supplies to become re-established – tip 'em in boys, carp always grow to a good size. Stupid, isn't it?

In established waters the carp will have to work harder some years to find sufficient natural food to satisfy their needs. In doing so their maintenance level will be increased. From the angler's point of view the effects of this might manifest itself in more carp being caught at a lower average weight or, if the fish are still growing, a poorer weight-for-length ratio than normal. A reduction in natural food might explain why the carp in a given water are easier to catch

A small south Yorkshire pond set in ideal surroundings. The land, a mixture of crops and pasture land, drains into the pond. It is very rich but vastly over-stocked

one season and harder in another. It follows that in a good year food-wise in the same water, where the resident stock have food well in excess of their needs, less energy is required to obtain sufficient sustenance. The angler, then, is offering baits to fish who already have enough. Although they are less inclined to feed those that are caught in an abundant year are likely to show a better-than-average weight for length ratio.

Nature has arranged a comprehensive food supply for aquatic predators like carp that is normally referred to as the food chain. A food chain is the basis of all life forms on earth, including Man. Each link in the chain has a life or death connection with the next; a few critical links removed from the chain could mean stunted growth or even death for the higher life forms. In a 'closed' environment like a still-water, the loss might affect all the higher life forms. Restoring these missing links could take several seasons, depending on the original cause of their destruction. Pollution is an insidious enemy that only occasionally causes a spectacular fish-kill, followed by the subsequent ranting and raving of the interested parties. In many waters of this highly industrialized country of ours pollution is present in amounts too small to cause a direct effect upon the fish. Instead there is a gradual, but sustained, attack upon the lower food chain organisms, quietly eradicating vital links in the chain, leaving no visible trace of the loss. The fish, deprived of a basic healthy diet, begin to suffer from mysterious diseases or become more prone to fungus or parasitic attack.

Any food chain always has plant life at the base of the production pyramid. Plants alone can thrive on sunlight, warmth and various nutrient salts. In a newly formed lake or pond the lake bed will be comparatively barren and before the water can become self-supporting it must first form the vital detritus on the lake bed. Gravel, sand and clay pits that have become flooded perhaps get the first layers of detritus from bankside vegetation. Aquatic plants absorb nutrients over the entire surface of their foliage and their roots serve mainly as an anchorage. Sand pits, in particular, are naturally acidic. The surrounding sandy soil filters out many of the dissolved salts that normally find their way into an enclosed still-water, thus removing some of the more alkaline elements. Most of the sand pits I have fished have had very poor weed growth and have shown an acid reading of 6 or 6·5 pH using litmus papers or BDH liquid methods of measurement. Such waters rely on material from the land entering the water so that bacteria can break it down to form the nutrients weed growth requires. It can take many years for decent weed growth to become established in these waters.

Once weed beds become well established there is a regular supply of material to form a rich detritus on the lake bed, which in turn forms a good feeding ground for the animal life there. Bacteria breaks down the composite animal and vegetable mix of the detritus, converting it back into simple mineral compounds that are released back into the main body of the lake to promote still more plant growth. Any new fishery formed from disused or worked-out gravel pits, etc. must go through this life-giving process before stocking if it is to be any good.

With each new order of aquatic fauna that enters the environment and survives in sufficient numbers to procreate, links are formed in the chain that allow a further increase in species and so a complex system evolves. The complexity of form and construction as the food chain lengthens means a reduction in numbers of each new species if the upward movement is to continue successfully. At the bottom of the chain are masses of weed and tons of detritus. It all starts here; tons of base material supplying reducing numbers of animal species up the food pyramid to end, in our example, with a handful of big carp forming the final link, or pyramid point.

Waters which contain big carp are often very clear and usually have prolific weed beds scattered around them. Some of them suffer badly at certain times of the year with massive algae blooms of one sort or another, while others seem to produce a fair head of 20 pound carp without ever colouring up. Good weed growth ensures a supply of well-oxygenated water and the removal of the carbon dioxide produced by bacterial and respiratory activity. In a secondary role it serves as an ideal hatchery, a nursery, a food supply and a hunting-ground for the wide range of larval, pupal and nymphal stages of the aquatic phase of the animals that use it.

A classical reversal of this can be seen in small ponds and lakes where the carp or other species are known to be numerous and stunted. These waters are perpetually coloured due to the clouds of silt being in constant suspension in the summer months and often in winter too. The diminutive fish are in a semi-starved condition, forever digging and sifting the sediment in an effort to locate some untapped food source. The teeming hordes are caught in a vicious circle. Desperately committed in their search for food they create such disturbances that the continual clouding prevents the necessary stability for weed growth or food chain development. The fish are destined to remain in a stunted and often diseased condition unless some are removed.

Before we look at the range of food available to the carp, we might briefly look at the way it is able to locate and select the various items.

Sight is one of the primary sense organs in most animals, yet there is some doubt as to the part vision plays in the carp's normal feeding. There is no evidence to suggest that the carp's eyes have any special ability to see well in the poor light conditions of its underwater environment. Neither the eye size nor the density of light-sensitive 'rods' are specially adapted to cope with muddy or night-time conditions. A carp will use its eyes to locate a piece of floating crust in daylight, though floating crust is hardly a natural food item. But the carp is just as able to find the crust in total darkness – through a dense weed-covered surface too. As carp often feed well at night in many waters we must conclude that sight plays little part in food location in these situations.

Smell and taste seem far more important. These two senses, while being distinctly separate to us, are possible much more closely linked in a dense medium like water. We can only guess at what the two senses might be like to a fish. But it seems logical to suppose that they are very similar in effect, except that the olfactory sense (smell) is a more sensitive form of taste, being able to locate minute traces of food at some distance. Smell and taste appear to have a more vital role than sight in food location and the angler would do well to heed this when considering bait samples, particularly in well-coloured waters. A carp has many smell- and taste-sensitive receptors grouped around the head, lips and mouth so obviously these particular senses are of extreme importance. I can remember catching several dace from the River Idle some years ago. The fish were completely blind, having a rough crystalline crust over both eyes, so opaque that no iris detail could be seen. One would expect that in a fast-flowing river like the Idle blind fish would be in considerable trouble. But, so far as I could tell, there was no difference in condition between those that could see and those that could not. All were caught from a fast run near the far bank too, so the blind fish were quickly able to locate and intercept a fast-trotted maggot.

Another vital survival mechanism is the sense of touch. The carp has four sensitive barbules with which to probe for live organisms such as annelid worms, bloodworms and other silt-based animals. These barbules are also well endowed with sense receptors. This probing ability is perhaps the major reason that carp are able to grow quite well, even in relatively poor waters. Apart from the tench and the gudgeon no other still-water fish has the ability to feel for movement in the silt. These two species offer no threat to the carp although the carp can seriously affect their survival. The tench and gudgeon are limited in their physical ability to probe deep into the silt. But the carp not only has longer barbules, it is also able to push its head several inches into the sediment, giving sufficient penetration to reach most of the living organisms present and thus robbing the other probing species of their basic food source.

The sense of hearing might also play some part in food location where the larger food items are concerned. The carp has two forms of hearing. It has an inner ear system, connected via the swim bladder, to give a limited form of hearing covering the low- to mid-range frequencies up to around 2000 cycles per second. It also has a lateral line hearing system responding to very low frequency and pressure waves caused by vibrations and other moving bodies within the environment. Hearing might at first seem to play little part in food location. But sound travels well in water and a carp that has located a good food supply and is chomping up crustaceans or other molluscs produces a sound which other carp can detect and home in on. In this direct way hearing plays a part in food location. I do not imply this as proven fact, but apart from mating – which then assumes a carp must also be able to make a mating call! – there seems little need for a hearing system as complex as the inner ear mechanism. It is doubtful that such an advanced system would be required entirely for balance as other fish manage quite well without the complicated Weberian structure, so food location is another possible reason for the sensitive mechanism.

It is possible that the carp has a sixth sense; the ability to detect electrical charges. All living bodies have a small electrical field around them – an 'aura' if you find that explanation easier to follow. A means of detecting an electrical charge at close range would be invaluable in an environment where the intended meal relies on concealment as a means of survival. While such a sense might appear extraordinary to us as land-based animals, the problem of detecting an electrical charge in water is less involved than in air. There are enough dissolved mineral salts in a natural water to ensure quite good close-range electrical contact between fish and food. Fish are extremely sensitive to small electrical charges, as the success of electro-fishing clearly proves.

The carp is equipped with a very substantial set of teeth to deal with the wide range of food the average lake contains. These are situated in the throat, or pharynx, and are called pharyngeal teeth. These are contained in two separate lower 'jaws', each containing five heavy teeth with flattened tops. On the flat tops are dozens of small rasp-like edges. The lower pharyngeals appear to have no meshing ability and function by pressing upwards to crush food against a bony structure which forms the upper pharyngeal half. The lower teeth appear to be independently controlled and able to break food into quite small pieces. The carp has no proper stomach in which to store food and food well ground-up by the pharyngeal 'mill' is ideally suited to the primitive digestion system, ensuring reasonable conversion.

Let us now examine the natural food a carp eats.

We must first look at the most basic component, without which there would be no life on this planet – vegetation. From the angling point of view we can lump all the mass of underwater vegetation under the general heading of 'weed'.

There seems to be some doubt that the carp can extract anything of value from eating weed. It is said that the simple digestive system is unable to break down the individual cells of the weed because they contain a considerable amount of cellulose. The carp would need to produce a special enzyme, from bacteria within its gut, to break down the tough cellulose outer covering of the cells. It is generally accepted that the fish's digestive system cannot contain sufficient bacteria to produce these enzymes. This is like you or I trying to suck a sweet without removing the wrapper. It would need

Close-season work is very important. Here small roach and rudd are being removed from a syndicate water to make more space and food available for carp. Ernest Colley, holding the net, seems to have forgotten he's fully clothed in the excitement!

a lot of sucking to remove the covering and until we did the sugar and taste agents inside would be unobtainable. The molecular enzymologist says the carp has not enough equipment to deal with weed as a diet. I had some correspondence with Nick Craven of Bristol University on this subject in the letter columns of *Angling*. Nick is a molecular enzymologist and the above is my own simplified interpretation of his very interesting comments.

One cannot really argue with the findings of a professional on complex subjects like enzyme production from micro-organisms. Yet, as a carp angler, I have an uneasy feeling that something is not quite right with the above explanation. Carp eat enormous amounts of weed during the summer. In four different waters I have seen carp eat filamentous algae, Canadian pondweed, hornwort and curly pondweed. And when I say eat I really mean *eat*. In one instance a bed of curly pondweed, about 60 square yards in area, was almost totally eaten in a five- to six-week period. The most carp I counted at one time was nine and they were slurping down the weed like there was no tomorrow! This was during the very hot July – August period of 1976. Nick did say that some weed might be digested in warm water conditions; perhaps this is the explanation as I have never seen carp so preoccupied with weed-eating during cooler conditions.

I did suggest in the correspondence with Nick that carp might eat weed for its animal rather than vegetable content. During summer the average weed bed has a very high animal population. There will be thousands of eggs being deposited by many aquatic species; thousands of immature larvae and nymphs browsing on the weed, all of which provide good-quality food. So perhaps here might be another reason why carp eat so much weed? This answer would be quite logical. The carp eats the weed and is able to digest the animal content while the weed passes through chewed but undigested. Weed so treated would find plenty of eager lower-order diners who could digest and thrive on the diet. Nothing is wasted in a natural environment so this line of thought fits such a sequence of events.

But despite this rational explanation I still feel there may be another explanation. The percentage of meat in relation to veg. would be low indeed and it might be that more energy would be used than gained, making a negative conversion whereby the carp is losing weight with the effort of eating!

The true herbivores like sheep, cows and even elephants need to eat for a major part of the day to survive on vegetation. Even these animals must eat a fair amount of meat in the form of snails, slugs, worms, spiders and their egg clusters. However no one suggests these animals rely upon this meat intake, for they have warm bodies and specialized techniques like cud chewing which give better bacterial production and more time for efficient digestion. Their teeth are also well adapted, the rear ones being flattened with ridges running along them to help break down the tough vegetable fibre of a self-supporting plant. One of the major differences between herbivores and aquatic omnivores like carp lies in the two forms of vegetable matter they consume. The submerged plants are not very fibrous in nature because their weight is supported by the surrounding water. Land plants have to be self-supporting and are therefore considerably more fibrous in construction. This fact alone must improve both the digestibility and the 'chewability' of the aquatic vegetation. Secondly, it could be argued that the carp's teeth are more suitable than a cow's for tackling a vegetable diet. Whereas the cow is required to crush and pulp tough, fibrous grass, the carp's teeth crush and *shred* relatively brittle aquatic vegetation into tiny fragments *at one go*, not needing to re-cycle a fibrous mass for additional chewing. We could simulate a cow's treatment of grass, for example, by bashing a cabbage stalk with a hammer. While, if I surmise correctly, the carp's treatment of aquatic vegetation would approximate to rubbing a potato with a coarse rasp.

Whichever way the fish or animal chews its food, its digestive enzymes are still faced with the 'sweet in a cellophane wrapper'. The essential difference is that the carp's 'sweets' are very much smaller than the cow's. Because of this a greater initial surface area is presented to the digestive enzymes in the carp's intestines, which in theory would present less of a digestive problem. It could be that the carp's chewing action is sufficient to break down the cell walls of the vegetable matter, even if the fish's gut does not contain the right kind of digestive enzymes to break them down.

Because so much scientific research has still to be carried out on fish like the carp I prefer to keep an open mind on subjects like the nutritional value of weed. Many of the lower-order aquatic animals are entirely vegetarian and are able to grow and thrive, regardless of water temperature, on a diet of weed. It therefore seems odd that a much higher-order animal like a carp cannot, at some period in the season, make full and proper use of an abundant and prolific food like weed.

Carp certainly seem to make the most of what fare a water offers. Take a pond stocked principally with roach, which, until recently, rarely grew larger than 6 ounces. In a pond like this where I fish the carp have grown up to 15 pounds in twelve years, while fingerling carp introduced in 1973 are making (in 1976) between 2 and 4 pounds. Although the water is really too overcrowded for maximum growth, the weight gain of these fingerlings suggests that there is no shortage of food – for the carp that is. That the roach are stunted indicates that either the survival rate at spawning is high; the fish are a 'stunted' strain; or the food needed to make the roach grow large just is not there. These factors and the lack of effective predation results in overpopulation. That the original carp have grown only to 15 pounds in twelve years is not any real guide to the food potential of the water. This is a reasonable growth rate, for the stock may not have grown any larger in a richer water. We do not know anything about the strain of these original fish and it could be that they only had average growth potential. The fingerlings we have introduced came from a parent stock that is known to have grown to more than 20 pounds and if the growth continues at the present rate these fingerlings could reach double figures in their sixth year.

This same water also contains rudd which, unlike the roach, have made better growth, the larger ones being close to 2 pounds. Within this environment we can see that a large proportion of any food items living in free water are going to be eaten by the roach and rudd before the carp get a look in. This, however, presents no problem to the carp since the richest part of the lake is available to the probing species, while being denied to the roach and rudd. The detritus houses a large number of animals, some of which I have briefly mentioned in the bubbler chapter. Many of these animals live in a tube or tunnel, the walls of which are probably stiffened with body secretions to give stability in the soup-like environment. One group **is the annelid worms, comprising some twenty-five species and including the well-known tubifex worm. This group of worms offers an ideal food supply to the carp as they can grow up to 3 inches or more in length.** It was once thought that bubbling carp are feeding on bloodworms. But it is just as likely they are feeding on annelid worms, which would help explain why brandlings and lobworms are such successful baits for this type of fishing.

The bloodworm is the larval stage of the midge *Chironomus* of which there are a number of species. Some are free swimming, others live inside plants, while the ones of interest to the carp live in the mud. Bloodworms, although only about half an inch in length, are gregarious, living in seething, waving, masses that offer good bulk return to a probing carp.

Other bottom-living animals that live on or just in the sediment are the caddis fly larvae. There are nearly 200 species of caddis flies, though not all live in still-water. Many that do are vegetarian and browse on the dead vegetation on the lake bed. They are equipped with a crude form of protection, a case. The case structure is as varied as it is interesting. Different species make use of sand particles, tiny sticks, bits of weed and all manner of things. Some I saw looking like a tiny willow leaf. The first time I saw a 'willow leaf' walking along the bottom I thought I was having hallucinations! This particular species was a common one with the imposing name of *Molanna angustata*. It is doubtful if the larger carp would deliberately hunt these larvae out, although being slow-moving bottom dwellers must mean they are occasionally eaten by carp. Carp would have no trouble crunching them up, case and all. Trout swallow them whole.

The dragonflies are another potential food source, but being carnivores they are present in smaller numbers than the herbivores. There are forty-three species in all, though many are localized and it is unlikely that you would find more than two or three species in your particular lake. Carnivores are generally more active than herbivores, yet to survive they must live in the same areas as the vegetarians. Although they are more mobile some will obviously end up in the carp's gut.

Snails also provide the sort of 'mouthful' that would interest a large carp. Of the smaller ones the ramshorn (*Planorbis*) and pond snails (*Limnaea*) could easily be cracked by the carp's pharyngeals. The larger ones, particularly *Limnaea stagnalis*, might be more than the carp could manage. I have seen fingerling carp eat small snails of this species, leading one to think that big carp might also be able to deal with the strong shell of an adult snail. Alternatively, a large carp might swallow the snail whole, digest the flesh, then regurgitate the shell. Carp have the ability to empty their stomach in this way through a process known as 'anti-peristalsis', which is a rippling movement of the intestines. I have a feeling – without actually knowing – that this form of digestion is in regular use in the sea, accounting in some degree for the large number of unbroken empty shells that litter most beaches.

Together with the snails we must include other molluscs like the orb shells or pea mussels, and the freshwater mussel. The shells of these species would offer no problems to the carp. Only the larger swan-mussels, which are too big for the carp to get into its mouth, would offer any difficulty. However, it is common to find, when clearing excess weeds, empty shells 6 inches and more in diameter. We can only guess at how they came to be in that state. Some say that carp are able to extract the flesh of these big molluscs – I would have to see it to believe it! Like all other animals the swan-mussel has to die some time. When it does, the muscles holding the two shell halves will relax, giving access to the carnivore, or more likely, the process of decomposition which will quickly disintegrate the fleshy body.

There is no room to mention the many species that live directly and indirectly on the rich feeding supplied by the detritus – the mayflies, the water bugs, the water beetles, many of which have nymphs and larvae that find a living on the lake bed and offer high grade feeding to the carp. Some are herbivores, some are carnivores, but so far as the carp is concerned all are grist to the mill. A growing carp will put on about a pound of body weight for every 6 or 7 pounds of this quality food it eats.

In large lakes, where the food supply often exceeds demand, some interesting patterns emerge season by season. My friend Fred Simson came up with a good theory after two years of watching and wondering on a large Cheshire lake. He said that the carp seemed to have three basic occupations. One was rolling about on the surface – the usual leaping and rolling seen at some time at most carp lakes. The odd fish could be caught from these places but he was unable to get to grips with the better carp and came to the conclusion that these places were 'playing' areas. Another occupation was swimming. That may sound a little silly until explained. What Fred meant was that he often saw carp swimming to or from the sporting areas. When they were doing this they could rarely be tempted by anglers' bait. Fred decided that when they left the place they were rolling in, it was for a particular feeding area. Conversely, when they approached it they had just fed. The big problem on large waters is finding the feeding area. After two years' observation Fred finally pin-pointed an area a long way from the sporting and rolling place. During this period he had caught odd fish, just enough to keep interest alive. The lake record stood at 18 pounds for something like ten years and while Fred and his companions had caught some nice carp, they had not caught anything approaching this weight in spite of seeing much larger fish.

Leaving what seemed an obvious swim, Fred turned his back on the rolling carp and moved to the suspected feeding area, hoping that the third occupation – feeding – would take place there. The new swim was not an easy place to fish, requiring accurate casting to a confined swim area, not difficult during the day but tricky at night. Fred reckoned he had a 10 or 12 yard area to play with; any more than that would put him outside the feeding spot. Fishing at range in large shallow lakes is often difficult and one particular problem on this water was thick floating algal scum which had already caused the loss of several good fish. It was September before Fred got the chance he had been waiting for – a clear cast to the hot-spot without floating algae carpets interfering. In several visits during a two-week period, Fred broke the lake record three times, ending with a magnificent 21 pound 5 ounce carp. Anyone who really understands carp-fishing will know what this success meant to Fred. To me it was a touch of quality carp-angling, the reward for many hours of careful observation. He was right about the confined feeding area too, for his friends fishing near-by swims did not have the same success. Since then fellow Hallamshire Group member, Mick Dougill, who is one of Fred's constant angling companions, has put the lake record above 24 pounds.

Fred was unaware, at the time, that I was working on the same sort of problem at another lake in a different county many miles away. My approach was from the opposite end of the problem. I knew that certain swims were feeding areas, so much so that if you were not in the hot swim you might just as well go home. There were usually plenty of carp rolling at the shallow end of the lake but they were not easy to catch by any method. I had noticed, when fishing 'hot' swims, that it was rare to see any surface activity of note. When you were getting runs fairly often and the carp really had their 'heads down' the only indication of carp in the swim was the run itself. On one occasion, in a two-hour morning session, I caught five carp and lost one at the net without seeing a roll, a vortex or even bubbler activity. It was not until 1973 when I found similar things

Portrait of a hot-spot

were happening at the lake I was then fishing that I tried to rationalize why carp could be seen rolling elsewhere when only two or three swims were producing fish. I managed to establish a number of points which lend weight to Fred's theory. Here is what my observation revealed.

Observation is often easier on small ponds and lakes than on big waters. Because of this I was able to establish that many of the most productive 'hot-spot' areas on this particular water were eventually completely eaten out. When the water settled in late autumn and there was less activity, it was possible to see a large sand or gravel patch reflecting light from the lake bed right where the hot-spot had been. The rest of the surrounding lake bed had the usual dark, muddy, look of undisturbed detritus. Further evidence was obtained the following season, when the former hot-spot proved to be very 'cold'. At the start of each new season it would be some time before a new hot-spot would emerge in the form of regular catches of carp from a completely different swim. It is often hard to pin down these fairly confined feeding areas. Carp will be caught at various spots around the lake and it is not until someone makes an exceptional catch that the hot-spot is isolated. Even then, to fish it correctly, you have to get the range right. I recall one hot-spot, on a generally accepted long-range water, which was only about 15 yards from the bank. The carp usually fed there at night. Other anglers fishing the water noted fish were being caught in the swim. But, because they never saw the actual capture of the fish, had no idea at what range the fish were being caught. When their chance came to fish the swim they would assume the carp were feeding at long range. Unless they were forewarned they would spend a lot of time fishing over the carps' heads, catching nothing. It sometimes happens the other way and the feeding spot is at long range. I have been caught out many times fishing the margins when I would have been more profitably engaged in fishing at long range. These days I like to hedge my bets where possible.

It would appear, from the observations that I have made at various waters, that certain areas of lake bed contain a good food supply, perhaps of a particular species of aquatic life. Some, but not necessarily all, of the carp become used to visiting this area at regular periods to feed. While one group of fish visit one feeding area another might be doing the same elsewhere in the lake. There is nothing of a fixed nature about the groups that use a particular hot-spot and carp swimming a long way from a recognized feeding area will tag on to any general 'drift' when the feeding urge takes them. A known fish might be caught two or three times from one hot-swim and suddenly turn up right over the other side of the lake in another. I think it was Dick Walker who said that 'carp are creatures of habit' and it does seem that visiting certain swims becomes ingrained in their behaviour. As the summer progresses these good feeding spots slowly become eaten out. The regular activity taking place results in much of the detritus being put into suspension in the water. If the lake has only a shallow detritus of 6 to 8 inches at the feeding place, the regular attentions of big fish like carp will result in the true lake bed being reached. If you look in these places when the light conditions are right you can often see the different colour of the bottom. Only the top few inches of detritus has any food value to the species that live there. If the feeding area is over thick mud it is often difficult to see when it has been 'eaten out' because there will be no appreciable colour change.

Carp will regularly return to a feeding area, even into winter, until it is eaten out. Once the rich detritus has been dispersed however, it might take two or three seasons before it is once again able to support a good food supply. The carp must look elsewhere for productive feeding and the following season a new hot-spot will emerge. This sort of evidence fits the natural pattern of things well. While the carp are really 'hammering' one part of the lake bed, totally annihilating the life-supporting qualities of the area, life is continuing undisturbed elsewhere, allowing the many species to procreate and ensuring survival in depth for future years.

What I have said about feeding hot-spots is intended to apply to waters where the stocking density is on the low side in relation to the size of the water. As any carp angler knows there are always some reliable places, in any reasonably well-stocked pond or lake, which produce a fair number of carp during the season. But there is one essential difference which both Fred and I are trying to point out from our separate experiences. The location of a natural feeding area will produce far better results than the rolling and sporting areas that draw carp anglers like a magnet! The advent of particle baits has now superseded natural hot-spots to some extent. But you still have to bait a place where the carp will actually stop to feed – since what you are trying to do with particles is create your own hot-spot in a known position. The location of natural hot-spots is still important where long-range fishing is involved as the effectiveness of particle baits is limited by the difficulty of feeding them accurately into a small area at long range.

The commonly held beliefs about the annual available food supply are also open to question. General opinion has, for years, been that there is an excess of food in summer and little or nothing in winter. A short study of aquatic entomology soon reveals some major flaws in this belief, at least as far as fish beyond the fry stage are concerned. I hope to show that a good deal of the so-called 'rich summer feeding' offers no direct sustenance to the larger carp, thus conflicting with much of what has been said in the past.

No one can doubt for a minute that summer is a time of plenty. There are leaves on the trees, flowers, fruits, berries and nuts. The air is full of flying insects too and the heavy drone of rapidly beating wings can be heard in the quiet country places. Taking toll of this summer harvest are many birds, some of which migrate thousands of miles to take advantage of the insect horde. At night the bats take over where the swallows and swifts leave off, so you can see that there is a 24 hour food supply available for any animal at the time it requires it. Now it so happens that a high percentage of the fly life that sustains the summer migrants and the bats originates from the ponds and lakes and rivers and streams and ditches of this fertile land of ours. When this mass of once-aquatic life is in the air one has to wonder at how tremendously prolific the average water is, and in doing so also think how depleted it must be now that these billions of insects have left their aquatic environment for an aerial one. From May onwards many of the larger food insects are reaching maturity and are in the final stage of their underwater existence which they are about to leave. A very short period, during which most of these insects mate, is spent in the aerial environment. Those that survive the predation of bat and bird return to lay eggs in the water. Some of them get eaten before depositing their eggs, others successfully lay thousands of eggs.

During the early summer then, the larger carp have lost much of the mature food supply that was available in the early spring. In exchange there is an influx of minute eggs, larvae, pupae and nymphal stages. These are ideal food for the growing fry hatched in late spring – which is why the annual cycle is staged in this way. Fortunately for the larger carp, the in-depth food supply includes quite a few insect species that require two or more years to reach maturity, providing some reasonably sized items of food during this period. Add to this the short-cycle gnats, midges and mosquitoes of the *Diptera* order, the annelid worms and the molluscs, and it can be seen that food is available at all times. However, it must be realized that through much of the summer there is a big reduction in 'carp-size' food, and the carp has to expend more effort to satisfy its needs. If, temporarily, the need exceeds the supply, then there is always plenty of weed to eat, which might be another reason why carp eat so much of it at times!

The plankton, zoo-plankton, diatoms, rotifers, daphnia, cyclops, eggs, immature insects and algal explosions of summer offer no direct food supply to the mature carp as has been suggested. All of these tiny organisms are present to supply the needs of the young offspring of both fish and insect.

Before we leave the subject of food supply let us briefly look at the aquatic life cycle of a typical fly such as the damsel-fly. The eggs of this species are deposited by the female in June or July. When they hatch the tiny nymph, being a carnivore, must begin to hunt even smaller living animals in the eat-or-be-eaten environment of the underwater jungle. When it has grown a little the inflexible external skeleton becomes a tight prison preventing further growth until a split occurs and the nymph climbs out of the old skeleton and is 're-born' with a new growth potential. This disengagement from the old skin takes place several times during the aquatic period. The nymph must get on with the business of growing, all the time selecting victims – including its own species – of an ever-increasing size. So it will grow through late summer, autumn and winter to be ready, with wing 'buds' showing on the outside of its skeleton, in late May of the following year. After swimming to the surface or crawling up an emergent weed stalk the mature nymph case splits. Blood

This large gravel pit at Brandsburton is being drained for reworking. Although it once contained double figure carp, an environment like this isn't really suitable for growing outsized specimens, as it is too deep and has little weed growth. Scale can be judged from the large oil drum in the water (centre)

pumps through crumpled wings and, in an atmosphere a hundred times less dense, a mate is sought to continue the cycle.

Many of the fly species follow this sort of reproduction cycle, differing only in the length required to reach full maturity. So you can appreciate that the so-called carp food shortage of winter is based upon assumption. It assumes that what is taking place on land is also taking place under water. In fact the reverse is true. Food has to be available to support the huge range of species that spend winter in the water. Winter and spring must really be the time of plenty in an aquatic environment or why else would the swallow and swift leave for warmer climes? And why is the bat forced into semi-hibernation? While the birds fly with excited screams in bright African sunshine the bat clings seemingly dead, yet alive. Meanwhile, the bulk of next year's food supply – the life-giving sustenance of bat and bird – is growing ever larger, snug within a winter environment that fluctuates by only a few degrees.

But soon the warming rays of the sun will wake the bat from limbo; soon the swallow, swift, martin, reed-warbler, fly-catcher and a host of other birds who rely on the annual emergence of the aquatic legions will arrive; and soon the inbuilt biological clock of the aquatic cycle insects, set eons before man planted his clumsy, destructive foot on earth, will begin to tick off the metamorphic minutes to emergence. No food in winter? Rubbish! Although the natural winter cycle means there is less demand on the food supply, the enormous individuality present in the strains of king carp almost guarantees that some will require a regular intake of food. It is no coincidence that these 'year-round' eaters are often the biggest carp in the lake.

9 Tackle

A public house; a group of anglers at a meeting, pints of beer in hands. Come with me to chat to my friend over the other side of the room and as we go just listen to the general conversation: 'Fast taper' ... 'through action' ... 'on the mark four "glass"' ' ... 'good fish' ... 'really wound down to the butt' ... 'found Platil line good' ... 'I use Maxima' ... 'thin wire' ... 'Gold-strike' ... 'strong' ... 'take a lot of sharpening' ... 'Walker' ... 'Mustad' ... 'great reel' ... 'machined gears' ... 'no roller in bale-arm' ... 'buy one now' ... 'must look into it'. And so it goes on, snatches of conversation heard from bright-eyed and often animated anglers as they relate their experience with this or that piece of tackle or enact the landing of a big fish.

Rods are perhaps the most-discussed item of tackle and the least understood. I have lost count of the number of times I have seen rods 'waggled' and action curves put into them against ceiling or floor: the mock strikes; the tips held, usually by the bloke who has built the rod, as he encourages a friend to heave on the butt, impressing him with the power of the rod. All good stuff that makes a meeting enjoyable but useless for testing rods. You can assess weight, balance, finish and discuss the merits of any departure from standard constructional techniques, learning quite a lot in the process. But the real test of any rod is how far it will cast a given lead or bait; how it will perform on the strike at range; and how well it handles with a good fish on. Things that no amount of waggling or mock striking or bending will reveal. All they do is subject the rod to excessive stress that can result in breakage or damage to the tip ring.

Some years ago I remember having a conversation with a well-known angler for whom I have a great respect. We were in a pub in company with many other anglers and my respected friend had certainly seen off many more pints than I could possibly hope to match. The conversation turned to fishing for carp with Avon type rods and 5 pound lines; a form of fishing we had both done with considerable success. Enthusing about the great sport offered when a double was hooked, my friend went on to talk of the problem of trying to get the fish up to the surface when, as often happens on light tackle, the fish just circles round and round under the rod tip, tired but not played out. At this point I chipped in enthusiastically, saying that the light rod had not got enough 'poke' to get the fish up to the surface due to the angle involved. You cannot get any 'butt' in when a fish is in the margins directly beneath the rod. Instead of the expected nod of agreement from the well-known angler, I was pounced upon and told that I was quite wrong. According to him it was the line that was not strong enough to allow sufficient effort to be applied to bring the fish up. There were other people listening to our conversation and, not wishing to cause any embarrassment, I shut up.

You can try it for yourself, as I already had before that conversation, and prove that it is rod and not line that lacks 'power'. Put up an Avon rod with 5 pound line. Tie a weight of about 3 pounds on the line, then lift the weight by the line to see that it can be done. Now place the weight about 8 or 9 feet away and with the rod tip over the weight, try to lift it off the ground. Do it very carefully, though, because you will find that an Avon rod is unable to shift the weight from this angle and the rod is more likely to break than the line. It is doubtful if a carp can ever pull its own weight and most breakages on running fish are due to the accumulated effect of the fish's weight and speed. A tired carp circling under the rod end might only exert a pull of $1\frac{1}{2}$ pounds on the line but an Avon rod will not move it – a standard carp rod would.

I have not a lot to say about rods and their different uses for several reasons. Many excellent books on carp-fishing have already covered the subject well, often to the extent of discussing the design of rods to suit a particular form of fishing. To design a rod requires a clear idea of what the rod has to do. To reach this point implies many hours spent using unsuitable rods. The so-called 'designs' which carry an angler's name are, with a very few exceptions, not 'designed' at all but selected from the wide range of standard blanks available to anyone. There is nothing wrong with this way of 'designing' a rod providing, as is usually the case, the angler involved is a recognized expert at the branch of the sport the rod is intended for, and has tried a number of blanks in his search for the right one. The chances are that the rod which emerged from such trial would be every bit as good as one arrived at by mathematical design. While a designer now works with the more predictable fibreglass, he still has to get the taper and wall thickness right. The spigot joining the two pieces, the number of rings and their type and positioning will also affect the action. Whether the rod has been designed or arrived at by a process of elimination, the angler in question will have decided the best compromise. Such rods can normally be bought with confidence.

An angler's choice of rods is usually decided by the type of fishing he does. But sometimes they can be a reflection of his personality. I once remember seeing four matched rods and reels set up with such accuracy that when I bent down in my position, some 30 yards away, and 'lined them up' it was difficult to decide just how many were there. Another chap I knew fished for carp with a 12 foot fibreglass match rod – it was the only rod he owned. It had but five rings throughout, the first one being halfway up the middle section, though it was possible to see from a few pieces of ragged binding where the other rings had been fitted. He used an old centre-pin reel that let out a tortured squeal from worn bearings that had not seen oil for years. With this totally inadequate tackle he caught two of the three carp taken during one summer from a difficult lake. Of course he did not worry about the state of his tackle or the ultra-cult approach and spent more time watching carp than repairing faulty gear. Pity about the state of his tackle, though. The larger of his two carp went 17 pounds and he might have bettered that had not the tackle let him down. Somewhere between the personality that insists upon four sets of matched rods and reels and the one which uses totally inadequate tackle must lay the perfect carp angler.

I like to keep my own rods in good repair and would call myself all sorts of unmentionable names if I lost a carp through avoidable tackle faults. I have six rods from which to select for the waters I fish. I usually take three to any given water – two for use, the third as a spare in case of an accident. None of the rods are matched pairs because it is rare for me to fish two rods alike. Instead I prefer to fish one rod in a recognized swim with a 'going' bait and use the other for experiment. Some of my friends like to use three rods but there is no clear evidence that three rods gives the angler any advantage. I think this is because every carp angler, subconsciously perhaps, has in his mind a position to cast his main outfit, followed by the second one and so on. Experience has taught him the most likely places and that is where the 'best' outfit goes. Occasionally you will pick a carp up on a rod that is fishing almost unattended but my own experience is that the most runs come to the main outfit. It is all a matter of personal preference and if you are happy using one rod or four, then do it by all means. But do not get caught in the trap of slavishly following fashion at a particular water. Once you start to worry about not having the 'right' tackle you will be lost. Carp are caught by observing what is going on in the water and the latest up-to-the-minute ultra-cult gear will not improve your catches while you are fussing about trying to make things look 'nice' on the bank. You can catch carp with any old rod providing the old rod is able to put a bait where the carp are. Only at extreme range is it desirable to use the more specialized fast-taper rods to improve hook penetration. Most of the other carp fishing situations can be covered with anything between an Avon or standard carp rod.

Most carp anglers make a rod or two at some time, a job made simple now there is such a range of glass-fibre blanks available. I have made all my own rods apart from one and once, for the fun of it, made a built-cane rod from scratch, splitting the bamboo cane and deciding the taper required. It came out very well for a first attempt. The joints were hard to see and after hardening it had a nice 'steely' feel to it because I had left all the outer layer on, as Dick Walker advised in his book *Rod Building for Amateurs*. It was totally unsuitable for the heavy gear I wanted to use it with at the time, though it handled nicely with light lines in more open swims on other waters. Finishing home-made rods can also give a great deal of satisfaction. I like to use a finish that is semi-matt and obtain it by mixing 40 per cent gloss and 40 per cent matt polyurethane with 10 per cent white spirit. It normally needs at least six coats before I am satisfied with the finish and if the sheen produced by this mixture is not quite what I want, a little more (10 per cent) of the matt or gloss is added, depending upon which is required, as the successive coats are put on. Some anglers do not like matt finish because it is said that it is not waterproof. This might have some truth if the rod is coated only a couple of times, but the built-cane S/U carp rod I made in 1966 is finished with six coats of matt polyurethane and neither the cane nor the pure silk binding show any deterioration at all. Mind you, it has been treated with the loving care a good rod deserves.

Reels are much more standardized than rods, the Mitchell 300 being one of the most common in use for many years. The more affluent members of the group I belong to gradually changed to the Abu Cardinal range of reels several years ago; they had suffered line damage when pressuring fish close in, pike in particular, with non-roller bale-arm reels. Later, others obtained a roller conversion to fit the Mitchell 300 reels they had and now appear quite satisfied with the reel. The Mitchell 300 was not really made for the heave-ho situations a specimen hunter often faces. It first started life as a match reel but somehow became universally adopted by the big fish man. It is a beautiful reel and now it is available with a roller bale-arm the line 'stripping' problem should cause no further trouble.

Dick Walker, whose writings in the late fifties greatly influenced my approach to the angling scene – specimen hunting in particular – convinced me that a roller in the bale-arm was essential if line damage was to be avoided and to give 'feel' like a centre-pin reel. In the early sixties I used Intrepid Elites and actually wore them out without any complaint during the years of good service they gave. I have the higher-geared Intrepid Super Twins now. One is smooth on recovery but the gears in the other make quite a racket and have done since new. Pity really, since the reel suits me well and the roller in the bale-arm has never given any trouble, which I feel is import-ant where you have to pressure a carp while still giving line grudg-ingly. I find the higher-geared reels a big help when fishing at long range. A reel of less than 4:1 gear ratio can make the recovery of 50 to 60 yards of line seem a long task. Another advantage offered with high-ratio gearing is that bombs of up to half an ounce can be quickly lifted off the bottom and planed along the surface without winding like a demented organ grinder. This is particularly useful when there are patches of sub-surface weed or clumps of that tough, stringy, algae between you and the distant spot you are casting to.

But the main advantage of high-geared reels is that they allow the angler to play a fish effectively from the reel handle. Some may scoff at this method but, believe me, it works.

The text-books usually advise the angler to play a fish from the reel clutch. The clutch is set at a pre-determined position, which is

Trevor Moss, specialist tackle dealer, returns a 20-plus carp. He sells the right gear and knows how to use it!

often arrived at by sticking the hook into the eyelet or belt buckle on the rucksack and striking at the load while adjusting the clutch accordingly. This looks good and I have done my share of it at various times. But very few clutches retain the initial setting for long due to the different expansion rates of the materials used for constructing the average reel. Where you have a combination of plastic for the clutch/line spool assembly and steel and diecast materials for other parts of the reel, all within a design that relies upon a critical adjustment of the internal frictional properties for safe, reliable operation, the odds are that the temperature changes under fishing conditions will seriously affect the original setting. Most metals expand when heated, whereas many plastics are either unaffected at reasonable temperatures or contract slightly. Under normal fishing conditions that carefully adjusted clutch setting will either be too slack or too tight within a couple of hours, depending on whether the temperature has risen or fallen. The best fixed-spool reel I have ever owned had a metal spool. The clutch action was very poor when I bought the reel but some experiment with different materials between the fixed and driven plates of the clutch system soon had it to my liking. This reel could be adjusted at the start of a session and rarely required touching again as it seemed to retain the original setting indefinitely, even between sessions. I assumed that this reliability was due to the metal spool and spool carrier spindle having a compatible expansion – contraction rate.

The higher the gear ratio of a reel, the slower the reel handle turns in retrieving or yielding line. The main advantage of high gearing is that it allows the experienced carp angler to screw the clutch hard down and to play the carp from the reel handle. By experienced I mean any carp angler who has caught carp at different ranges and has a fair idea of what to expect in the opening seconds of the fight. I always yield line to a running fish by backwinding on the reel, except when I am margin fishing. The few times I have hit a real 'flyer' I have just let go of the reel handle until the fish slows down, usually after only a few yards of line have been taken. The only time I use the clutch now is when fishing very close in with 5 or 6 pound lines and Avon type rods. The clutch is set very light and as soon as the first wild run is over the clutch is screwed down tight.

There are sometimes looks of disbelief from other carp anglers when I mention playing doubles on 5 pound line with the clutch screwed down. People tend to become brainwashed into thinking that use of the clutch system is the only way to play big fish. It is one way to play big fish; using the reel handle is another. I have played fish from the reel handle for the last seven years and, in my opinion, this is the best method. In fact, the method is quite sound when you look at the forces involved when playing a fish.

Let us assume a carp is exerting a force of 4 pounds on the line as it swims away after being hooked. Using a reel that requires one turn of the handle to cause the bale-arm to revolve four times, means that any force the fish is applying to the line is also geared up by four times. If we ignore the slight frictional loss caused by the gear system, a force of 4 pounds on the reel spool becomes 16 pounds on the reel handle. In snaggy swims where heavier rods and stronger lines are used the force at the spool can easily reach 6 pounds and something like 24 pounds on the reel handle. This amount of pressure is still within the limits of the tackle and the easiest way of relieving it is to backwind the reel. Using a slipping clutch under the same sort of conditions has several disadvantages. First the forefinger must apply considerable pressure to the clutch to put the same pressure on the fish. If you have a rod with standard slip-on reel fittings the front one sometimes comes loose as the butt flexes. Even with screw fittings only three fingers can hold the rod and there is little grip on the rod handle from the angler's thumb. By ignoring the clutch the angler has a much firmer grip on the rod handle. When a clutch is giving line there is no indication of the amount it has yielded. But when you get used to using a locked clutch system you will find yourself counting the back-turns and allowing about 2 foot for each. This is a big advantage once the fish has boiled or rolled in a tight swim as it gives some guide to the amount of line taken from the spool. I do not claim that anyone can become so accustomed to catching big carp that he will be able to judge distances and calculate backward turns to the nearest inch. But I do think that after a few years at the game your tackle somehow becomes an extension of your own body. When you are playing a fish you suddenly feel, 'That's enough.' If the fish is given any more line he will be in the snags or whatever and you clamp down on the reel handle. The carp, who has had to fight very hard for what line he has taken from you, has little momentum to help him. I have seen mid-range doubles roll over backwards, even on lines as low as 6 pound breaking strains, when you finally stop them in this way. Since I started using this method of playing carp it has been well tested by a good range of double-figure fish taken on both heavy and light tackle. I have not been broken by a carp, except for a couple of times when I was taking a chance by fishing right among some snags. But there have been many times when the extra control gained by backwinding has helped me land fish which would otherwise have been lost in snags.

If I were asked to design a fixed-spool reel it would have no clutch or ratchets of any sort. The money saved from these unwanted and often defective devices would be spent in trying to design a reliable ball-bearing roller for the bale-arm and, if possible, improve the gear system without going to the expense of machined gears. The gear ratio of this imaginary reel would be 5:1 and the winding knob spindle would be strengthened where it joins the handle to accommodate the additional forces applied at this point by the gearing. The result would be an ideal carp-fishing reel at a price within the pocket of any serious carp angler.

One piece of tackle that seems to vary almost as much as rods is the landing net. Landing nets generally seem to fall into three categories: the pessimist, with arms of about 24 inches; the realist, where the arms are 30 to 36 inches long; and the optimist, with arms of 46 to 48 inches long. It is surprising how a big carp will fit into the first category provided the net is sufficiently deep. I have seen near 20s slip into such a net with ease although the net is really too small for carp-fishing.

The realist will settle for 36 inch arms as a compromise between a size adequate for the largest carp he is ever likely to catch and a length that makes the net unwieldy. It really is amazing how a slight snag, catching the net mesh at a vital moment, can stop the net being lifted. Any momentary delay can lead to big fish being lost. It requires split-second timing to net a good fish cleanly. Most big-fish anglers develop the timing without being aware of their own accuracy: it is all part of the wonderful coordination between hand, eye and brain that comes with practice. The danger in missing 'first go' lies, not so much in touching the fish and scaring it, because the angler will be expecting a final surge from the fish and will be prepared to give line should this happen, but rather that the line might become snagged (links, bombs or even the hook) within the net frame or mesh. The art of landing any big fish cleanly is to be sure it is played out and coming straight in. Never be in a hurry to stick the net under it the first time it rolls and you will find that 36 inch landing net arms are ample for any carp while still retaining the sort of manoeuvrability that will often be needed at a critical moment.

An optimist with a 46 or 48 inch frame might have good reason for a net of this size. One or two of my carp-fishing friends have such nets because they switch to pike fishing in the winter. A good landing net is expensive and, as few of us can afford to have one for carp and one for pike, it makes sense to buy one with arms suitable for the long-bodied pike and make do with that. Big nets are fine for landing pike in the generally more open swims where they are sought. But in the overgrown, tree-lined and often confined swim of the carp angler they can be an embarrassment. With the average 5 foot net handle the overall length is nearly 9 feet and that piece of twig that snapped off in the autumn gales and has become lodged in the silt takes some shifting with a 9 foot arm extension!

Most landing nets are commercially made although one does see quite a few home-made ones. The home-made ones tend to be soundly, if crudely, constructed and are often a little on the heavy side. Many commercial types are light but will not stand more than a few seasons' use without showing some defect. One of the most common is the failure of the pivoting parts due to electrolysis taking place between different metals. This can happen with nets where copper rivets are used to hold the alloy frame together. I have used one net frame for nine or ten years and it is still as good as new. It is rust-proof, corrosion-proof, strong, light and has reliably hinged joints that do not seize up. Let me hasten to add that the design is not mine, but that of a Mr Tyas who taught a tackle-making class at night school at the time I made my landing net.

The entire apex assembly is constructed from stainless steel – all small scrap pieces that were obtained at no cost. There is a fair amount of work involved as it took me about four evening sessions to make the metal parts, though this was largely due to having to wait for machinery that others were using. Some allowance must be made for the time that has passed since the frame was constructed. It was the fashion at that time to use laminated arms; mine had five laminations of a fine-grained wood called 'Ramin' and six laminations of thin fibreglass cloth, giving a combination of section strength and lightness that I have yet to see equalled in similar arms. The materials for the frame cost me about 50p. Tubular fibreglass is the rage now and using this material would reduce the construction time. When I constructed my net much of my time was spent on the

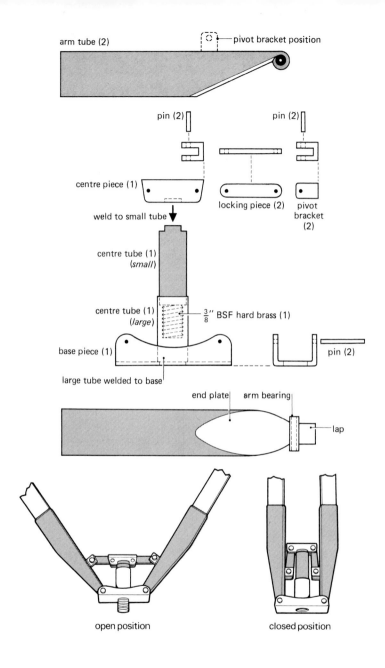

Figure 9 Arm tube bearing detail. The arm bearing is secured to the arm tube by first forming a lap around the bearing and then welding. The lap piece is an integral part of the arm tube. Open and closed drawings show fabricated arm tubes for laminated arms. Assembly of round type for fibre-glass arms is identical. (Both types are mentioned in text.) Note how screw thread is protected in closed position

square-sectioned pieces which receive the arms. These were fabricated from stainless sheet and then brazed together. Using tubular
steel, of a size to suit the glass arms, would cut the construction time
considerably and the dimensions given in the drawing are to suit this
form of construction. The dimensions are not critical in themselves
but accurate construction of the two halves is. Fit the arm tubes in
place at the required angle and rivet them with stainless rod. Then fit
the central part. When the frame is completed and the net fitted you
just open it, press down on the central pivot assembly to lock the net
open, then screw on the handle. The result is a most effective,
life-time, landing net that anyone could make with a little guidance
from a metalwork teacher.

After completing the landing net frame I took it to the next
Hallamshire Group meeting, and four group members immediately
enrolled at the night school to make similar frames. Two made
tulip-shaped arms for the frame, which is done by fastening the
laminate to a suitably curved former before the adhesive sets. I
made a second set of metal parts for a landing net for 'spares' but as
they were still waiting to be used four years later I gave them to my
good friend Bob Ford, who soon had them together and was very
pleased with the result. Afterwards I made the built-cane rod from
tonkin poles, mentioned earlier in the chapter. Making this rod gave
me a great deal of satisfaction even though it did not turn out as I
had intended. This was partly because the canes which had been
ordered were for 12 foot three-piece rods and because I had problems in getting the taper right the first time. A 10 foot two-piece rod
requires poles over 5 feet long and the available poles were only 4
foot 6 inches, which meant that the rod had to be fitted with a plug-in
butt to obtain the required length. That the taper was not right the
first time is nothing to be ashamed of; even Dick Walker and his
friends did not get it right the first time or the most famous carp rod
of all time would have been the 'Mark One'!

I have mentioned the evening class simply to illustrate how such a
class can open up a new field of interest. With expert tuition the
angler will be amazed at his own abilities and may be able to make
items of tackle which are superior in quality and far cheaper than
their shop-bought equivalents. I can, for example, make a decent
job when working with wood, but, give me a task in metal, like
opening a tin of sardines and I am sure to break the key. There are so
many things you can do well with the right assistance and materials

both of which are usually available at night school. I saw a short-handled, folding, landing net for trout. It was made of stainless steel with arms that folded back parallel with the handle. To open it needed only a touch of a button; to close, an upward flick of the wrist. The mechanics were simple and foolproof – another Tyas construction of class design. It did not stop at net frames either. Mr Tyas also taught us how to make netting and I made a net to fit the frame. If you find yourself with a similar opportunity, take it, for surely you must come out better informed at the end of it.

Another easily made item of tackle that I have used for the last ten years with complete satisfaction is the hook box illustrated. The box part is made from one of those flat cigarette tins that held fifty cigarettes. Any suitable flat metal or plastic container will do but it should, preferably, have a hinged lid. The insert is made from expanded polystyrene – a ceiling tile is ideal – and the fitting is very easy. Open the lid, place the bottom section face down well inside the edges of the tile and press down firmly. A clear outline of exact size will be left in the polystyrene. Mark and cut the hook slots and those for file and tweezers; cut the slots out with a sharp knife held low, as this makes the cutting easier. After cutting the slots out, carefully cut round the impressed outline and push-fit the polystyrene into the bottom of the tin. For the larger sizes of hooks, like sizes 2 to 6, it is advisable to retain the angled pieces removed from the hook slots. After fitting the hooks in position these angled pieces can be used to wedge them in place. These larger hooks, unless **wedged, can tear loose in the general rough-and-tumble of a season's fishing. You need not bother with smaller hooks as these do not have enough weight to tear loose when you jump from a fence or wall, or fall down the bank with the rucksack on your back!**

Some hooks have been in my container for years and the protective varnish is still good with no sign of rust. Make one of these very simple hook containers and give it a few seasons' trial. I'm confident you will agree that this form of hook storage is superior to odd packets in the pocket or a jumbled mass of mixed sizes all rubbing together in one small box. These are generally rusty because the

The cigarette tin hook box showing hooks, tweezers and file. The tweezers are used for individual hook selection. Note second triangular section placed on lid to show the shape the hook slots are cut to

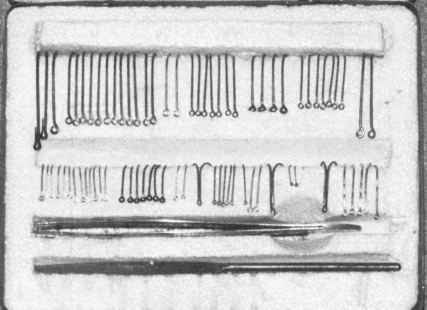

varnish has been removed or, worse still, covered in oil to stop rust forming.

I had intended to discuss the maintenance and repair of the well-known and much-used 'Heron' bite indicator, including converting it to an electronic system instead of the standard buzzer and bulb. The topic is, however, both complicated and lengthy. Instead, for those who have had some electronic experience at school or college or who have access to advice on the subject, I have included

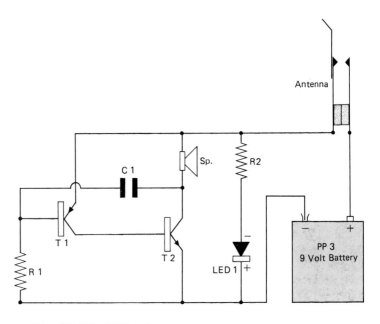

T 1 = 2 N 1309 PNP Transistor
T 2 = BC 107 NPN Transistor
R 1 = 100 k ohms
C 1 = .05 mfd. (see text below)
R 2 = 470 ohms for 20 m/a LEDs etc.
LED 1 = 20 m/a light emitting diode
Sp. = 25 to 80 ohm impedance speaker

Figure 10 Circuit for self-contained bite indicator. This circuit has proved extremely reliable over many years of use in all weather conditions. It will operate with a wide range of speaker impedance but one chosen from the above range will give the best results. The value of R_1 and C_1 may require some change to suit the actual speaker chosen to arrive at a suitable tone. Get the oscillator working first and then alter components if tone isn't to your liking. Increasing C_1 (0·1 mfd) or R_1 (200 k) will make tone lower and vice versa

two circuits that have seen many years of use, proving completely reliable in all weather conditions. One circuit is for the self-contained type of indicator that is becoming increasingly popular while the other is suitable for converting a 'Heron' or similar design of separate head indicators. Both feature a parallel wired circuit for visual and audible indication, giving improved reliability.

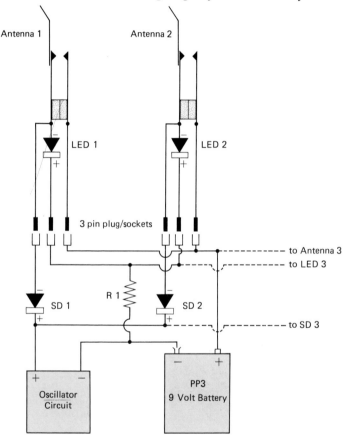

LED 1 and 2: Light emitting diodes
SD 1 and 2: Silicon diodes
R 1 is 470 ohms for 20 m/a LEDs; 220−330 for others.

Figure 11 Parallel wired circuit. Circuit for parallel light and sound with separate heads and bank box. Leads from heads are twin-screened cable and should have a minimum length of 3 yards. By using additional wiring (dotted) you can have any number of heads to one oscillator

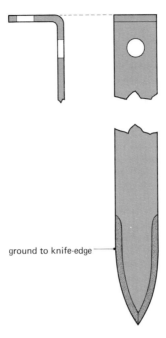

ground to knife-edge

Figure 12 Dagger-type bank stick detail. The material is 1 by $\frac{1}{8}$ inch mild steel. The length is decided by whether you use the high or low style of rod positioning

Although I do not have sufficient space to cover indicator construction fully, there is room to look at the item of tackle that supports them – bank sticks. Most bank-stick designs available commercially are of round section. Why I do not know, because they are most unsuitable for the wide range of bank conditions an angler will meet. In fact some critics of the self-contained bite indicator say the all-in-one indicators are too heavy and large, thus causing the bank stick either to fall or be blown away. This sort of criticism is unjustified. Self-contained bite indicators are only about twice the size of a separate head indicator and normally weigh between 4 and 5 ounces. Such criticism also completely ignores the design of the bank stick – it is like blaming the tyre when a wheel falls off your car. Good bank-stick design depends on two things: a knowledge of the range of conditions under which it is required to support a rod and a little common sense.

Many years ago I made what I call a 'dagger'-type bank stick which has proved to be extremely versatile and stable in use. It is constructed from steel strip about 1 inch wide and an eighth of an inch thick – the actual dimensions are not critical. You will see from the drawings the advantages it has over the more conventional round type when in use under common bankside conditions. Other, less readily appreciated, advantages are that the flat top allows

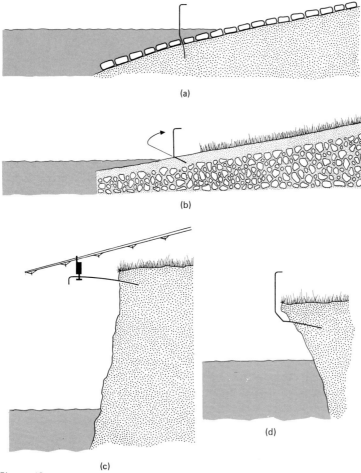

Figure 13
(a) Stone-paved or concrete bank with expansion cracks
(b) Hard, stone-lined bank with only a few inches of soil
(c) High vertical bank where the rod would be well above water normally
(d) Loose undercut bank

A pair of 'dagger sticks' in use with a twitcher-hitter and standard bite indicators fitted

much more effort to be applied when pushing the bank stick into the ground without the risk of hurting your hand in the process. The flat strip form of construction allows the stick to be inserted into expansion cracks in concrete banks or stonework. Even if these cracks are at awkward angles the bank stick can be bent, at right angles if necessary, to make it vertical without loss of stability; something that is hard to achieve with round-section types which usually fall over if bent more than a few degrees. My own dagger sticks were originally made to allow secure rod support at a water that had concrete banks with cracks running at all sorts of crazy angles. It was virtually impossible to get any real security with standard bank sticks and, even after much scrabbling about to insert them, the rod end was invariably five or six feet above the water. The dagger-type bank sticks solved the problem completely. Another advantage is the wing-nut head-fitting arrangement where the indicator head can be rotated to any horizontal angle and locked in that position. Although the dagger sticks were made for a particular water I have found them so versatile in use that they have now superseded the round ones, which are left at home. The people who argue that self-contained indicators are too heavy and too bulky, thus contributing to bank stick collapse, conveniently ignore the weight of the rod which, when fitted with a reel, is about five times heavier than the indicator. The rod/reel outfit also offers about ten times the horizontal cross-section of an indicator to winds blowing from either side; another point ignored in the blowing-over argument. Facts speak for themselves. If a bank stick falls over in use it has not been properly inserted in the first place and no amount of argument can escape that fact. Like most carp anglers I have fished in the full range of weather conditions this country offers and in spite of using self-contained indicators exclusively I have never suffered from bank stick collapse while using dagger-type bank sticks. Try them for yourself. They are so easy to make and so effective in use.

10 Nylon lines

In 1969 I lost a carp that was possibly the largest I have ever had the good fortune to hook. My line broke as I tried to stop the fish entering a very big weedbed. No doubt my inexperience in handling very big carp could be blamed to some degree though, at the time, I blamed the 12·8 pound breaking strain Platil Strong line I was using. A whole season had passed, almost, before the chance came to get a hook in that fish. The loss caused a great deal of soul-searching and I decided to take a close look at the effects of stress on nylon line. I tested the line I had been using and found it broke consistently between 7 and 8 pounds' stress when knotted with a five turn half-blood knot. This is a very low breaking strain considering that the line had a rating of 12·8 pounds breaking strain. Even allowing for wear and tear it seemed to me that something more basic than my incompetence lay behind the breakage.

A few months later, Eric Hodson, who was then secretary of both the National Association of Specimen Groups and the Hallamshire Group, obtained several brands of line from the importers and manufacturers. These samples were in 'factory-fresh' condition and required testing for breaking strain, diameter and any other things of relevance to the angler. Eric asked me if I would care to undertake the tests as he was already engaged in testing swivels and Sintox rod-rings. Still brooding over the loss of the big carp I seized this chance to improve my understanding of nylon lines.

I would like to make it quite clear that the results I obtained from my tests were based on my own testing methods and routine. That some lines appeared to give better results than others could possibly be explained if a different test routine was followed. However, every effort was made to be impartial during the tests, even to my refusal of the Group purchasing more lines from its own funds to fill in the gaps between some brands. I argued that it would be unfair to buy lines from a retail source since we had no way of knowing how long the retailer had had the lines in stock or if, during that period, there had been any change in composition or manufacturing procedure. The list of lines given is intended to be used as a comparison guide between brands, showing the various inherent characteristics. That some brands appear in a wide range of breaking strains and others in only a few might reflect upon the generosity or confidence of the supplier. That we received so much free line – some of it very expensive – shows that the tackle-trade is not as black as it is sometimes painted.

From the test point of view, the requirements were reasonably easy to fulfil:

The rated breaking strain printed on the spool had to be compared with the breaking strain obtained from the test equipment.

The rated diameter on the spool also required comparing with the actual line diameter.

If possible the relative striking power and relative stiffness of the various brands ought to be compared too if a fair assessment of line performance overall was to be obtained.

As I was to be involved in many repetitive tests obtaining the first two requirements another, better-qualified, group member took over the more difficult task of assessing relative striking power and stiffness. When the time comes to consider these two points I will let his pen do the explaining.

The first essential of any test programme is that of obtaining reliable results. Where comparison between different brands of goods is concerned it is even more important to try to maintain a strict test procedure. To try to overcome human error I made a machine to measure the breaking strain. This helped tremendously in applying a smooth increase in tension though, of course, there is room for human error in the accurate tying of the knot. I experimented before the actual tests and found that really accurate breaking points resulted if I followed a set procedure when tying a knot. The line would break, over and over again, at the same amount of stress. I would have liked to have employed the popular half-blood knot in these tests but it couldn't be tied with any reliability on the large-diameter 'eye' of the test equipment and kept slipping. I used the 'blood-bight' knot, which has the same efficiency rating of 85 per cent, instead. Separate comparison tests between the two suggested there was little difference in the overall

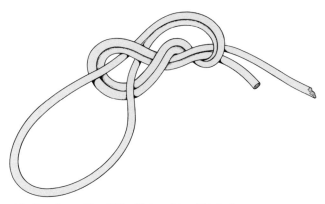

Figure 14 Test knot. The 85% efficient blood-bight knot

performance. A further advantage with the blood-bight was that it could be tied accurately before connecting the line to the machine, whereas the half-blood required tying directly to the machine, resulting in greater chance of error.

A Moore and Wright 1 inch micrometer was used to test the maker's claims about the line's diameter. By taking random

Testing nylon lines

Brand name	Rated breaking strain (lb)[1]	Measured breaking strain (lb)[2]	Rated diameter (inches)[3]	Measured diameter (inches)[4]	Relative strike power (lb)[5]	Relative stiffness[6]
Platil	1·8	2·0	·005	·005	0·75	19
Standard	2·9	3·3	·0065	·007	1·13	40
	4·4	5·6	·008	·0085	1·31	95
	5·3	6·0	·009	·009	1·19	96
	6·0	6·6	·0095	·010	1·88	188
	8·2	8·8	·0115	·0115	2·50	330
	9·5	9·6	·0125	·0125	3·25	507
	10·4	11·2	·013	·013	3·25	548
	12·3	12·0	·014	·014	3·25	636
	15·4	16·7	·016	·016	5·25	1343
	22·0	24·3	·020	·021	7·25	3200
Platil	1·8	2·0	·005	·0055	0·63	19
Soft	4·4	3·3	·008	·0085	1·38	100
	16·7	14·8	·016	·017	1·88	542

Brand name	Rated breaking strain (lb)[1]	Measured breaking strain (lb)[2]	Rated diameter (inches)[3]	Measured diameter (inches)[4]	Relative strike power (lb)[5]	Relative stiffness[6]
Platil	3·3	3·6	·0055	·0065	1·13	48
Strong	7·3	5·7	·0085	·0095	2·88	260
	9·2	7·2	·010	·0115	2·88	380
Damyl	5·0	4·2	·008	·0083	0·63	44
Royale	10·5	9·1	·012	·0125	2·06	322
Pescalon	2·0	1·6	·005	·0055	1·13	34
	5·0	5·8	·008	·009	2·50	203
	10·0	8·3	·012	·012	4·25	611
	14·0	11·8	·014	·015	6·75	1510
Luron	1·5	1·8	·005	·0055	0·56	17
	4·0	4·3	·008	·009	0·81	66
	7·0	6·0	·011	·012	2·19	315
Perlyl	3·0	3·4	·007	·0075	1·25	70
	9·0	7·7	·011	·012	3·0	432
Sportex Fluor	12·0	8·3	·012	·0125	4·75	741

1. Manufacturer's rated breaking strain (printed on spool).
2. Measured breaking strain with test machine (rounded off to one decimal place).
3. Manufacturer's rated diameter printed on spool (in some cases converted from metric measurement to inches).
4. Measured diameter (at random on 10 yard test sample).
5. Relative striking power in pounds. This is the force at the hook for a strike that takes in 10 per cent of the line.
6. Relative stiffness in bending. The figure gives a relative value of the stiffness of the line. The lower the figure the more supple the line.

The 85 per cent efficient blood-bight knot was used for testing all lines.

measurements along a 10 yard test length, the uniformity of the line's diameter was also checked. It could be claimed that such a measuring system might compress the line, causing inaccurate readings. But, as many of the samples had a diameter greater than the maker's claims, this is unlikely. Throughout all the testing routine great care was taken to ensure each sample received the same treatment.

When studying the various breaking strains, both rated and measured, it is important to compare the diameter of similar lines before deciding the potential of a given sample. The striking power and stiffness must also be taken into account. Both are important factors that have some bearing on the fish picking up the bait and the success of the strike. My friend Ron Barker, who calculated the striking power of the test lines, comments as follows:

To set a hook in a carp requires a substantial force even with a good, sharp hook. In close-range fishing, where there is not much line out, the power of the strike is controlled primarily by the angler and is moderated by the action of the rod. The effect of the line is minimal. In the case of long-range fishing, however, the situation is very different. Consider fishing at 30 yards' range under good conditions with a fairly tight line. Assume a fish picks up the bait and moves away from the angler. The bail-arm is engaged and the strike is made, all in one movement. In making the strike the rod is swept back from the horizontal to just past the vertical. With such a movement a typical 10 foot carp rod will take up, at the most, 3 yards of line. The force of the strike will be controlled almost entirely by the properties of the line. The force will be the same as that which will stretch the line by 3 yards in 30 yards or 10 per cent. This was measured for all the lines and the results are given in the table.

It will be seen that there is a considerable variation for a given breaking strength and that the soft lines are very poor in striking power whereas the so-called 'strong' lines are very good. It must be emphasized that these results would be very much lower at a 5 per cent extension which corresponds to taking in 3 yards of line at 60 yards. The situation gets progressively worse as fishing distance increases.

It should be pointed out that a line which shows a lower measured breaking strain than the maker's claim is not necessarily a poor line. Providing the line breaks with reasonable consistency at a similar breaking strain each test, then it can be considered a reliable line that has been slightly overrated. The reliability of a line is vital from the angler's point of view. A line rated at 10 pounds breaking strain that fractures at a 15 pound pull on one test and 5 pounds on the next is useless. It may have an overall breaking strain of 10 pounds but the angler is never sure when the 5 pound break is due. Conversely, a line rated at 10 pounds that breaks consistently at 8 pounds must be considered very reliable, for it gives the angler the opportunity to become accustomed to the amount of stress he can safely apply before it breaks. So much emphasis is placed upon the maximum breaking strain of a line in relation to its diameter that its overall reliability is sometimes overlooked. Let us take a closer look at what is involved here.

During the preliminary tests ten fractures were considered for each line, the mean of the ten then being calculated to obtain the overall 'measured breaking strain'. However, it was found that many lines were breaking within 0·25 pound of the maximum so often that ten tests per line would not only have been excessively repetitive but, more importantly, would only have made any difference to the fractions involved. The carefully tied knots and the smooth pull of the machine made it possible to reduce the number of fracture tests to three per line. For instance the Platil Standard 5·3 pound line broke at 6·0, 6·25, 5·75 pounds, in that order, for the three test fractures. The 10·4 pound Platil Standard broke at 11·25, 11·0, 11·25 pounds and so on. These are examples of a reliable line characteristic that many of the tested brands possessed. The Platil Soft 4.4 pound did not show the same consistency, breaking at 4·25, 3·0 and 2·75 pounds respectively. The 16·7 pound had similarly inconsistent results with a maximum variation of 4 pounds. Platil Strong had good consistency but averaged over one thou' thicker than stated. The 'Strong' 7·3 pound and 9·2 pound lines had rather poor overall breaking strains. Obviously I cannot go through each line, though I have a full set of test results for each, including the actual fracture point and whether it occurred on the line or within the knot structure. But two other samples to round-off the breaking strain tests. Luron '2' 4 pound broke at 4·25, 4·25 and 4·25 pounds; a very consistent and reliable line that possesses a rather low striking power. The Sportex 'Fluor' did not perform well at all. Rated at 12 pound breaking strain it gave fracture tests of 7·5, 6·75 and 10·5 pounds. It was so inconsistent that I did a lot of additional tests to overrule any question of unfair comparison. My conclusion was that there had either been a mix-up when the spool label was printed (12 thou' diameter for a breaking strain of 12 pounds is considerably overrated when compared with similar lines) or the whole spool of line was faulty. The former appeared the most likely.

At this point I must hand you over to Ron Barker again for the line suppleness tests. To assess suppleness in nylon line requires the use of mathematical formulae but, as Ron points out, it is the conclusions that matter.

As has already been argued the amount the line stretches for a given loading can be as important as its breaking strength. A further very important property of the line is its suppleness or softness. All anglers must have been infuriated at some time by a stubborn line that spills off the spool in coils when fishing with the bail-arm open. A stiff line can also make good bait presentation more difficult.

Now it is a fundamental fact of nature with monofilament line that a supple line will be stretchy and have low striking power, while conversely, a line having a high striking power and low stretch properties will be stiff. This is because suppleness is just another way of saying ease of bending and bending is a combination of stretching one side of the line and compressing the other.

When solid materials are deformed by the application of a stress the deformation can be either elastic or plastic or a combination of both. In elastic deformation the material will return to its original size when the stress is removed, whereas in plastic deformation the material will retain its new shape after removal of the stress. A good example of an elastic material is a coil spring of a spring balance which, when used correctly, would always return to zero. If, however, the spring was overstretched it would not return to zero and there would have been some plastic deformation. A good example of a material exhibiting almost pure plastic properties is soft lead as used in split-shot.

Now nylon behaves elastically almost to its breaking point and can be considered to be purely elastic in its behaviour as a monofilament line. As an elastic material it can be studied using the same mathematical formulae as are used to study the behaviour of engineering structures. Where suppleness is concerned we are interested in the elastic strength in bending. We have already measured the elastic strength in tension for consideration of striking power and with the known line diameter we have all the information required to determine relative stiffness or suppleness. For those who are mathematically inclined I will go through the maths but this is a mere detail, it is the conclusions that matter.

The formulae for the elastic deformation of a cantilever of circular cross section is:

$$\frac{P}{D} = \frac{3E\pi d^4}{64\,l^3}$$

where

P is applied bending force

D is displacement resulting from applied force

E is elastic constant (see below)

d is diameter of cantilever

l is distance from fixed end to a point of applied force

$\frac{P}{D}$ is just another way of expressing relative stiffness and it will be seen that it is controlled by elastic strength × the fourth power of line diameter.

The elastic constant E is derived from measurements in tension as follows:

$$E = \frac{\text{stress}}{\text{strain}}$$

where stress $= \dfrac{\text{applied load}}{\text{area of cross section}} = \dfrac{L}{A}$

and strain $= \dfrac{\text{increase in length}}{\text{original length}} = \dfrac{l_i}{l_o}$

$$\therefore E = \frac{L\, l_o}{A\, l_i} \qquad \text{or} \qquad \frac{4\, L\, l_o}{\pi d^2\, l_i} \qquad \boxed{1}$$

Now stiffness $S \,\alpha\, E\, d^4$.

or from $\boxed{1}$ $\quad S\,\alpha\, \dfrac{4\, L\, l_o\, d^4}{\pi d^2\, l_i}$

$$\therefore \quad S\,\alpha\, \frac{L\, d^2\, l_o}{l_i}$$

If we select a fixed value of $\frac{l_o}{l_i}$ (stretch) as we did for assessing relative striking power then relative stiffness is proportional to the load required times the square of the line diameter. This was done for all the lines tested and the results are given in the table and are also presented graphically in Figure 15.

The conclusions of this study are very simple. For any desired value of measured breaking strain the angler has a choice of lines varying in stiffness by up to a factor of two to one. But the soft lines are stretchy and have poor striking power whereas the lines having a high striking power are stiff. As discussed later the stiff lines also have the disadvantage of reaching the breaking point after only a small amount of elastic extension.

The amount of elasticity in monofil line can be a good or bad factor depending on your particular style of fishing. At many ponds and lakes there is no longer a choice. Although you may get greater enjoyment from presenting baits to carp you can see, pressure on the water usually means fishing at range. But if there is the opportunity to fish the margins the high-elastic quality inherent in some lines offers an additional safety factor where fast-moving, margin-hooked carp are concerned. Long-range fishing requires a different approach and we require a low-elasticity line for optimum transfer of striking force.

I carried out some checks on the elasticity of various lines to find

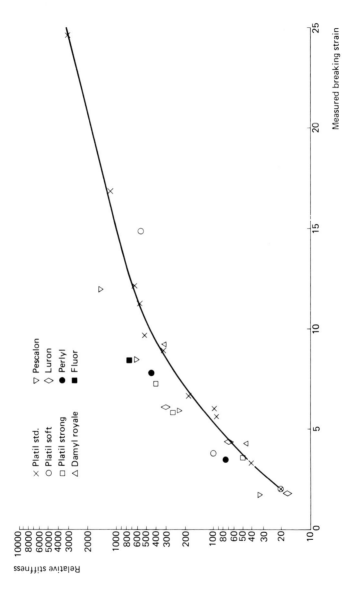

Figure 15　Graph showing relative stiffness of the lines subject to test

the different brand characteristics. This was not part of my test schedule as Ron's 'Striking power' and 'stiffness' tests were really doing the same thing. At the risk of repeating Ron's comments, my findings regarding the stretch quality in nylon line may be of additional interest.

There has been considerable comment about line elasticity at various times in the angling press, particularly in connection with long-range fishing. Where percentage stretch is quoted in an advertisement it probably refers to the amount of stretch, or elongation, measured at the breaking point. This figure is only a guide from the angling point of view, for if a strike took up all the stretch in a line there would be no fish to play at the end of it. The line would have broken. In practice we must be prepared to downgrade the percentage stretch quoted to avoid breaking on the strike. This is not something you can measure as you play a carp but it is something to keep in mind as you pressure the fish. My elasticity tests were aimed to establish just how the line-stretch was proportioned as stress was applied to it, up to and including the actual point of fracture. I do not intend to list all the elastic properties of the brands of line tested, but a range of between 7 per cent and 25 per cent was recorded, the average being around 12 per cent to 15 per cent.

I found the way the line stretch took place as the tension was increased of particular interest. There appeared to be three distinct phases. At first there was a steady movement of the marker which indicated the stress applied when the line was put under tension. This movement continued until the marker indicated the tension was about half the rated breaking strain of the line. Then, as further tension was applied, the marker remained almost stationary. Instead the line itself began to stretch. After the major stretch period had been passed and most of the elasticity had been taken up, the marker began to move once more until the line eventually broke. I found that the applied tension had to be increased very carefully during this final phase. If not the line would break prematurely before the optimum breaking strain was reached. It was as if the molecular structure of the line could not stand any increase in acceleration of the tensioning device and the molecules, already fully stressed, lost adhesion and slipped apart. This should be borne in mind when playing a carp: when the rod is hard round and you are really pressurizing the fish, the average line will be well into the second phase, perhaps near the limit of elasticity and about to enter the final phase. Any struggles by the fish represent stress accelerations that could cause premature line breakage. Additional care is required, for example, while trying to stop a carp reaching a snag. Side-strain on the fish might have to be transferred from one side to another. Unless this is done smoothly breakage may occur.

The low-stretch lines were received with indifferent acclaim when released on the market. Some leading anglers were full of praise for them while others had bad experiences, swearing never to use them again. The average angler never really got to grips with this latest aid to angling. There is no doubt that the reduction in line diameter helps to improve casting range, or that the low elasticity improves hook penetration. The Platil Strong averaged about 7 per cent stretch on my test equipment, whereas the 'Standard' line was approximately 10 to 12 per cent. But do not forget these figures were fracture point measurements; something in the order of 5 per cent and 9 per cent respectively is nearer the amount for practical use. My strain observations with these lines indicated that they went through the same three phases of strain action as ordinary lines, except that the sequence was compressed into a smaller area of movement. The third phase, in particular, was very compressed and in practice would be quickly reached by a heavy-handed angler. This is really the crux of the matter. An angler who gets on well with low-stretch lines may have the gentle touch; one who complains they are 'below standard' might well be guilty of applying too much 'stick'. My tests revealed no inherent weakness in the lines, suggesting that the essential factor was to choose the correct type of line for a particular type of fishing. Choosing 7 per cent stretch line for margin fishing is just not on; neither is the choice of a 20 per cent stretch line for long-range work. Reverse the roles and you are in business.

The higher-elasticity lines like Golden Marlin and medium ones such as Turboline and Hardy Jet are really ideal for power carp-angling such as fishing near snags or weed and lily-pad beds. Many anglers have a set of rods for long-range work and a set for general carp-fishing. But usually their reel spools are filled with one kind of line which varies only in breaking strain. A few extra spools to carry lines of different elasticity seems a worthwhile investment. It would give the angler greater versatility and justify his expenditure on different sets of rods and reels.

Split-shot is sometimes blamed for line breakage. Some anglers opt for soft shot to avoid line damage while others prefer hard shot, saying they want the shot to stay in position. Research suggests that a standard knot would fail long before a line-break at the point where a shot was fitted. This applies whether the shot is hard or soft. When a hard shot is clamped on the line it squashes it to some degree, giving rise to the belief that because the line is thinner at the shotting point, it must be weaker. However, although the line is now flatter, it is also wider than the normal section. Therefore the cross-sectional area is virtually the same. The line is not weakened, it has merely been subject to a change in shape. My own preference is for soft shot on the grounds that should a hard shot slip in use, damage might be caused by the sharp edges of the 'split'.

One other point of considerable interest to many carp anglers is the knot used for tying the hook to the line. Manufacturers often claim that their particular line has good 'knot strength' without giving details. We must assume that this is intended to mean that a knot will not seriously affect the overall breaking strain of the line. This is true to some extent, for the tests generally showed good knot strength, with many breaks occurring above the claimed breaking strain rating even though an 85 per cent efficient knot was used. In theory a 10 pound line should always break on the knot at 8·5 pounds when using such a knot, and lines of greater or lesser breaking strain ought to show the same degree of efficiency. The majority of the lines tested did break at the knot, though some broke well above the rated breaking strain and others below it. This might be due to the way a particular manufacturer rates his line or a differing set of test conditions, but it can be very confusing for an angler. My own advice is to compare the breaking strain claimed with the line diameter printed on the spool; my preference is for those that are more conservatively rated.

The only information I have to hand concerning knot strength does not clarify the situation a great deal either. This is a copy of a test report issued by the Perlon monofilament company. In a section on mechanical and technological properties it states: 'Perlon has a wet strength equal to 80 per cent of the dry strength'. In other words it loses 20 per cent of the rated breaking strain when wet and a 10 pound line will break at 8 pounds. Then it gives the knot strength as: 'dry, approx. 60 per cent; wet, approx. 50 per cent'. But it does not state whether the 50 per cent relates to the previous dry breaking strain or the wet figure. In one case a wet 10 pound line with knot would break at 5 pounds and in the other 4 pounds. These figures appear very conservative to me and I have never tested a 10 pound line from any manufacturer of note that has even remotely approached these low figures.

Knots and nylon have always fascinated me and consequently I have spent a considerable amount of study on them. Having completed the allotted tests on the nylon lines as requested, I carried out further study on knot performance as a matter of personal interest. This revealed some information of practical value in carp-angling. I found that a knot of 85 per cent rating tied badly, i.e. not wetted and pulled down tight, would break at a much lower figure than the rated breaking strain. Perhaps the anglers who claim to have 'been smashed like cotton on 10 pound line' are really guilty of bad knot tying? With the right knot and a good-quality nylon a 10 pound line will take enormous stress before it breaks – you virtually have to point the rod at the fish before the break occurs. It was also interesting to note whether the break occurred at the knot or elsewhere on the line. With lines below 5 pound breaking strain there seemed to be a fifty–fifty chance of the break occurring at either the line *or* knot, whereas with heavier lines the break nearly always occurred at the knot. This suggests that either the thinner lines are subject to varying strength or that they react less predictably than the thicker ones when knotted. I think the latter is the most likely explanation. I think that the knot action on nylon lines below a given diameter becomes less predictable. I spent a considerable amount of time looking at fractures that had occurred inside the coiled turns of a knot. To do this and to examine and compare knot fractures, I used a powerful microscope. This allowed me to obtain a reasonable idea of what caused a knot to fail and, at magnifications in excess of 400 times, a fair insight into knot action was acquired.

Most knots used for tying nylon line rely on an ever-increasing 'grip' as the stress is increased. When tension is applied to the line the coils forming the knot contract, taking an increased grip around the line running through the centre of the knot. A good example of this is the half-blood knot, where the outer turns bite into the central line like a circular vice. This vice-like effect puts incredible pressure upon the central line core, trapping it to stop the knot slipping. When the tension is increased beyond a certain point the pressure within the knot becomes so great that the line fractures. That is what my own observations seem to suggest anyway. When you consider that lines below 5 pounds break at random while lines above 5 pounds invariably break at the knot, it suggests that this theory could be correct. A line of less than 5 pounds breaking strain will break at the weakest point along its test length because insufficient stress is developed within the coils of the knot to break it at this, its potentially weakest point. In stronger lines the pressure is greatest at the knot and sufficient internal pressure is built up on the coils so that it invariably occurs at this point.

When you look at a knot break in one of the higher breaking strain lines under high magnification, two things are apparent. There is often some 'necking' in the line just below the break. This necking is partly due to the line being compressed by the circular

 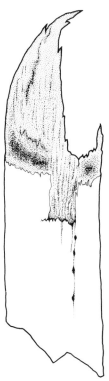

Figure 16 Typical knot fracture at approximately 120 times magnification. The line is Pescalon 14 pounds breaking strain, 0·014 inch diameter

Figure 17 Typical line fracture at approximately 120 times magnification. The line is Pescalon 14 pounds breaking strain, 0·014 inch diameter

constriction of the knot turns and partly because the line has taken up a different shape because of the stress to which it has been subjected. The end of the line, where the break has occurred, has a distinctive appearance. Sometimes it has a mushroom-shaped dome appearance; sometimes it is like the head of a nail with a flattened effect. But in each case the surface usually has a lumpy, fused, finish. A knot break (Figure 16) contrasts sharply with a break elsewhere along the line. In a line fracture you can still see some necking but the broken end has an entirely different look (Figure 17). This is a typical break with the fractured end consisting of a series of jagged spikes which indicate that the line has been torn apart.

It struck me that if a knot could be devised to overcome the constriction on the main line caused by the knot loops, then the effective breaking strain of the line would be increased. It would then be possible to use a line of a lower breaking strain. Reducing the breaking strain of a line also reduces the diameter of the line. This is important, since reduced line diameter increases casting distance. The thinner the line the more supple it is and the more natural the presentation of the bait to the fish.

It was some time before I came up with the answer. I was watching a film of a ship docking when I suddenly hit upon the solution. A rope was thrown ashore and was given a couple of turns around a bollard on the quay-side. The man holding the rope was then easily able to check the energy of a large ship with little effort, the load being absorbed in the two turns around the bollard.

This was the answer to my problem! If two turns were taken around the eye of a hook there would not be enough load left to allow the securing knot to bite into the line and weaken it. The two turn 'bight' was first tried with a half-blood knot. But as the knot bedded down prior to testing it damaged the line, making small circular kinks in it. After a little experimenting a simple slip-knot was used to secure the end of the line. The procedure is to take the line through the hook eye twice, finishing with a simple slip-knot to the main line. The knot is very easy to tie with a little practice. If you follow the illustrations you should have no kinking problems (Figure 18).

The next step was to test the knot to see if there was any improvement when compared with the 85 per cent efficient blood-bight test knot. I used the Platil Standard line simply because a wide range of breaking strains had been supplied. The increase in maximum breaking strain using this knot was very impressive. Here are the test figures for the higher breaking strain lines:

Spool breaking strain (pounds)	Blood-bight	Two turn slip-knot
8·2	8·8	9·9
9·5	9·6	10·5
10·4	11·2	11·6
12·3	12·0	13·2
15·4	16·7	18·1
22·0	24·3	28·1

Comparison between blood-bight and two turn slip-knot (Platil Standard line)

A separate series of tests were then carried out to see how often the fracture would occur in the knot. As you recall, the vast majority of fractures occurred within the knot with lines above 5 pounds breaking strain. I chose a 10 pound line for the test.

In all, twenty fracture tests were carried out using the two turn

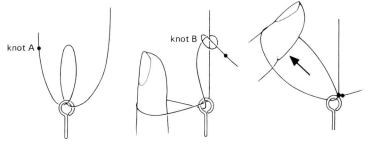

1. Twice through eye and tie knot A, pulling tight

2. Finger through loop then tie knot B and bed down to knot A

3. Hold hook in one hand moving finger in direction indicated, when both knots will slide to hook-eye

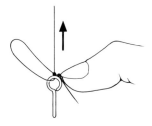

4. Still holding hook, place thumb nail on knots and gently pull the reel line

5. Make sure the line has bedded to the eye correctly, then snip-off excess

Figure 18

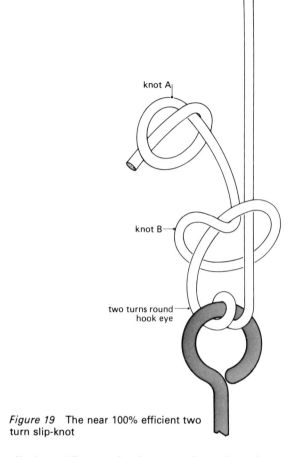

knot A

knot B

two turns round
hook eye

Figure 19 The near 100% efficient two
turn slip-knot

slip-knot. Nineteen broke somewhere along the test length and only
one broke within the knot structure. Here was a complete reversal
of the previous recorded results. Instead of a break almost always
occurring in the knot the two turn slip rarely broke there. The knot
was working as planned. The two turns dispersed the load around
the hook eye and there was no stress applied to the main line within
the knot.

The results obtained, using a wide range of different manufacturers' line, suggest that the two turn slip-knot must be rated as a
near 100 per cent knot. Simple observation of broken test lengths
knotted in this way confirms this. When line is subject to maximum
stress it loses the normal smooth, round, shape and becomes
deformed (plastic deformation). The elastic limits of the line have
been exceeded and a molecular re-arrangement has taken place.
The molecules in nylon line are mainly arranged along the length of

the line. But some are out of alignment and they shift with the stress. Once the elastic limit of the line is passed the molecules become trapped in their new position and are unable to return to their previous, unstressed, position. With top-quality lines there appears to be less molecular shift and the line does return to its original shape to some extent although it never fully regains its former roundness. This loss of roundness is worrying at first as the angler equates it with loss of breaking strain. I carried out several tests on such samples of line but found little evidence that they had been seriously weakened. Repeated stress on the line, like being snagged often and pulling for a break, will eventually affect the breaking strain and it is up to the angler to realize this. But my own conclusions suggest that a form of 'tempering process' had taken place, realigning the molecules in their strongest position. The result was not a stronger nor weaker line but a line with less stretch.

It is doubtful if molecular re-arrangement will cause problems under actual fishing conditions. However we must remember that if we are using a knot that has virtually the same strength as the line a break could, in theory, occur anywhere along the line. It would not be funny if you were playing a carp at sixty yards' range and the line broke at the rod-end! In practice it seems that any such break will occur near the terminal end of the tackle. I have used this knot since the early seventies and found that on the few occasions I have been irretrievably snagged the break has always been near the terminal end of the tackle. This end of the tackle is subject to a greater degree of damage than the remainder of the line. Since I began using this knot I can only recall losing three carp while in direct contact with them. Two were lost when the fish rubbed the line along a concrete shelf in the lake, while the other chewed through the line. I may not have caught as many fish as some other anglers, but the quantity and quality of those I have landed have been sufficient to test the efficiency of this particular knot.

I began this chapter by moaning about the loss of a big carp on Platil Strong 12·8 pound line. Let me put the record straight. The hook was secured to the line by a five turn half-blood knot which broke at between 7 and 8 pounds' pull when tested afterwards. Remember that the line had seen considerable, if careful, use between June and September, when the fish was hooked. When I tested the same line, but with the two turn slip-knot, it broke consistently at 11 pounds. I have every confidence with the performance of the two turn slip-knot. And it does seem that certain lines, such as the Platil Strong, need a special knot, such as this one, to display their properties to the full. I have tested various lines during the last few years and it seems that this knot is the most suitable, particularly for those with low elasticity.

Let me end with a few more comparisons between this special knot and the more common ones. Some results are from the original test report whilst others are given from various lines tested since then.

line	Rated breaking strain (pounds)	Knot-type breaking strain (pounds)	Two turn slip-knot breaking strain (pounds)
Platil Strong	7·3	5·7 (blood-bight)	7·5
Platil Strong	9·2	7·2 (blood-bight)	8·4
Damyl Royale	5·0	4·2 (blood-bight)	5·4
Damyl Royale	10·5	9·1 (blood-bight)	9·83
Hardy Jet	10·0	8·0 (6 turn blood, tucked)	9·2
Intrepid	10·0	10·2 (6 turn blood)	10·5
Micron Braided	20·0	15·5 (5 turn blood)	19·5
Golden Marlin	4·0	4·6 (5 turn blood, tucked)	5·7
Golden Marlin	8·0	7·8 (5 turn blood, tucked)	9·1
Golden Marlin	12·0	10·8 (blood-bight)	14·7
Centurian	10·5	9·7 (5 turn blood, tucked)	11·4
Turboline	11·0	10·4 (5 turn blood, tucked)	10·9

Comparison between two turn slip-knot and common nylon knots

The figures in the table appear to show that some lines are slightly overrated while others seem underrated. Some have good knot strength with a standard knot, others require a special knot to get the best from them. Recently there has been a change in the line ratings printed on spool labels. I think this has been done because of 'line-class' records. If you catch a sea fish on (say) 12 pound line-class tackle, the line you are using is officially tested if the fish is to be entered as a class record. The line must break below 12 pounds or you are automatically put into the next highest class. To ensure that an angler is not cheated of a possible record in this way, I think some line manufacturers slightly overrate their lines, thereby ensuring they will break below the stated figure when tested. That a line breaks below the figure stated on the spool does not mean it is no good. The important point with any line is the reliability and consistency of its point of fracture. The more consistent the figure at which it breaks during repeated testing, the more reliable the line.

The test results outlined are from lines supplied to me in new condition. All the breaking strain tests were done on a simple machine constructed for the job. We are not so much concerned with extreme accuracy in the tests, but rather more with comparisons between various brands and breaking strains. To this end every effort was made to ensure that each line received identical treatment. Without a machine it is almost impossible to obtain the smooth pull required without stress accelerations and therefore realize the maximum breaking strength of a line. You can test a line with a spring balance, using your hands to apply stress. But bear in mind that you are unlikely to achieve consistent results particularly with the stronger lines.

The idea of using the two turn slip-knot occurred to me as a direct result of my testing and examining nylon lines at high magnification. I make no claims of originality for it seems likely that others have already seen the problems involved and taken similar steps to overcome the knot's internal pressures. My comments on knots and line stress may well be common knowledge. All I have done is bring the facts to the angler's attention.

In writing of stress action, elasticity, suppleness, striking power and knot action in greater depth than usual, it is my hope that anglers who fish for any large species will have a better understanding of what is involved in the choice of nylon lines. The specimen-hunter has, after all, a vested interest in knowing what stress his line

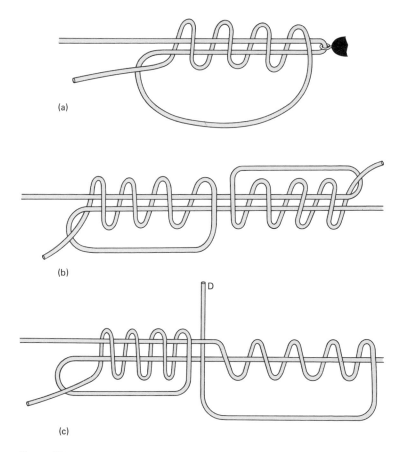

Figure 20
(a) Grinner knot for eyed hooks, swivels etc.
(b) Double grinner knot
(c) Blood-grinner knot. D is the dropper end. If the strands are of different thicknesses, the end D should be the thicker

These three knots were devised by Richard Walker who says, 'They are measurably stronger than blood knots and tucked half-blood knots; more reliable, because the ends are trapped by all the turns instead of simply being jammed between adjacent turns as in a blood knot, and satisfactory for joining strands that differ considerably in thickness.

'If you join different strengths of nylon with a blood knot, the jamming turns cannot apply equal pressure to the ends which are of unequal thickness. The thinner end is therefore not gripped properly and can slip out. If it does, the knot collapses. That cannot happen with a double grinner knot.'

My own tests on the grinner knot prove these claims and suggest a knot efficiency in excess of 90%.

is being subjected to while playing a large fish. The specimen-hunter may have put in many hours of fishing before he gets a chance to hook the fish he is after. Unlike the less selective angler, who is content with catching small fish frequently, he can afford to make fewer mistakes. The obvious way to minimize fish losses is to choose the right line.

Finally, we must look at the effects of sunlight on nylon line. It has been claimed in the past that the ultra-violet rays, part of the 'white light' spectrum we call daylight, can damage nylon line. In essence this is quite true. However, ultra-violet light offers no serious problem for the angler. Although ultra-violet rays will damage the nylon group of plastics, the damage is very small indeed – in fact 'minimal', as a scientist would put it. The amount of damage is in proportion to the amount of ultra-violet radiation absorbed by the line. This, in turn, is decided by the colour of the line. A clear, transparent, line offers little resistance to the light rays and a high percentage pass straight through, whereas a line that has been dyed, made translucent or delustred offers much more resistance and consequently a higher proportion of the damaging rays are absorbed by the line.

Existing evidence suggests that if a nylon fishing line was put into continuous outdoor use, it would take a whole year to reduce the tenacity – the ability of the molecules to hold together – by only 10 per cent; so small is the effect of the ultra-violet light. I have read of lines losing strength 'overnight' but have never had a first-hand experience of this phenomenon. That is not to say that I have not witnessed a loss of strength in a line. But, in such cases, inspection with a microscope has revealed evidence of physical damage to the line. Perhaps I have been lucky. I prefer to think that understanding nylon line in a basic, amateur, sort of way, and respecting its limitations, is why I have not suffered this mysterious weakening for which ultra-violet light is often erroneously blamed.

Nylon line is, perhaps, the most important single item of tackle the angler uses. It is subject to considerable stress and is less able to cope with extremes than is the rod or hook. There are many different brands of nylon line available to the angler. With a little understanding of the various properties inherent in a given brand the angler can further improve his chance of hooking and successfully playing a big fish. While suppleness, elasticity, reliability and diameter are the principal points in any line, few brands, if any, can supply all the characteristics required for all forms of carp-fishing. Because of this many good lines have been labelled 'rubbish' entirely through incorrect use. Choose wisely, use the right knot, and line breakages will be almost non-existent.

11 Hooks

One hardy annual topic on the fishing scene is hooks. Anglers argue about barbs; the temper of the steel, or lack of it; the carbon content; the length of shank; the shape of bend; the width of gape; the amount of reverse; the off-set; the eye size; the eye position – upturned, downturned or straight-eyed; the thickness, or thinness, of wire. All these things and more have received ample discussion in the angling press. So why bother to write a chapter on hooks if the subject has been so well covered? Well, the majority of comment I have read about hooks has been based on personal preference – although there is nothing wrong with that – or based on insufficient solid evidence, which under fishing conditions is not too easy to obtain. The fact that one type of hook obtains 100 per cent penetration during one session, while another sort only manages 50 per cent in a different session is no real proof that the first hook is better than the second. Many other factors are involved. Was the fishing range the same? Was the line the same? Were both hook barbs treated in an identical fashion during sharpening? And, a most important but not easily proved factor, was the carp facing or swimming away from the angler? All these things affect hook penetration, as does the character of the lake bottom. Whether it be clean gravel or sand, or littered with debris or silk-weed, each will have some bearing on the cleanness of the strike and the amount of hook penetration.

Quite a lot of moaning goes on between carp anglers about the temper of hooks. What angler has not listened to a sad tale of how a real 'lunker' was hooked, which, usually after a detailed account of the ensuing fight, managed either to straighten or snap the hook? The person relating the story rarely blames himself for the loss – it is always the poor hook-manufacturer who takes the stick. If an angler loses a carp because of hook failure he has only himself to blame. When you consider the low cost of eyed hooks it is not surprising that some fail. The fact that hooks are mass-produced and the process is subject to rigid control is no guarantee of a perfect product. There is always some human element involved and this means occasional slip-ups along the line. It is like the jokes made about computers – the ones where a bill is received for some astronomical amount. How people laugh, calling computers a stupid innovation. If a computer is correctly programmed it cannot make a mistake and if we wish to continue using the word 'stupid' then it must be applied to the operator who programmed it.

If we accept that not all fishing hooks are perfect, it makes sense to test each hook before use. Do this and you will not be the narrator of the sorry tale of a carp lost through hook failure. When I sharpen a hook it takes quite a while to get the barb and point just as I like it. I will often spend up to twenty minutes working with a file and magnifying glass before I am satisfied with the hook. I am sure you will agree that it would be stupid of me to spend all that time working on a duff hook, particularly when it requires only three seconds to test the temper before starting the sharpening procedure. A quick twist with a pair of pliers, which you need to hold the hook while sharpening, is sufficient to test for any fault in hook temper. During the years I have fished for carp I have made many mistakes. I could relate endless tales of woe but none would be about hook failure simply because I have never lost a fish through hook failure. When you contrast the strength and thickness of the average hook with the nylon line, to which it is tied, the line should always break before the hook fails. If it does not the fault must lie with the angler, rather than with the hook-manufacturer.

During the early sixties I bought a copy of a minuscule book, the title of which I have forgotten. If my memory serves me right, the author's name was Frank Oates. The 'book' was about the size of the average angling clubs' handbook and was, I think, a 'private' edition. It was full of common-sense statements that were the result of years of successful match-angling. One thing I remember to this day was the author's insistence that a hook should have a cutting edge to the point rather than the thorn-like point we normally associate with hooks. He likened the hook to a chisel and said that for good penetration the hook should cut its way into the fish's lip. His comments impressed me and I began to sharpen my hooks in this fashion, finding that the penetration was improved. At this point in my angling 'career' I was concentrating on catching chub,

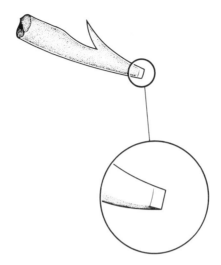

Figure 21 Standard hook sharpened to 'chisel' point

roach and trout, using the smaller sizes of hooks. Later, when I started carp-fishing, some of my larger hooks were treated in a similar way, having a chisel-edge instead of a point. There is no doubt that this method of sharpening a hook is the best. The chisel-edge pares its way into tough, leathery, flesh much better than a symmetrical point ever could. A point is able to force only a narrow, conical, wedge of flesh apart, and relies on a later, tearing, action to drive the barb home. With a cutting point to the hook the tissue is neatly severed, allowing the barb much easier entry. Flesh has some very elastic properties and it is easy to test them by pulling a hook point into the end of your thumb. The skin is thick enough to allow considerable penetration before blood is drawn. As you pull the sharpened point in you will see that the skin will begin to pile up in front of the barb and that little ripples will form in it. When you look at the angle of attack by a hook with line attached, and then study the near-vertical face of the barb, it is obvious that the elastic nature of the tissue will 'shoot' the hook out the moment tension is released unless the barb has entered. With the standard, untreated, barb of many of the larger hook sizes, the tissue would be unable to stretch enough, in spite of its elasticity. It has to be torn apart for the barb to secure a hold. This requires considerable effort, perhaps more than can be applied with an average carp rod except when margin-fishing. By reducing the thickness of the barb and making a cutting edge to the hook point, much less effort is required to drive the hook beyond the barb. The barb can be reduced by squashing it down a little with the pliers or by filing. I prefer to file the barb down as I am always afraid that it might crack if squeezed by the pliers.

With larger hooks it will also be necessary to increase the size of the chisel edge so that a deeper vertical cut will be made in the fish's mouth, allowing smooth entry of the thicker wire of the hook. This is where the problem starts, for size 2 and 4 hooks require a large cutting edge which, if not driven in cleanly, might create a long cut inside the carp's mouth. I have never used a chisel point on a hook larger than a size 6 for this reason. I have never noticed these long cuts inside the mouths of hooked carp. But the very thought that they might occur is sufficient to prevent me from sharpening large hooks in this way.

In 1967 I began using some hooks called 'low-water salmon hooks' for dense weedbed-fishing. I think Jack Hilton brought these hooks to the carp angler's notice in his great book *Quest for Carp*. Of course I had no way of knowing that Jack was using the same

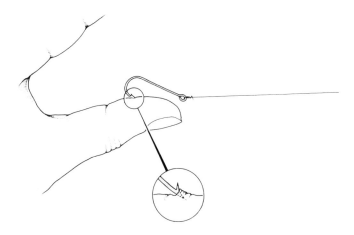

Figure 22 Standard untreated hook pulled into thumb showing tissue build-up in front of barb. The inset shows an enlargement of this – note near-vertical barb face

hooks, my choice was based purely on my local tackle-dealer's recommendation. I had gone to him looking for some really strong hooks to use with my S/U carp rods and 15 pound lines. He suggested low-water salmon hooks and, after inspecting them, I agreed! I liked the long shank and the looped eye that is bound and held closed by the knot itself, making it as strong as the line. The hooks proved to be exceptionally strong when tested and the long shank made for cleaner hooking and better penetration. It is not generally realized, but the longer the hook shank the greater the amount of striking force which is directly applied to driving the hook point home. The only thing that bothered me was the rather crude barb on these otherwise ideal hooks. It was not long before I decided to make a cutting edge along the barb. This has a double advantage since it also drastically reduces the height of the barb in the same operation. The result is a knife-edge, low-profile barb. When I first began treating barbs in this way I used to finish off the cutting edge, after filing, with a small carborundum stone to produce a smooth, sharp, edge. Later on, after comparing a filed barb with a honed one at high magnification, I came to the conclusion that the cutting edge along the barb was better left in a 'filed' state. The file left minute serrations along the sharpened edge, making it a more efficient cutting instrument than the smooth edge. Knife-edge hooks are now available from Mustad and might well have been available when I was experimenting with cutting edges. I have used cutting barbs ever since, finding their penetration and hooking power vastly superior to barbs treated in any other way.

The cutting barb has been criticized by anglers who claim that it is just as likely to cut out of, rather than into, the tissue. I know of one incident where this may, indeed, have happened. A study of the forces acting upon a hook when a strike is made may help clear up any misunderstanding. When a strike is made some of the force generated on the line is used in trying to pull the hook along, rather than into, the tissue of the fish. The angle of attack is reduced as the hook shank is lengthened. More of the force is then diverted to the hook point although this, in turn, leads to shallower hook penetration. The length of the hook shank needs to be within reasonable limits. If it looks unnaturally long anglers are reluctant to use such a hook, although it is doubtful whether a carp would be put off. Fortunately, a reduced angle of attack can be obtained by bending the hook point towards the shank reducing the gap, or gape as it is

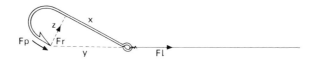

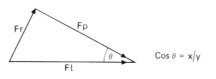

$\cos \theta = x/y$

on sample hook:

x = 16mm
y = 18mm
Cosθ = 8/9
θ = 28°
Fp = Fl Cosθ = 8/9 Fl

Figure 23 It can be shown that if *x* is increased relative to *z* the factor (i.e. 8/9) increases and the force F_r pulling the hook out of the fish is reduced.

A practical example using the factor obtained for a sample hook showed that if a force F_l of 4½ pounds was present on the line, the force at the hook point F_p would be equal to 4 pounds and the rejection force pulling the hook out (F_r) would be ½ pound.

A hook with a shank length longer than the sample would result in more of the force available being used to drive the hook in, while a shorter shank than the sample would increase the force F_r pulling the hook out

sometimes called. This slightly reduces the hooking power of the hook, but increases its penetration. Now, if you try to marry the two features – cutting barb and reduced angle of attack – in the same hook you can expect trouble, for both are modifications that are not readily compatible. This was the case I mentioned earlier where the barb cut out, and not into, the tissue. Here the hook point had been bent towards the shank by an excessive amount, reducing the angle of attack considerably – and the hook had a cutting barb as well! When you drastically reduce the entry angle the hook is liable to take only a small, shallow, hold in the tissue. The point still puckers up the flesh in front of it and, with a shallow attack angle, it drives straight through the small 'hill' of tissue with the minimum of effort. Consider then the effect of a cutting barb used under these hooking conditions. It very neatly cuts away the shallow hold that is obtained as the thin layer of tissue slides over the sharpened edge of the barb.

The angler should first decide the depth of hook penetration he requires for his particular type of fishing and then choose a suitable hook. A hook with a shallow entry angle, compressed barb or barbless, is better suited to long-range fishing as it only requires small effort to find sufficient hold. It can be used for any form of carp-fishing in snag-free water but should never be used in conjunction with a cutting barb hook which has had its gape appreciably reduced. For 'tree' swims, thick weedbed swims or any snaggy swims where it is often necessary to hold a hooked fish hard, use a standard round-bend hook with a cutting barb. The angle of attack in a standard hook is fairly steep, facilitating the deep penetration necessary to cope with these swim conditions. This is where a cutting barb comes into its own, parting the tissue behind the point and allowing easy entry of the barb and thick hook wire. There is no disputing the efficiency of a cutting barb, particularly where big hooks, used at ranges of up to 30 yards, are involved. Under such conditions I have often landed carp on a size 2 hook and found they were double-hooked. The hook has penetrated on the strike and, during the fight, the hook point has gone right through the lip, turned and re-penetrated the lip in another place. When this happens the fish should be unhooked by cutting the line and easing the hook out by gripping it at the bend. The two basic rules can be summed up as follows. For shallow hooking, requiring little strike force, use hooks with low attack angles and with reduced barb profile or no barb at all. For deep hooking use standard, round-bend, hooks with a cutting-barb to assist penetration.

Anyone who has experimented with pulling hooks into different materials soon realizes the problems involved. When you start looking at the angle at which a hook hangs when attached to the line and the force available to drive it downwards, against the resistance of the barb, it is a wonder that full penetration ever occurs. The first thing you notice, as you stick a hook into any material, is that the barb is on the wrong side of the hook. Instead of being sited on the leading-edge of the bend, it ought to be on the trailing or reverse side. Moving the barb 180 degrees from the 'inside' to 'outside' position has several advantages. Firstly, there is no barb to present a near-vertical face to the 'ripple' of flesh pushed up in front of the point – just a smooth metal surface that allows easy entry. Secondly, as the tension applied on the hook is increased, the elastic qualities of flesh create a hole behind the point of entry. This allows free

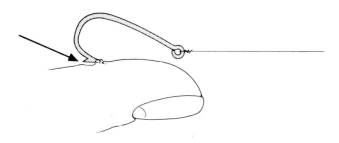

Figure 24 Enlargement of reverse or outside barb concept. Note that tissue 'hill' has no barb to overcome and that the barb gains free entry via hole left by tissue displacement (arrowed)

access for the barb without extra effort. I saw these double advantages in 1970 and modified some number 2 Mustads so that the barb was on the outside of the bend. Before modifying the hooks I had a word with a metallurgist friend who advised me of the possible short-comings of treating hooks in this manner.

When steel is softened in a normal atmosphere it oxidizes, causing pieces to flake-off, and making the material thinner. There is also a possibility of the wire changing in character from the original specification. To overcome this the softening and re-hardening would have to be carried out in a strictly-controlled atmosphere. The average bloke is not likely to have a controlled furnace in his kitchen. But, according to my expert friend, this oxidization was unlikely to cause serious problems as long as the heavier-gauge wire hooks, like size 2s, were treated. With this advice I went ahead and found that softening and re-shaping the hooks to an outside barb offered no problems. When I came to re-hardening the hooks I ran into difficulties. Many of them were too soft or too brittle, resulting in only a small number of usable ones from a given batch.

This high failure rate worried me, so I consulted my friend again to find out where I was going wrong. The following is a combination of my method of tackling the job and my friend's advice.

When you try to soften a thin wire hook the obvious way is to heat it over a gas flame or blowlamp until the hook becomes red hot. After it has cooled you are rather surprised to find that the hook is still hard and not easy to bend. I realized that the thin wire was cooling too fast and looked for a way to overcome the problem. One alternative was to use a shallow tin lid with a quarter-inch layer of 'Polyfilla' in the bottom. The hooks are placed on this layer of powder and another layer of similar thickness is placed on top of them. The whole lot is then heated until the Polyfilla glows red-hot. It is then allowed to cool naturally. I found the hooks were then quite soft, being easy to bend, and that only a very small amount of oxidization had taken place. My metallurgical friend confirmed that this was a good method as it slowed down the cooling rate and, to a point, supplied a crude form of controlled atmosphere to help reduce oxidization.

The next problems to overcome were in the hardening and tempering of the hooks. This was where my metallurgist friend's advice was invaluable.

He suggested that after the hooks had been re-shaped with the barb facing outwards they should be individually heated until red hot and then dropped, as quickly as possible, into a bowl of water. You must have the water close to the heating device. Do not try taking a heated hook to water some yards away – it will cool before you get there. When the hooks have been dropped in water they are very hard and brittle, breaking at a touch, so do not try bending them at this stage.

Then comes the trickiest part of the whole operation – tempering the hook. The hooks must be tempered until they are in their original tough, springy, state. This means re-heating them so they are neither too soft nor too hard. Obtaining the correct temper by heating them over a flame is a hit-and-miss affair. To obtain more consistent results, my friend suggested that the tempering be done in a domestic oven. He calculated that the hooks would be correctly tempered if they were 'cooked' for half an hour at 200 degrees Centigrade. This works out at just under 400 degrees if your oven is marked with the Fahrenheit temperature scale. Results became far more consistent with this method, although some slight adjustment of temperature and 'cooking' time may be necessary to arrive at the best possible temper.

Many anglers will not be sufficiently interested in the advantages offered by the outside barb to bother with modifying standard hook patterns. However, I know from correspondence on the subject that most carp anglers are sufficiently interested to spend a few hours experimenting with the idea. This sort of experiment is ideal for winter nights or close-season periods, providing hours of absorbing work.

I have found that the outside barb hooks have terrific hooking power and I have never had a carp slip the hook while using them. Their only disadvantage is that they can only be used in the larger sizes. It is frequently necessary, during the summer, to scale down bait and hook sizes to tempt a carp. A No. 2 hook is particularly limited under these conditions, particularly if the lake bottom is very soft. Particle baits, like sweetcorn, are often fished with one or two seeds on a No. 2 or 4 hook. But the situation is different when you have to present one piece of bait in an area frequented by carp. With particle baits you saturate an area, placing your bait among the free offerings. The chances are that a carp would not even notice a 2/0 sized hook under these conditions. Presenting a small bait at long range is a different proposition. It is virtually impossible to saturate a small area effectively at long range and a big hook will be too conspicuous. I am certain that hooks with outside barbs would be invaluable to carp anglers if the hooks could be manufactured in a wide range of sizes. This hook, used with a cutting barb, offers secure, deep, hooking with absolutely no chance of the cutting barb doing anything other than assisting penetration. The first decent fish I caught on such a hook was a 12 pounder. It was hooked, an inch inside the right-hand side of its mouth, at a range of 45 yards. The hook had driven straight through the tissue, emerged outside and turned, giving a double hook hold that had no possible chance of failing.

Testing the penetrative qualities of various hook modifications has some limitations. The peculiar, elastic, resilience of tissue is hard to re-create and many of my first tests were carried out by sticking a hook into my thumb. You have to be a masochist to put up with this for very long and, in any case, no true comparative figures can be obtained for complete penetration. I stood outside a fishmonger's one day looking at the cod laid on the marble slab. A cod's head would offer an ideal test-bed for hook penetration tests and I mulled over how I would rig up the test equipment. It was no good, though, I just could not face what was entailed. To secure the head would have meant driving a 6 inch nail straight through it to hold it to the test bench. The thought of repeated tests, all carried out with a pair of large eyes, clouded in death and apparently watching every move, was more than I could stand. But reasoning out what was required from the tests showed that there was no need to go to these extremes. The aim of the tests was to compare the force involved to pull a hook beyond the barb. It did not really matter what material was used providing only comparison force was being sought. I used the same hooks for all the tests – Mustad No. 2s of the No. 7947 pattern. These are long-shank, forged, round-bend hooks. I used them in four different forms: standard, unsharpened, condition as bought; a cutting-barb with reduced barb profile and honed point; outside cutting barb; barbless with honed point.

The first tests were tried with a rubber compound material and proved to be inconclusive. The material seemed to tear at the same tension no matter which hook was being tested. For the second test I used some good-quality cork and for the third test some cork–rubber compound material. Both tests provided some useful information and are detailed in the table.

Pull required to sink hook down to the bend (pounds)

Hook type	Cork	Cork–rubber compound
Standard unsharpened	6·3	6·3
Outside barb	3·3	4·5
Cutting barb	2·8	3·17
Barbless	3·3	4·5

Comparison of hook types

The tests were carried out in a dry state. Under fishing conditions, the less dense tissue of the fish's mouth and its extra lubrication would mean less effort would be needed to achieve the same degree of penetration.

I also carried out some strike simulation tests to compare standard, unsharpened, hooks with low-profile cutting barbs. I used a measured length of nylon line with a hook tied on one end and a stop on the other. A sliding weight on the line was released from measured positions. It dropped down the line, hit the stop and drove the hook into the test material. The weight had to be dropped only once to drive the cutting barb hooks fully home. Four or five drops were needed before the standard, unsharpened, hooks achieved the same amount of penetration. These results are not surprising. It is logical that a lower barb, with reduced cross section, will require less effort to achieve full penetration. Yet to find such improvement after a little work with a file was encouraging.

The test figures show that the cork–rubber compound material is the denser of the two, as more effort is needed to drive the hook into it. The test on the standard hook, where the two test figures were identical, shows that an untreated hook relies on tearing the material apart to allow barb penetration. These figures are the mean of several, measured pulls. The cutting barb actually severed the material and the figures show that the cork severed more easily than did the cork–rubber compound sample, which had some of the elastic, resilient, qualities of tissue.

The test results of the outside-barb and barbless hooks might surprise a few people. The tests gave me a chance to see exactly what happens when hook penetration takes place. With the majority of round-bend hooks the pulling force involved is dispersed, evenly, along the leading-edge of the hook point. As both hooks had the same profile at this point penetration was obtained by equal amounts of force. But the outside-barb hook has an added advantage. No extra force is needed to drive the barb home and, once home, it provides extra security. Unlike the barbless hook it ensures the hook will not fall out should the line go slack when a fish is hooked. Under most conditions the angler will do his utmost to avoid a slackening of line while playing a fish. But there are times, such as when a fish becomes snagged, when he has no alternative. Under these conditions a barb is a definite advantage, even though carp will eventually rid themselves of even barbed hooks.

In the case of the cutting-barb hook it is vital that only the third of the barb nearest the shank is specially filed to give it a cutting edge. If this is done the point of the hook will enter the tissue and

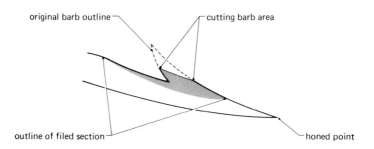

Figure 25   Enlargement of cutting barb principle

overcome the tendency to pull forward, making a cut along the tissue. Only when the hook is well set and pushing downward will the cutting barb begin to work, easing a path through the tough tissue for the increasingly thick hook wire. For this reason I like to see a long, low-angled, barb on a hook. The short, high-angled, barb hooks tend to open up a deep, shallow, cut instead of sinking into the fish's mouth when the barbs are filed to a cutting edge.

When I refer to 'deep hooking' I don't mean hooking a fish in the back of the throat or gullet, as in pike-fishing. The terms deep and shallow hooking refer only to the angle of attack at which the hook enters the fish's tissue. The steeper the angle of entry, the deeper will be the hold if full penetration takes place. The shallower the angle, the less secure the hold. The wise angler will choose a hook to suit the swim he is fishing. If it is the old heave-ho technique you are better off with round-bend deep hookers. If it is a more delicate style of fishing where 4 or 5 pound lines are adequate, then a light hook-hold is permissible and shallow hook-hold will be adequate.

I have seen carp anglers using dozens of different types of hook patterns bent to every conceivable angle to reflect the angler's individual views on hook patterns. This is good, for it shows that the angler is thinking about his fishing and trying to put his ideas into practice – but for this there would be no advancement at all. Yet hook-manufacturers have been making hooks for hundreds of years and in that time must have learned most of all there is to know about hook design. It is reasonable to assume that the old, round-bend, straight-shank hook would have disappeared years ago if there had been any real value in bending the shank at one angle or another.

The most common example of hook modification is to bend the point towards the shank to get lighter and easier penetration. So doing reduces the hooking potential because the gap between point and shank is smaller. The easier penetration has been obtained at the expense of some hooking power. It would be more sensible to use a smaller hook with thinner wire and corresponding gap distance which in turn would aid easier penetration. A thin wire hook is not much good for a 'tree' swim, but it is surprising how much stress a small hook will take when driven home correctly. For years I have regularly used size 8 and 10 hooks and, on many occasions, have applied maximum pressure on the hook-hold with my $2\frac{1}{2}$ pound test-curve rod without the hook giving way. There is no magic about this. It is simply because the hooks have been tested before fishing and have penetrated properly, right up to the hook-bend. It takes tremendous effort to straighten or break a hook – even a small one – when it is correctly driven in. I am sure that many fish lost through hook failure, particularly when large hooks are concerned, are lost simply because the hook has not penetrated correctly. The whole of the stress is placed on the still-exposed bend.

For general carp fishing at ranges of up to 45 yards the type of hook used is not particularly important, provided that it has been sharpened. At greater range the hook becomes more important and must be really sharp with some barb reduction for clean penetration. Many anglers believe that even if the barb does not penetrate on the strike it will be pulled into the fish's mouth during the ensuing fight. Some even go as far as to say a hook never penetrates fully on the strike. Who can argue? My own experience suggests that there is no substitute for a clean, hard strike. I have lost very few fish when the solid thump of contact has stopped my rod half-way through a strike. Like most carp anglers I have lost my share of carp but on the strike and not through a faulty hook. It would be nice if every run was matched by a perfect strike. Perfecting the perfect strike might be possible if every run was identical. But they are not and it is nearly impossible to guarantee sound hooking under all conditions. Losing a certain proportion of fish during a fight is inevitable and not necessarily attributable to bad angling. It happens to us all at times. The only thing to do is to experiment with different hook sizes or types of rod and line to try to minimize these losses. To lose carp through hook failure is much more serious. When this happens the angler must blame himself and accept that the loss could have been avoided had he taken the right precautions before tying on the hook.

12 The bait syndrome

In the early years of carp-fishing, thirty years ago, many different baits were successfully tried by anglers. Carp are omnivores and not particularly fussy about their diet. Provided that they have not been caught too often on a given bait, they seem prepared to accept anything from pure vegetable to raw meat. The old Carpcatchers Club established that they could be caught on a wide range of quite unusual baits. One has the impression, though, that many of the baits mentioned in the earlier carp books were never taken seriously, or the anglers in question would not have continued to use and advise bread, worms and potato. It is understandable that anglers in those early days were relatively unwilling to experiment with new baits. Little was known about the species and anglers preferred to spend their precious sessions fishing with proven baits. Potatoes were, of course, a relatively new bait at the time; a poor bait in my humble opinion despite all the carp which they have accounted for over the years. Their only virtue is that unwanted fish left them alone. The situation now is different in that carp are more widespread and more people fish more often for them – so much so that the same carp are frequently caught on the more common baits and soon become suspicious. Carp anglers, having become used to catching carp on a particular bait, soon began to experiment when things got difficult.

Although the early carp-fishing pioneers, to whom we owe so much, knew that carp would eat all manner of things they over-looked the potential of some of the less-used baits. The newer generation of carp anglers, faced with pressure that the pioneers had never known, began to experiment with different bait concepts that became known as 'specials'. Thus the bait syndrome was established and less adventurous anglers saw good carp being caught on baits that were quite obviously not bread, worms or potatoes. The heavily-fished southern waters appear to have suffered worse from the bait secrecy which developed and we heard of baits being stolen while anglers were playing fish; binoculars, formerly used for fish-spotting, were now used for 'bait-spotting' as the more progressive anglers caught carp on specials. Since that period there have been two significant bait advances. One took the ordinary baits, some of which were mentioned in the bait chapters of the earlier books, and used them in a way that had not been tried before; the other was a bait concept so unique that the arguments still rumble around as I write this book. Two anglers must receive full credit for providing the general body of carp anglers with these advances. I feel very fortunate and privileged that both Rod Hutchinson and Fred Wilton have agreed to write of their respective experiences with particle baits and high-protein bait. Because both gave unselfishly of their hard-won information, my own comment on baits will be confined to a small section at the end of this chapter.

First then, Rod Hutchinson, who has used many different sorts of particle baits and made exceptional catches from a variety of ponds and lakes. Here he presents information not previously published and gathered from the sort of waters that you or I might fish any weekend. It makes fascinating reading.

Particle-bait fishing *by Rod Hutchinson*

During the middle sixties, carp-fishing underwent several changes, the most important being the use of meat- or fat-based 'special' baits and the extensive use of long-range fishing techniques. The new baits, often used at long range, opened up a number of carp waters where before, few fish had been caught. Hitherto unheard-of catches were made and, quite rightly, both technique and baits received great publicity. There were, however, waters which did not respond to these new bait techniques, waters where the carp seemed well-nigh impossible to catch. The waters which did not produce 'the goods' were usually very clear waters with prolific weed growth and very high concentrations of natural food. Why the specials did not work on these waters is very much a matter of conjecture. It can be said, and has been, that in such waters where the carp have always had plenty of readily available natural food – snails, molluscs and all forms of the aquatic cycle fly life – balls of paste and specials are just not recognized as food. In other waters which do not hold such large amounts of natural food, most things are tried for their edibility. It has even been suggested that carp in some waters are more intelligent than carp in others. I think it more likely that carp in the more barren waters just have to be less cautious in their approach to foodstuffs in order to feed.

It was for the waters saturated with natural food that the particle-bait approach was evolved. In such waters the carp were preoccupied with small natural foodstuffs, such as bloodworm, snails, leeches or various pupae. Ideas had previously been put forward to catch such preoccupied carp, ideas such as nylon stockings filled with bloodworms, or snails used for hookbaits. My main arguments against such ideas are that we are only presuming that the carp are feeding on bloodworm when it could be any of a 101 tiny species of animal life. We do not really know if we are offering the carp the food with which it is preoccupied at the time. Bloodworms do not have individual appeal, they will be found in tight concentrations and taken in by the mouthful. How do you get the carp to your bait? As it has no attraction of its own, you are counting on your hookbait landing in a concentration of bloodworm. Just casting around after bubblers is not really the answer as we cannot be certain our hookbait is right.

The logical answer to it all is to get the carp preoccupied with small foodstuffs of your own. By doing this you are creating your own abundant feeding areas and with the food of your choice. There are a certain amount of small foodstuffs which carp just do not seem to like and no amount of groundbaiting really gets the carp feeding, although occasional fish may turn up. In my experience, green peas, nuts, most citrus fruits such as blackcurrants and redcurrants, are among the foods on which you just cannot get the carp preoccupied. Why I just do not know. Take green peas, for example. When I first thought about their lack of success, the answer appeared simple. Were not fish often killed by the residue from pea vining? Then, lo and behold, I read of roach being caught on peas from swims alongside a canning factory in Ireland! Work that one out if you can. By the same token, it would be easy to blame the citrus fruits for their acid content. But are not sultanas and currants citrus fruits? and both of these work well as particle baits. True, both are dehydrated, but once in water the fruits swell up and must I think have a large acid content. Carp-fishing is full of such inconsistencies which help keep the would-be successful angler on his toes.

Back to baits that do work and the simple theory behind

Rod with a fine pair of upper twenties

particle-bait fishing. My first experiments were with hempseed. I am talking now about what I regard as particle fishing, that is using tiny foodstuffs of the same size which are mopped up like small natural food. I had previously baited up with large baits of the same size such as potatoes and even boiled pullet eggs. But these baits are eaten individually and so receive individual inspection, unlike tiny baits, and so do not come under the same theory as the small baits.

The intention with hempseed was to put in sufficient quantities as to make the seeds a natural food to the water, indeed the most abundant food. Hopefully the carp, when they fed, would become preoccupied with the bait. The intent was to have seeds wherever the carp went to feed, so that every time they took in mouthfuls of mud they would take in seeds and, unlike the lake's natural food, the seeds would be everywhere, not just in pockets and set areas that had to be searched out. Once the fish were feeding on the baits, your groundbaiting was narrowed down into concentrations of your choice. That is the area of your swims.

When I first told people I was trying hempseed, I was asked the usual question: 'Do the carp think the seeds are snails?' The answer is: 'I don't think they do.' They are merely eating a readily available foodstuff. You might as well say when a carp eats snails it thinks it is eating hempseed. An angler I respect once told me he thought fish ate cheese because they took it as a piece of mussel flesh. Again you might as well say when a fish eats mussel it thinks it is eating a big piece of cheese.

The point I am trying to make is that carp and fish in general will eat all manner of foodstuffs just because they are edible and presented in a natural manner. You do not have to pretend or try to imitate some natural foodstuffs. Once enough food has entered a water, it will be regarded as a natural food, in its own right. I am sure this is what happens on many of our match rivers where, I believe, maggots and casters are looked upon by the fish as natural food.

Looking back on my first experiments it is clear that I started at the wrong end of the scale as far as bait sizes are concerned. Between hempseed and conventional-sized baits are hundreds of readily available foodstuffs which fit the particle theory, i.e. all the same size and flavour. Baits ranging from the size of broad beans, going down through smaller beans such as haricots and soyas. Various types of peas (not green) such as chic and maple peas. Sultanas and currants, sweetcorn, macaroni, etc. The list is vast, and one point soon emerges after fishing the baits for a time. The more visual the bait, the quicker it is picked up by the fish and the shorter its reign as a successful bait. I think this is because the larger a bait the more visual it is. But the larger baits are more like conventional baits and soon come under suspicion. A bait's visual appeal depends on two things, its size or colour. Obviously the size of baits like broad beans and kidney beans makes them highly visible and it would appear that smaller baits in 'warm' colours are also highly visible. I have had greater success from beans dyed various colours from yellow to red than with the natural, white, beans. To our eyes the natural white would appear highly visual. Another inconsistency, or is the carp's reaction to colour different from ours?

Contrary to popular belief, baits which have visual qualities do not usually need the mass groundbaiting I have recommended for other particle baits. Indeed the baits regularly catch carp the first time they are used with no more than a pint or two of the given bait scattered around the hookbait. Mass groundbaiting of the entire lake certainly would not have any detrimental effect, it is just unnecessary. To be successful without mass baiting, you must be fishing swims that hold carp or which carp frequent regularly. Otherwise there is nothing to draw the fish to your hookbait.

The particle technique was originally intended for big fish on hard waters. Now it is used on all manner of carp waters including the so-called 'hungry' waters. On these waters, where the aim is just to catch carp and not try to sort out the bigger specimens, I would opt for the visual particle baits every time. In my opinion, carp in such waters depend to a very large extent on sight-feeding, and so should be quickly on to the baits.

The more visual a bait the shorter its success is likely to last. How long it is successful will depend upon the particular water. The hungrier the water, the longer a bait is likely to last. For example, within three months of sweetcorn being used in Redmire, a water with prolific weed growth and food stocks, carp were actually bolting at the sight of the corn. At Cuttle Mill Fishery, a hungry water, sweetcorn still turns up occasional fish three years after it was first used and carp still twitch at most sweetcorn hookbaits.

On the harder, clear, waters the more visual type of particle bait will soon be fished out and smaller, dark-coloured, foods, groundbaited in large quantities, will be the order of the day. There are hundreds of baits suitable for this mass bait-fishing technique, the largest being maple peas, going down through various peppers; a large range of dari seeds and a huge array of cereal crops. Theoretically all the baits should be equally successful because we are now providing our own natural food and not appealing by visual qualities. But results have shown some mass baits appeal more than others. I do not know, for example, of anyone having really outstanding success using a mass bait of wheat, although buck wheat and malting barley have, on occasions, produced some really good catches. Yet to the human eye and senses of smell and taste, there appears little difference.

One problem with these baits is whether to cook them or not. I know that carp will eat them either cooked or uncooked. Although carp are well equipped with grinding teeth, capable of smashing snail and mussel shells and all manner of materials used in caddis jackets, I am inclined to think that cooking does add that little bit extra. Admittedly, when using the mass method, the cooked baits will be in identical numbers as uncooked baits and will be found by the same method of feeding – grubbing and bubbling. But it may be that cooking brings out additional odours which enhance the pre-occupation. This may explain why some of the baits work better than others. My best catches with maples and mini maples have been taken when I was using bait which had been cooked three or four days previously – bait which was giving off a smelly, milky, substance. Whether success is due to this smell, or because by the time the smelly milk is given off there has been a build-up of groundbait, I cannot be certain. I do know I feel more confident when the bait is smelling a bit.

The techniques, method of groundbaiting and hooking arrangements used with the baits, have been well covered in the angling press. What has not been discussed is why and when to use certain baits, once it has been decided whether a water will respond better to dark mass baits or the more visual ones. Say, for example, we decide to use the visual baits – which one should we choose given that none has already been fished out? The answer lies in the nature of the bottom of the lake and the corresponding type of feeding. Take two of the lakes I fish. On the first the main feeding areas are in shallow water less than 3 feet deep. The bottom is covered in filamentous algae which is up to 18 inches thick. The carp here feed mainly off the top of this algae, taking in mouthfuls of weed, snails and other animal life that lives amongst this weed. Four different particle baits were used on this lake before it became apparent just what type of bait was needed. Two of the baits, sweetcorn and red kidney beans, were successful. The other two, chic peas and maple peas, were not and caught no fish at all even though they were proven baits on other waters.

The reason for these results was the relative buoyancy of the baits. The sweetcorn, being light and holding a lot of liquid, rested on top of the algae as did the red kidney beans with their large flat flanks and large liquid content. The baits were readily found in the abundance needed to create preoccupation with them. The denser maples and chic peas, which are bought dehydrated and have to be thoroughly soaked before they will hold any liquid, had very little buoyancy. The majority of the bait went straight through the filamentous weed and was found in insufficient numbers to create preoccupation.

The second lake is actually the reverse being, to a large extent, of fair depth, 6 feet and more. Weed growth is also prolific but the weed grows straight up from the bottom, breaking and spreading out at the surface like 'dead men's fingers'. In this water the carp feed extensively among the roots of this weed, a situation that calls for a dense bait which will go through the surface weed barrier and get down in numbers to the carp beneath. In this water, where sweetcorn had failed, maple peas proved the ideal and successful bait.

It can be seen that to get the best from particle baits, much thought must be put into just which bait to use. It is not just a question of using a bait which has not been used before. On any one water there may be many different fishing conditions such as swims with silt, clay, gravel or pebble bottoms. White beans, which would show up on a silt bottom, would hardly show up on a pebble bottom. So, as with all baits, think what it is like down below before deciding which one to use. When using the tiny mass baits remember that a cooked bait will be more buoyant than an uncooked one. Do not forget either that maggots will work their way through weed to the bottom, while casters will rest on the weed.

I sincerely believe that particle baits will bring success on all waters. Their success is based on the necessity of introducing sufficient amounts into the water to provoke preoccupation among the feeding carp. The greater the problems in doing this, the more limited the angler's success. If no success is had after mass ground-baiting, then the wrong bait is being used. If the bait needs certain properties or characteristics and no natural equivalent is available then it is perfectly feasible for the angler to manufacture his own – a 'special' with a carefully controlled colour and buoyancy. The bait is then presented in particular form.

Some people have doubted my claim that full preoccupation is at times achieved. I first wrote about this state when most of my fishing was being done at Redmire, which I can now see is not a fair indicator on which to base or generalize views on carp-fishing. The lake is natural and the fish naturally bred. However the water has none of the problems the average carpman finds at his local lake – overfishing, noise, nuisance species and waterfowl. It holds more big carp than any water I know, so it is very difficult to relate what happens at the mecca of carp-fishing to the average water. Since I first wrote about preoccupation I have fished a large number of club and day-ticket carp waters, and I still firmly believe that full pre-occupation can be achieved.

In four consecutive visits to a carp water where you would usually be happy to get a fish and overjoyed if you caught a couple, I took five to $17\frac{1}{4}$ pounds; six to $12\frac{1}{4}$ pounds; ten to $14\frac{1}{4}$ pounds; and four to $12\frac{1}{4}$ pounds. On another occasion I hooked the same fish four times and lost it. I was having difficulty in keeping the hook point clear, before I finally landed the fish. Having watched carp root, almost up to their tails, as they felt for bait and having seen a carp swim on its side to get under a flat boulder to get a visible particle, I am convinced that the carp can become preoccupied with particle baits to the exclusion of all other foodstuffs. The preoccupation may be short lived because the bait runs out or the weather changes and puts the carp off feed, but I am sure it does take place.

The smaller the bait, the more preoccupied the carp seem to get with it. I do not usually like to relate human behaviour with fish, but in this case I can see a great similarity. It is rather like a human eating peanuts. He would have to eat an awful lot to be filled up as would a carp feeding on small seeds. A human would be full up after eating one steak and a carp after eating two or three potatoes.

A carp might eat two potatoes before it is hooked on the third one it takes. If it is feeding on seeds, which it sifts out of the mud like natural food, it will consume dozens, perhaps hundreds, before it takes those on the angler's hook. Which bait would be treated next time with the most caution? I am quite sure with the tiny, mass-baited seeds, a fish does not know what it has been hooked on. There is nothing visual to which it can relate the experience of being hooked. I am certain that this is why the larger the bait the shorter its period of success.

Obviously a fish, feeding on tiny seeds, could pick up the hookbait first time. But the odds against this must be 1000 to 1.

Many anglers are concerned with the amounts of particle baits fed into carp lakes and that these baits are frequently uncooked. Some think that both could prove dangerous to a carp's health. I understand the concern but I believe the fears are groundless.

The amounts of tiny massbaited seeds used by anglers must be compared with the baits previously used by carp anglers. Back in the early sixties it was quite usual to bait a swim with half a dozen mashed loaves. This amount of bread is easily equal to a couple of buckets of seeds. An angler might go to extremes and put in half a hundredweight of seeds. This may sound a massive amount but it is nothing compared with the amount of bait used in an average match. True, most matches are held on flowing rivers, but bait will settle somewhere, be it locks, bends, gravel bars or depressions. These rivers have been under this pressure week in, week out, for years without wholesale fish fatalities being put down to overfeeding.

The fears about uncooked baits all seem groundless as all the natural food of fish is uncooked. I believe a carp's throat teeth are capable of crushing all the foodstuffs I would recommend for particle baits and some, such as maples or chic peas, can be really hard. It may well be that not all the baits are crushed by the teeth and that many are swallowed whole. But any undigested food would be passed out again as a carp's digestive system is a continuous process. To quote Fred J. Taylor: 'Hard maize seems to come out pretty much the way it went in.' I am however convinced that the majority of hard food is first crushed. The carp has evolved over millions of years and those throat teeth have a specific purpose – to crush hard food items, namely snails, caddis and molluscs. I have kept carp in sacks after capture and many of them have regurgitated food. All this food, although often still recognizable as a specific item, has always been crushed. Much of it has also been uncooked which suggests the fish have had no problem in crushing even the hardest items.

Another fear which I believe is unfounded is that hard baits could swell inside a fish's stomach. For one thing any baits which do get by the throat teeth without being crushed are just not in the stomach long enough to expand – even if the stomach was full of the water needed to make this happen. Even if the process of digestion is not as continuous as we think and that the baits have been eaten faster than they can be digested, a situation which I do believe occurs at times, it is highly unlikely that baits will be in the stomach as long as an hour. But baits need several hours of soaking before they begin to swell. It should also be remembered that the gastric juices and enzymes in the stomach aim to break down food rather than swell it up.

I still have a preference for cooked, rather than uncooked, baits. But only because I feel there is more chance of catching fish with them. The smells and scents of cooked baits enable the carp to home in on them so much more quickly. The sooner a fish goes from one mouthful of seeds to another, the sooner preoccupation is achieved.

I cannot finish this chapter without giving my opinion on the tackle set-up used for fishing particle baits. Another carp angler has claimed: 'Gorging is a problem with particle baits.' What he should have said is: 'Gorging is a problem with particle baits if the wrong terminal tackle set-up is used.'

The whole feeding pattern of a carp eating particle baits is entirely different from the way it feeds on conventional baits. Conventionals, such as potatoes and specials, are taken individually and so receive individual inspection. If the conventional hookbait is to behave in the same way as the free offerings, the carp must be able to pick it up and take it into its mouth without feeling resistance. All previous tackle set-ups (other than tight line twitcher set-ups) were evolved with this in mind. The use of these set-ups such as free-lining, long-link legering, and sometimes even float-fishing will, if used with particle baits, result in gorging, and the hook being bitten off. It is common to hear of anglers receiving nothing more than a few twitches and, when winding in, finding their hooks gone. To overcome this the majority of anglers do one of two things, both of which come from the conditioning of using conventional baits most of the time.

They either try to omit resistance completely, by free-lining or lengthening hook lengths and leger links, in order to get better bite registration; or they go on to a twitcher set-up in order to hit those twitchers. What usually happens is that the first method produces even more bite-offs, while the second produces lots of foul-hooked, or pricked, fish. The frenzied way in which carp feed on particle baits makes it folly to strike at twitches, as fish are continually going over and under lines, catching them with their tails and dorsals. The angler has created a highly concentrated feeding area with his bait somewhere in the middle of it. It stands to reason that he will get lots of twitches which are not bites.

The only solution to this problem is to leave twitches alone completely. Use a terminal set-up which will create resistance when a fish takes in your bait and so frighten it into bolting to produce a run. In the last three seasons, using these set-ups for all my carp fishing, I have suffered no bite-offs whatsoever. The set-up is a $\frac{1}{4}$ or $\frac{3}{8}$ ounce bomb stopped between 3 inches and a foot from the hook. If the bottom is fairly weedy, the bomb may be on a link which is never longer than 2 inches. If the bottom is clear the bomb is put directly on the line. Should the water be one where bite-offs occur regularly or where the hook is found well down the throat even when a bomb is used directly on the line, then use a drilled-bullet or a coffin lead directly on the line and no more than 3 inches from the hook.

It all sounds crude, I know, but these set-ups produce the results. Although it is totally alien to previous thinking on carp set-ups, do not forget that it is only during the last few years that carp anglers have accepted the use of any lead, at all, on the line.

To sum up let me say that particle baits can bring spectacular results without danger to carp waters, but they have no magic ingredients which guarantee fish. To be successful and to realize the potential of the baits, the angler must put as much thought to his angling as he would with any other bait. There are no short-cuts to consistent success. But, if the right bait has been chosen and the baiting-up done properly, I believe particle baits will catch carp from any water in the country. For while I could put forward reasons why conventional baits may be refused I can see no logical reason why well-presented particles should be. The idea is to create a food carp accept as natural. That involves putting in enough of the tiny mass baits to make it so.

I think everyone will agree that an awful lot of thought and practical fishing experience has gone into the above account. Once more I must thank Rod for his contribution – a contribution so expert that I could not possibly have hoped to match it with my limited knowledge of particle baits.

Now to my second guest writer, Fred Wilton, who has had ten years of experience in the development of high protein baits.

Fred's theory about high protein baits was first brought to the carp angler, some years ago, in a series of articles published in *The Carp* – the British Carp Study Group quarterly magazine. The articles set the carp-angling world on fire and since then the subject of high-protein bait has continued to cause controversy between the angling world and the professionals who have dismissed Fred's theory as rubbish. There is one thing that no one can deny. The people who have followed Fred's advice are continually writing to thank him for the big fish they have caught using high-protein baits. The concept was unique when introduced and here Fred tells the story behind it, giving enough information about proteins and vitamins to allow anyone to make and use the baits.

High-nutritive-value baits *by Fred Wilton*

The use of high-protein baits is based on my belief that fish have an ability lacking in humans, namely the ability to recognize the nutritive value of foods they have eaten and digested, and that this ability is combined with an instinctive urge to eat the most nutritious foods available to them. This area of fish behaviour is not well documented and large numbers of people, including some well-known anglers, find it impossible to accept my ideas. I can only say that throughout more than ten years of experimenting with these baits my observations have only further convinced me that the original concept was correct.

Although these baits are usually referred to as 'high-protein' baits, it would be more accurate to think of them as 'high-nutritive-value' baits, because to be effective the bait must be digested and absorbed by the carp. It is the final nutrient absorbed from the gut that will decide the degree of effectiveness of the bait, rather than its original protein content. Most people talk of protein as though it was one substance but this is not so. There are a very large number of proteins, each different from the other, but all being made up of simpler compounds called amino-acids. Not all of the twenty-two amino-acids are found in every protein; some lack one, some lack several and the amounts of each amino-acid can very widely from one type of protein to another.

During digestion the links joining the amino-acids together are attacked by enzymes produced by the digestive system. The protein is gradually broken down into its constituent amino-acids. These are then absorbed through the wall of the gut and joined together again to form body proteins. But, as the body proteins will not be made up of exactly the same amount of each amino-acid as the food protein, the 'change-over' will not be 100 per cent. This change-over is helped, to a certain extent, because almost half the amino-acids are interchangeable, so that a surplus of one can be broken down by the body and reassembled to make up a deficiency of another. But the rest, the so-called essential amino-acids, are not interchangeable and can only be used in the quantities found in the food protein.

The degree to which a food protein will make body proteins is called the 'biological value'. So that a protein which will replace an equal amount of body protein is said to have a biological value of 100, whereas one that would only replace half of its own weight of body protein would have a biological value of only 50 and so on. We can see that it is quite possible for two baits, both with the same percentage of protein, to be completely different in effectiveness if the protein of one is of a higher biological value than the other. Therefore, if we are to make the best possible use of this type of bait, we must not only aim at a high protein content, but also see to it that the protein is of high biological value too.

Unfortunately very little research appears to have been done on the biological values of proteins in respect of the carp, so really accurate assessments are not currently possible. However, as a general rule, proteins of animal origin have higher biological values than those from vegetable sources. Where possible then, we should make more use of animal proteins rather than vegetable proteins; if vegetable proteins must be used, then we should favour those like soya-bean protein, which has a relatively high biological value, in preference to proteins like gluten which are fairly low.

The high percentages of protein I include in baits has caused a fair amount of controversy. Some people argue that such a high-protein diet is not needed by carp, while others believe it may even be harmful. Yet if we look at the role that proteins play in all forms of animal life, their importance is obvious. Proteins are essential parts of every living organism and all animal tissues, with the exception of fats, are composed of proteins of one sort or another. All the actions of the body, whether voluntary like walking or swimming, or involuntary such as breathing, are controlled by enzymes or hormones which are themselves protein based. And whereas proteins can be broken down by the body and used for energy if insufficient fat or carbohydrate is available for this purpose, the body has no

One of Fred Wilton's angling companions, Robin Monday, with two chunky carp caught on HP baits – 23 pounds 5 ounces and 19 pounds 12 ounces

means of manufacturing proteins from fats or carbohydrates if they are in excess and protein is in short supply. Because of this I was convinced that if carp were able to recognize the nutrient value of their diet, protein was so important that it was certain to be one of the major areas of recognition. As to the possibility of high protein percentages actually being harmful to carp, I suggest that the natural food of a carp disproves this idea completely, consisting largely of tubifex worms, bloodworms, shrimps, snails and other small water creatures. The importance of these various animals in the carp's diet is shown by the fact that it is the waters where these food forms are found in the greatest numbers that produce the biggest fish. As all of these are animal forms and we know that all animal tissues, with the exception of fat, are composed of protein, we find that the natural diet of a carp is a high-protein diet. It is also interesting to note that as the proteins are of animal origin, the natural diet of a carp is a high-protein one, with the protein being of 'high biological value'.

This then is the diet against which we are competing when we try to persuade a carp to take our baits rather than its natural food. So what else does this food contain besides protein?

As we have seen a very important part of a carp's natural food is made up of living animals and it is a fact that all animals require vitamins in order to live. Differences do occur between species as to those vitamins which can be synthesized by the body and those that must be obtained from the diet. But regardless of whether the vitamins were synthesized or obtained from food, they will be present in the animal's body at the time the carp eats it and so be made available to the carp. Also available will be the minerals the animal contained along with the fat and glycogen which served as the animal's energy store. So when we look closely at a carp's natural food, we find that it is a diet containing a high percentage of high biological value protein; all the vitamins essential to life; plus minerals, fats and a very small percentage of carbohydrate.

In my opinion if we want a bait that will consistently be readily accepted by carp this is the basic specification to which we must work and is, of course, the basis of all high-protein baits. In a properly made high-protein bait we have all the dietary factors of a carp's natural food, but in a form over which we have control. We can decide its shape, size, texture, colour and smell and, if we choose heavily to prebait a given area, we can cause an increase in the food value in that area similar to that which would occur if an explosion of natural food had taken place.

I believe that the greater the nutritive value of the bait the greater is its attraction. The most attractive bait for carp will therefore consist of the optimum amount of all the nutrients: protein, vitamins, fats and carbohydrates, with the protein content having a biological value for carp of 100. This then would be the carp's most preferred food and therefore the Ultimate Bait.

Making high-protein baits has its problems. But I believe that anyone who overcomes these will find the results well worth the effort. Almost all the really effective high-protein baits in use today have a protein content of 60 per cent to 70 per cent and this is almost invariably achieved by using casein in one form or another. Here lies your first problem. Casein is a high-biological-value protein obtained from milk, either by precipitation with an acid or by a process using rennet. This latter process gives rise to rennet casein or as it is more frequently called 'calcium caseinate', which can be obtained from most chemists under the trade name of 'Casilan'. It has two drawbacks. Firstly it is somewhat expensive, and secondly it cannot be used in really large amounts as it tends to thicken the skin of the bait. Acid-precipitated casein is usually sold in minimum quantities of at least one hundredweight and so is usually cheaper than the small brand-name packs. But, unlike Casilan, its quality is not consistent so, in general, I would advise newcomers to stick with Casilan. Later, if you feel like gambling on acid-precipitated casein, here are some of the problems I have come across. Some types work extremely well; some less well; and some not at all. I believe this is caused by differences in manufacture which alter the casein's digestibility as far as carp are concerned. As the bait relies for its effectiveness on the nutrients absorbed by the carp, the less digestible it is the less effective a bait it will be. I know of no hard and fast rules regarding this and even if one lot of casein works well, there is no guarantee that the next batch, from the same supplier, will do the same. At the moment acid-precipitated casein is something of a gamble.

Having found your supply of casein or settled for Casilan you next have to decide what other ingredients to add to it. Firstly, you need a supply of vitamins and minerals. The most widely used for this purpose is 'Equivite', this being a food supplement intended for horses and can be ordered from any large branch of Boots the chemist. The rest of the dry ingredients is a matter of personal choice. But always bear in mind that the higher the protein's biological value, the more effective it will be. Among the ingredients available are the following:

	Protein value (per cent)
Textured vegetable protein	50–60
Soya flour	40
Wheat germ	30
Gluten (sold as gluten powder or wheat gluten)	80

These are all readily available from health food stores. Textured vegetable protein requires grinding into a powder as it comes in fairly hard, large, pieces. This is quite a useful ingredient, made from soya protein, but try to obtain an unflavoured variety such as natural 'Protoveg' so that the final smell of the bait is not interfered with. There is another ingredient I like to use, called 'Lactalbumin' (sometimes spelt Lactalbumen). This is another protein obtained from milk and, like casein or Casilan, it is approximately 90 per cent protein. If you can get it I would recommend its use in conjunction with casein or Casilan, as a mixture of the two has a higher biological value than either on its own. For simplicity always work in 10 ounce totals as this makes it much easier to calculate the approximate percentage of the dry mix. For instance here is the make-up of dry ingredients for a bait I have used with great success in recent years:

Ingredients	Protein content
5 ounces casein (90 per cent protein)	(5 × 90) 450
1 ounce Casilan (90 per cent protein)	90
1 ounce lactalbumin (90 per cent protein)	90
1 ounce gluten (80 per cent protein)	80
1 ounce soya flour (40 per cent protein)	40
1 ounce Equivite –	—
total	750

Divide the total by 10 to obtain approximate protein percentage of the dry mix: 750/10 = approx. 75 per cent protein percentage.

I have set this out in detail so that it is easy to understand how the protein percentage of baits can be calculated. The above could have been improved by replacing the gluten with another ounce of casein, which, although it would have raised the overall protein content by only 1 per cent, would more importantly have raised its biological value. However, the casein being used at the time was very expensive and the above recipe is a compromise. You will notice also that, despite having access to casein, I still include 1 ounce of Casilan in the bait mix. This is done to help bind it, as casein tends to make a somewhat crumbly bait. Gluten is also a very good binding agent but you must bear in mind its lower biological value. If casein is available then it is fairly easy to make baits of up to 76 per cent protein such as: 7 ounces casein; 1 ounce Casilan; 1 ounce soya flour; 1 ounce Equivite. But with only Casilan available the scope is somewhat more limited owing to its tendency to coagulate. It should be possible, though, to make bait mixes of around 60 per cent, such as: 4 ounces Casilan; 4 ounces Protoveg (finely ground); 1 ounce soya flour; 1 ounce Equivite. But remember these are only given as examples and have no particular significance. You can make baits containing all sorts of protein percentage simply by rearranging the ingredients. But always bear in mind that success depends on the nutrient value the carp absorbs.

Having decided on your choice of dry ingredients you now have to decide on a smell factor for your bait. This serves two purposes. Firstly it enables the carp to find your bait more easily and, secondly, it enables the carp to differentiate between your bait and any other. This last point is vital as, when a carp finds one of your baits for the first time, it has no way of knowing that it is a highly nutritious food. It is simply picking it up and eating it out of curiosity – just as it would any other new and apparently edible object. *It is only after digesting and absorbing the bait that the carp will register it as a nutritious food.* And the carp will register a nutritious food with a particular smell. From then on, although the fish will seek out the bait as a rich source of nutrients, it will trace it by its smell and pick up any bait which has that smell. So it is very much in your own interest to ensure that the smell factor you use is one that no one else is likely to use on your water, and to tell only your trusted friends. This is not being unnecessarily secretive – as some people have suggested – it is purely a matter of common sense. The alternative is to establish a good bait only to find your efforts interfered with by someone else groundbaiting with the same smell in an inferior bait. Or worse still, some unscrupulous (pronounced 'unscrupu-louse'!) angler putting the smell into breadpaste and using it on the hook to catch fish at your expense. Believe me both have occurred in the past and once the fish finds that particular-smelling piece of bread is not nutritious you will have to find a new smell factor and start prebaiting all over again.

You now have all your ingredients itemized with the exception of eggs. These are used because baits mixed with eggs and boiled lightly have a skin which stops unwanted fish, such as roach and bream, nibbling them away. The skin also ensures that your bait will remain firm in the water for many hours and, in warm weather, it will remain intact long enough for the products of bacterial action to cause it to float to the surface and so give you some idea of how your groundbait is being received. If you see none on the surface it can mean that the fish are eating it. Eggs are a very nutritious food, so do not be misled, as so many people seem to be, into believing that the high water content in eggs will lower the nutrient value of the finished bait. The effectiveness of the bait depends on the nutritive value of its dry content. With the water removed eggs have a protein content of about 44 per cent. For those who are still worried, this means that a bait whose dry ingredients have a 60 per cent protein content, will still have a protein content of approximately 57 per cent in its finished form when the eggs have been added.

You will probably find that six standard eggs per 10 ounces of dry mix is about right. But, if more are needed to get the right texture for rolling, do not hesitate to use seven or even eight. Mix the dry ingredients together thoroughly and whisk the eggs well. If the smell factor you choose is in a powder form it should be mixed in with the dry ingredients. If it is a liquid it should be whisked in with the eggs. You then mix the whole lot together and roll into balls of whatever size you wish to use. Then put them, a few at a time, into boiling water for approximately one minute to form the skin; longer if you want a tougher skin. It is advisable to put the rolled baits into a sieve or small chip pan basket before putting them into the boiling water. It is then easy to put them all in together and, providing you only cover the bottom and do not pile them up, each one will get identical treatment.

It is essential to prebait with these baits – my own preference being for two or three baitings of say 100 balls, rather than putting in dribs and drabs. Remember that, as these baits are highly nutritious, they are an ideal food for bacteria and therefore go bad very quickly. So always bait up and fish with the freshest baits possible, for the carp will reject them long before you are able to detect there is anything wrong with them, and groundbaiting with 'off' baits will quickly 'spike' your results. If, for any reason, you manage to put the fish off your bait, the easiest remedy is to stop using that particular smell and, still using the same ingredients but with a new smell factor, prebait again. The carp will accept the bait as a totally new and highly nutritious food.

There is another way of using a high-protein bait and this is in a 'floater' form which is presented like floating crust. To do this mix the dry ingredients as for bottom baits but include a level teaspoon of baking powder to the mix. You then mix this with twice the number of eggs, put the mix into a cake tin and bake it in the oven at gas mark 2 for approximately two hours, leaving it to cool in the oven. You should then have what looks like a well-risen cake. If you have not, ask the wife to try instead! When you remove the crust you will find a porous inner, looking something like sponge-rubber, which, cut into pieces like crust, will make an excellent floating bait that will have the same smell as any bottom baits you have been using.

I think there is little else for me to say except that in my own mind I am completely satisfied that high-protein or high-nutritional-value baits, whichever term you prefer to use, have proved very effective in use and have accounted for hundreds of good carp up to well over 30 pounds in weight.

I hope I have cleared up any misunderstandings about the baits and their uses. I also hope that these baits will help the reader to catch more fish and derive more enjoyment from his fishing.

I found Fred's theory and bait ingredient description thoroughly absorbing. Like Rod Hutchinson he has put a tremendous amount of time and thought into the subject. Between them these two anglers have provided a way to success for hundreds of carp anglers and we owe them both our sincere thanks for passing on their respective information.

My approach to the bait scene has, for years, been confined almost entirely to the 'smell' factor. I believe that a carp's sense of smell and taste is much more important than sight under most feeding conditions. I am pleased, therefore, to see that Fred attaches considerable importance to a smell factor in his high-protein baits and that Rod also remarks that he has more confidence in the particle baits when they are smelling a bit and exuding a milky liquid. I have always selected baits primarily for their smell and secondly for food value. This food value aspect had nothing to do with Fred's theory of high nutrition; this never entered my head until I first read of high-protein baits. It just seemed to me that a good bait should smell good, taste good, and give some sort of satisfaction to the fish. The fish would then want to eat it in preference to its regular, natural, diet. I can see now, from Fred's reasoning, that a good smell and taste in a bait like luncheon meat can also mean that it has high food value too.

One of the most successful baits I have ever used in this respect is a particular brand of luncheon meat. Now, I know that luncheon meat generally is old hat, but this brand is worth a try on any water for it has caught literally hundreds of carp from waters that have already been fished out on luncheon meat. It is called Bacon Grill and I owe my introduction to it to my friend Fred Simson. We were concentrating on luncheon meat as a bait at the time and I think Fred just bought this sort as a tin of bait rather than something special. He soon realized, though, that it was a superior bait to the average luncheon meat. It has a smokey-bacon sort of smell and taste which is quite unlike any other tinned meat I have smelt or tasted. Another point that might also tie in with the high-nutrition theory is that the label on the tin states that the contents are 90 per cent meat. If you have used luncheon meats a good deal you will know that some of the cheaper brands contain quite a lot of fat and cereal. Some can actually be used as floating baits, with a quite small cube supporting the weight of a No. 8 hook! Bacon Grill is a little expensive when compared to some other brands, but it has never failed me and has caught carp from every water I have fished. It has also caught carp for many of my other friends who have given it a fair trial on their waters.

There are many meat pastes that have attractive smells. Liver paté and liver and bacon paté are both good. Sutherlands make a wide range of paste spreads that can be mixed with fine groundbait and flour to make very good paste baits. Their liver and bacon paste works well, as do the various ham and beef spreads, though I have never had much success with the fish pastes or turkey or chicken sorts. I have also tried pieces of cooked chicken and turkey (only at Christmas!) without taking a single carp on either, though winter fishing is not really the time to try new or unusual baits. Another bait I tried in winter was caviar. My neighbour is Polish and he had a

Sorry about the face but this is my best carp! Caught on Bacon Grill, it weighs 26¼ pounds

small tin of caviar sent him for Christmas by his relations in Poland. He said it was the very best quality and brought me a generous portion to eat. The eggs were about three-sixteenths of an inch in diameter and had a beautiful reddish gold colour. One smell of the sickly aroma like cod-liver oil told me that, caviar or not, I certainly was not interested, but the carp might be. Anyway I tried them for several sessions but did not catch any carp. Not a viable proposition anyway at £10 a tin!

One bait that will catch carp is peanut butter. There are two sorts, 'smooth' and 'crunchy'. Both work well but the smooth sort makes a better paste. It was the unusual smell and oil content that first attracted me to the bait. I could imagine bait samples giving off lots of lovely, oily, aroma in the water, drawing carp irresistibly towards it! The food value of peanuts is also high. You can mix it several ways to make a good paste bait, but it is wise to include a small percentage of ordinary butter in the mix. The butter slows down the rate of disintegration considerably. I normally mix two lots; one with butter for hookbait; the other without for free offerings which I want to disintegrate as an attraction to the fish. The way I make paste is simple, if messy. Take two thick slices of bread, either brown or white, and remove the crusts. Butter each piece, like a normal sandwich, spread the peanut butter thickly on each slice and put the two together. Work the bread between your hands, adding a little water at a time until you have a ball of paste. Then add as much peanut butter as you can by pushing holes in the paste and kneading it into the paste. My friend, Barry Varney, used brown flour for his mixture and had two carp from a fairly difficult water the first time he tried it. Other friends have successfully used ordinary white flour, but do not forget to add the ordinary butter to the hookbait mixture; it will ensure the bait remains intact for eight to ten hours in water. The best carp I have caught on the bait is 15 pounds 13 ounces. Some of my friends have done better and I recall Barry getting one of 18 pounds 2 ounces shortly after beginning to use it.

There are a number of other baits I have used with varying success over the years but I have not the space to discuss them in detail. Ordinary bacon is a good bait in waters where you have to wait a long time for a run and which contain a lot of small fish like roach.

Barrie Varney with an 18 pound 2 ounce mirror caught on peanut butter

The bacon really wants to be a bit 'high' as it has not much smell otherwise. Best fish on bacon so far is 17 pounds. Another good bait that seems to be overlooked these days is cheese. I have found it ideal for fishing a water that is stiff with small roach that pester with continual twitches on particle baits and have paste or luncheon meat baits off the hook within seconds of them reaching the bottom.

After a bit of experiment I found the best sort of cheese was red Leicester. There are several others that would doubtless work just as well. The main requirement is that the cheese is firm, hard and even and not crumbly. I prefer to use small baits on a size 8 hook. This allows more free offerings of a similar size to the hook bait to be cut from the block of cheese and used to build up a carpet of food around the hook bait. If small fish are a nuisance I end up using big 'blocks' for both hook and free offerings. These blocks are 1 inch long by about $\frac{3}{8}$ inch square. A long-shanked No. 2 hook is carefully worked through one edge halfway along the length, leaving as much of the hook exposed as possible. Cheese appears to work best when it is really smelly. Cheese which has been in the bait box a month or more and covered with the green bacterial 'overcoat' seems very attractive to carp. It often pays, when small fish are a nuisance, to mix up some flavoured groundbait as a free offering. I make it from old bread, soaked in cold water, and worked into a mash. I then add powdered Parmesan cheese and fine groundbait to make the mixture into a throwable consistency. Large amounts are thrown into the swim and followed by the free offerings and hook baits.

The roach or other small fish seem to leave the hard cheese alone, concentrating, instead, on the bread mash. The resultant activity sends the powerful Parmesan cheese smell in all directions. It is generally not long before a carp picks up the smell and homes in on the baited swim, where it finds the big lumps of smelly cheese waiting.

I had some nice carp a couple of summers ago using this technique. The small water I was fishing had produced only a handful of doubles over several years. The pond 'record' was a carp of 10 pounds 6 ounces. My smelly cheese produced carp of 10 pounds 3 ounces; 11 pounds 6 ounces; 15 pounds 1 ounce, as well as other smaller fish. This is my sort of carp-fishing and those three fish gave me a feeling of pride although they are not big fish by carp-fishing standards. To be absolutely fair, I must report that my friend Peter

A pond record, caught on a 'block' of cheese and a large eye paternoster rig

Author's son Andrew tries to find a hold on a nice double Dad's just landed (caught on liver pâté)

Evans also caught the 15 pounder a few weeks later from the same swim on a particle bait – maple peas to be precise.

Perhaps this is the ideal way to end a chapter which has contained so much of interest about particle and high-protein baits. The same fish caught twice within a few weeks; once on cheese, which has a reasonable protein content and once on particle baits. What could be better evidence to support the views of my two contributors?

Epilogue

And now the book is near completion. It is the work of an ordinary man of insignificant education. But needs must and it is the unrest inside – not simple egotism – that has made me write this book. There have been times of absolute joy in the period of writing and times of blank despair. Such internal conflict too; writing when the whole body cries out to be fishing and fishing when the mind wants to write.

But all that conflict is over now. Already in my mind's eye I can see that summer morning. The steaming cup of tea is halfway to my lips at dawn when a heron lands in the shallows opposite and stands, like a smoky-grey walking stick, rigid, upright. The minutes tick by; the heron watching me under my brolly, trying to decide if I intend harm, while I watch it, hoping, willing it to stay, each of us locked in frozen immobility. Then at last, with barely a perceptible relaxing of the rigid stance, the heron begins to examine the water in front of it. With head held in a high forward position this superlative angler starts to fish. A pace forward. Then another. A pause, followed by a slow tilting of the body as it pivots on the long slender legs. The neck begins to coil, snake-like, in a unified movement as the body angle increases, and at the last moment the head weaves quickly from side to side before – stab! One lightning thrust forward and a slow return with a small fish in the pointed beak.

I am watching, fascinated. Time has no meaning as I count six stabs and see six sticklebacks disappear down the long, slender throat, while drops of water fall from the tip of the beak as muscles in the neck rhythmically push the fish downwards. And in my entrancement, absent-mindedly I continue the half-finished movement of raising the cup of tea to my lips. The heron responds with a coarse 'Kraark!' of alarm. Slender legs thrust the heavy body upwards and blunt wings beat, driving the bird into a vertical take-off to clear the barbed-wire fence of the opposite bank. The heron flies off to land in the field 200 yards away, where it stands in the upright, alarmed stance, its bright beady eye looking straight at me. Finishing the movement I find my much-relished dawn cuppa has gone cold; a loss fully compensated by observing the beautifully synchronized and deadly accurate fishing of this shy, drab bird.

The vision fades to be replaced by another mental image of a fishing bird. With a 'Peep! Peep!' the flash of iridescent blue speeds past only inches above the water and climbs steeply to land on the branch of the tiny beech tree. The tree grows, bonsai-like, with exposed roots scrabbling over the equally tiny island supporting it, giving the impression of a frantic search for nutrients to support and boost its diminutive growth. Once, long ago, the roots had found enough food in the hard-packed clay of the island to allow a large branch to grow out over the water. But the effect of producing this branch, which is as long as the tree is high, seems to have been a sapping of the island's resources, leading to a stunting of the tree. It was on this branch the kingfisher landed and is now perched, gazing

A pretty North Lincs club water

downwards to the water 10 feet below. Suddenly it drops with a flutter of wings and lands in the water with a splashy, belly-flop of a dive. It all seems so clumsy for such a resplendent bird and unrewarding too. After four of these 'dives' the bird finally emerges with a small fish. Flying back up to the branch it begins to rap the fish on the hard surface to kill it. How strange the ways of nature; the kingfisher, painted with colours of such splendour, is so much less efficient than is the drab grey heron.

Now the image changes again as my memory savours another highlight from the store of carp-fishing memories. It is a clear summer night and I lay relaxed by the side of my rods, waiting for the run that usually comes between 10.30 and 1 o'clock. Gazing upward the dark luminance of outer-space reveals the spectacular universe, spread in all its glory as far as the eye can see. Countless millions of stars, all shimmering with that cold, fluorescent blue that belies the intense atomic heat providing the light rays.

What number of planets circle each one?

Some are bound to have many more than our small sun, which is but a minor sun in a moderate galaxy. But there, above, are suns that would make our nice homely sun look insignificant by comparison. However could man be so egotistic and ignorant as to once think that this speck of dust called Earth was the centre of the entire universe and all that incredible mass revolved around it? My thoughts come in short pulses, with long intervals between: All those suns up there.... All the planetary systems that surely must revolve around them.... Perhaps a hundred or more around one of the really big ones.... Why, life must be universal.... Common in fact.... Yes, of course it will.... The chances are that given the same elements to work with things will have progressed in a similar way to life on Earth.... It seems unreasonable to accept that intelligent life has the form of a shapeless blob, so beloved by fiction writers – it must be like us or how could a complex civilization exist?... Men up there in their millions.... Perhaps they go fishing! They may have carp swimming in their lakes too! Have they got commons and mirrors and leathers? Lovely deep, fat fish with golden sides and smoky-blue backs! Wonder how big they grow! Do they have war and peace, governments, politicians, religion?... A God?... A Christ? Do they deal out wholesale death to all the species that inhabit their planets?... Perhaps, with luck, they may have evolved beyond that stage....

A carp rolled gracefully right over my baits, bringing my thoughts sharply back to earth. It has happened a hundred times before but it does not prevent a quickening of the pulse or still the tremble of anticipation at the thought of the expected run. Will it be a double or an average fish? Who cares as long as it is a carp that will give a good account of itself. And as I wait, hand poised over the rod, deep down in my head I can hear disconnected snatches of an old classic sung by Bing and Satchmo.... 'Gone fishin'.'... 'There's a sign upon my door.'... 'Gone fishin'' ... ' 'stead of just a-wishin'.' Pure magic that is waiting to be experienced.

So with relief or regret, it is difficult to decide which, my pen will soon be at rest. All that remains is for me to wish my reader good fishing and meaningful observation. If a small part of what has been said within these covers makes your sessions more enjoyable my self-imposed task will have been worthwhile.

Index